Joel and Ethan Coen |

Contemporary Film Directors

Edited by James Naremore

The Contemporary Film Directors series provides concise, well-written introductions to directors from around the world and from every level of the film industry. Its chief aims are to broaden our awareness of important artists, to give serious critical attention to their work, and to illustrate the variety and vitality of contemporary cinema. Contributors to the series include an array of internationally respected critics and academics. Each volume contains an incisive critical commentary, an informative interview with the director, and a detailed filmography.

A list of books in the series appears at the end of this book.

Ethan and Joel Coen
(Courtesy of the
Academy of Motion
Picture Arts and
Sciences)

Joel and Ethan Coen |

R. Barton Palmer

**UNIVERSITY
OF
ILLINOIS
PRESS**
URBANA
AND
CHICAGO

Library of Congress Cataloging-in-Publication Data
Palmer, R. Barton, 1946–
Joel and Ethan Coen / R. Barton Palmer.
p.   cm. — (Contemporary film directors)
Includes bibliographical references and index.
ISBN 0-252-02936-4 (cl. : alk. paper)
ISBN 0-252–07185-9 (pbk. : alk. paper)
1. Coen, Joel—Criticism and interpretation.
2. Coen, Ethan—Criticism and interpretation.
I. Title. II. Series.
PN1998.3.C6635P35   2004
791.4302'33'092273—dc22   2003026970

For my sons, Jeffrey, Colin, and Camden,
who share my love of the movies

Contents

|

Acknowledgments |

This project would have been neither conceived nor completed without the advice and support of the series editor, James Naremore of Indiana University. I am grateful to him and also to Matthew Bernstein of Emory University for their careful reading of my initial draft. Incorporating their many wise and pertinent suggestions for revision has removed many an embarrassing error and oversight from the final version. My graduate assistant, Jennifer Lightweis, helped me identify numerous infelicities of form and style. Carol Betts of the University of Illinois Press read the manuscript with great care and saved me from many errors. The Academy of Motion Picture Arts and Sciences library and film stills collection contributed film stills and photographs; I am grateful to Barbara Hall and the many others on the Margaret Herrick Library staff for their kindness and assistance. Gratitude is owed as well to Michel Ciment, Hubert Niogret, and *Positif* for allowing me to translate and publish three of the interviews they have done with the Coens during the past fifteen years or so. The Calhoun Lemon endowment and the Psaras Fund contributed money for travel and other incidental expenses. I thank them for their generosity.

Carla Palmer lent her enthusiasm for and interest in Hollywood film to this enterprise and graciously tolerated her husband's preoccupation with the necessary research and writing. I have learned much over the years from our conversations about the movies. During the last year, we have shared many a pleasant hour in front of the VCR debating the complexities and mysteries of the Coen brothers' oeuvre, from which I have greatly profited.

Joel and Ethan Coen

Any book proposing as its subject the oeuvre of a contemporary film director must confront the somewhat uncomfortable fact that such an approach is rather out of fashion, at least in the academic discipline of cinema studies. For the last twenty years and more, film scholars have in various ways challenged the so-called "auteur theory," which is the view that the personality, interests, and vision of the director can be considered, in significant and substantial ways, as shaping his or her films as a unique body of work. In contrast, contemporary film theorists of a postmodern bent have increasingly echoed the cultural critic Roland Barthes's theory of "the death of the author," proclaiming a historically conditioned fiction any notion that texts, literary or cinematic, exclusively owe their form or meaning to some "originating" individual.

Within cinema studies, the standard view has now become that the principal usefulness of the film "author" becomes its ascription of the inevitable complexity and diversity of an industrial product to the creative urges of one person. The auteur theory, then, is not imagined as speaking uncomplicated truth; rather it may be conceded a certain utility within the context of cinema culture, where authorship functions as a shorthand method for explaining how films come to be what they are and come to say what they seem to say. As a result of the postmodern challenge, the auteur theory does not have the academic respectability it once had. Today film history is no longer organized, except in small part, by the concept of the great director.

An auteurist approach, however, is arguably called for in the case of Joel and Ethan Coen, a writing/directing brother act. They have exercised nearly complete control over the ten "small" Hollywood films they have released through 2003. At the very least, considering the Coens as their author (sharing creative responsibilities, Joel and Ethan can be considered for critical purposes to be an "individual") offers a revealing perspective on a body of work that has made a considerable impact on the contemporary scene. The productions of the Coens bear an obvious imprint that is personal, at least in the sense that it may be traced across their various films and made the proper object of a critical analysis. And yet, even though the films themselves strongly announce their authorship, the Coens have chosen to occupy a kind of anti-authorial position within the industry. This strange fact bears some further comment.

It is an interesting paradox that as the place of the director within academic criticism has become less prominent, directors have become increasingly important figures within film culture in the broadest sense. Many directors (Steven Spielberg and Martin Scorsese are notable examples) are as well known to the general public as anyone in the industry has ever been, except perhaps for major stars such as John Wayne and Tom Cruise. More important, perhaps, is the emergence within the Hollywood cinema of the last two decades of a new role for the director, which has become, in Timothy Corrigan's words, "a *commercial* strategy for organizing audience reception . . . a critical concept bound to distribution and marketing aims that identify and address the potential cult status of an auteur."[1] This is nowhere more evident than in "the contemporary status of the auteur as star" (105). What role does this new class of stars play within the contemporary industry? Corrigan believes that directors' "commercial status as auteurs is their chief function as auteurs" (105). This is not to say, of course, that at other times during the history of the American cinema some directors have not attained a genuine stardom. D. W. Griffith, Frank Capra, and Alfred Hitchcock (just to choose the most obvious examples) were relentless self-promoters and managed, often in the face of considerable institutional pressure, to attain a celebrity that rivaled that of star performers. What is new today is that, in this post-auteurist age, it is much more common (and sanctioned) for directors to cultivate a public prominence.

Indeed, star directors now find their greatest importance in the promotion and marketing of the films they help manufacture. The moral and professional danger of such a development is, perhaps, obvious: today's directors are "always on the verge of being self-consumed by their status as stars," as Corrigan points out (106). The films of auteur-stars can, in short, become more or less dispensable with regard to their celebrated position within contemporary American culture. For most viewers, the cult status of Steven Spielberg, for example, makes irrelevant any substantial consideration of the problematic relationship between his more "personal" projects (such as *Schindler's List*) and those undertaken more strictly for commercial reasons (such as the *Jurassic Park* "franchise"). All the films signed by Spielberg contribute to his celebrity—and his "bankability" within the industry.

Though surrounded by the many luminaries among the ranks of contemporary directors who eagerly cultivate their public images, Joel and Ethan Coen have refused to become auteur-stars in any way. In fact, opposing the trend identified by Corrigan, the Coens have done their best not to be well-known "personalities." Instead, they have put all their energies into making movies that are interestingly idiosyncratic, smart, and more than a little enigmatic. In other words, their small-scale productions (which they write, cast, direct, and often edit) reflect deeply their shaping influence, yet make no reference to some media-crafted image of their makers—for the Coens have allowed no such image to take shape. No doubt, the Coen brothers have emerged to celebrity of a sort if only as "names" to be reckoned with in an American independent cinema movement that has flourished spectacularly since the 1980s. No enthusiast of the contemporary Hollywood cinema is unacquainted with their signed work, whose virtues and originality have been recognized by critics, their peers, and those who love independent films. And yet no better indication of their ambiguous place in contemporary filmmaking is the fact that *Fargo*, while winning numerous awards from the Academy and other juries, is one of their smallest, most idiosyncratic and personal productions. It is a film without stars that lacks any connection to a "pre-sold" property and affords nothing in the way of merchandising possibilities. *Fargo*'s place on the American Film Institute's list of Hollywood's top one hundred films of all time affirms that the Coens' success is viewed by those within the industry as transcending their prominence within the popular wave of "independent" filmmaking during the last two decades. Yet who would be foolish enough to affirm that this film is typical of its time?

The Coens have resisted the pressure that inevitably comes from such success to create something like a bankable "brand name" by working mostly within the confines of two recognizable genres, film noir and comedy. Furthermore, they have shown little interest in graduating from small-budget work to better-funded productions of greater scope and wider commercial appeal. To be sure, one recent release, *The Man Who Wasn't There*, "stars" Billy Bob Thornton, a "hot" actor who is not a member of their stock company (members of which fill the secondary roles in this project), while one current project, a remake of the British classic comedy *The Ladykillers*, features Tom Hanks, one of Hollywood's top performers. Both projects, however, remain otherwise quite limited in scale. Perhaps more important, the Coens' oeuvre of distinguished small films, though unified in ways discussed throughout this book, is characterized by a calculated dispersal of energies. Such dispersal invites interpretation as a deliberate refusal of the position of the classical auteur, who is generally understood as a unifying force imposing a personal and singular design on a variety of materials.

What matters most about the Coen brothers is that they have made some of the most provocative and engaged films to appear in the New Hollywood era. And yet their work has not been much taken up by those within academe. In part, one suspects, this is because they have not played at being "authors" as other contemporary independent directors have, notably perhaps David Lynch and Quentin Tarantino. My hope is that the discussion to follow will demonstrate that their films demand and repay serious study. This book emphasizes the engagement of the Coens with postmodernism, broadly considered, as the second chapter explains in more detail. This book, then, is not mostly about them (for which they will undoubtedly be grateful). Readers who are interested in more biographical details, production history, and star gossip than will be found here are directed to the six fan-oriented books that have thus far appeared (details can be found in the bibliography).[2]

The Coens have consistently refused to be public figures who control the reception of their films by shaping carefully, in the manner of a Hitchcock or Welles, the images that filmgoers are meant to have of them as authors. They dislike appearing on talk shows, being "seen" at industry-sponsored events, or even granting interviews (which they often refuse, as they did when I requested one to appear in this book). It is significant, I think, that the Coens offer the fullest and most forthcoming accounts of their work to French journalists for the film journal *Posi-*

tif, which obviously has a limited circulation in the United States. A selection of these interviews, which I have translated into English, appears as the final section of this book. As their responses show, when questioned about their work, the Coens often seem to feign ignorance or a lack of interest, particularly with regard to questions about their engagement with classic films, literary texts, aesthetic movements (notably postmodernism), and even the philosophical concepts that seem prominently displayed in their films.

Thus, although the Coens are undoubtedly notables on the contemporary scene, their "celebrity" as a writing-directing duo could never "exceed" the movies themselves. The most predictable aspect of their filmmaking is its unpredictability (also one of their films' characteristic themes), its quirky and surprising engagement not only with Hollywood and American culture, but also with authors ranging from Homer to Clifford Odets to James M. Cain. Though witty, flashy, and filled with inventive visual jokes, their films are (*Barton Fink* excepted) more accessible than arty, inviting the viewer's engagement on a number of levels. Consider *O Brother, Where Art Thou?* In a postmodern gesture of boundary transgression, this film draws in equal measure on both "high" and "low" culture, on, in particular, both the *Odyssey* and Preston Sturges's classic Hollywood comedy *Sullivan's Travels*. Yet the comic energies of the Coens' film, its startling visuals, and its sharply pointed if humorous handling of political issues (one striking sequence features a Ku Klux Klan rally staged like a musical number from a Gilbert and Sullivan operetta) were appreciated by many who remained happily unaware of its more rarefied literary and cinematic sources.

The first chapter of this study explores how the Coens developed their approach to filmmaking while completing their debut effort, *Blood Simple*, whose astounding success on the film festival circuit launched them on their commercial career in the early 1980s. The second chapter defines their engagement with the complex movement within the arts called postmodernism, while the remaining four offer critical analyses of the six other Coen films that, to date, have made the most impact on the American scene: *The Man Who Wasn't There, Fargo, Barton Fink, Raising Arizona, The Hudsucker Proxy,* and *O Brother, Where Art Thou?* Any discussion of the three remaining commercial releases to date, *Miller's Crossing, The Big Lebowski,* and *Intolerable Cruelty,* would add little of importance to the general account offered here of the Coens' place within the history of the contemporary American filmmaking scene. The brothers' reputation at this time, I believe, stands or falls on the basis of the seven films that will be given close consideration here. But first a brief overview of their career is in order.

Born (Joel in 1954, Ethan in 1957) and raised in the St. Louis Park suburb of Minneapolis, Minnesota, the brothers are the children of academics. Their father, Edward, was an economics professor at the University of Minnesota, while their mother, Rena, taught fine arts at St. Cloud State. The brothers, they have often confessed, found growing up in the American heartland boring. They spent much of their time watching television, particularly old movies, which became something of a passion, inspiring them to produce their own "remakes" with a neighbor who shared the expense of buying a used camera. Uninspired by what public education in Minnesota had to offer, Joel and, later, Ethan, persuaded their parents to send them to Simon's Rock, a school in Massachusetts. In an environment that encouraged independent study, they thrived. After graduation Joel spent four unhappy years in the New York University undergraduate film program, taking away little from the experience. Ethan found his college years at Princeton studying philosophy more rewarding.

After graduation Ethan joined Joel in New York City, where he had broken into the film industry as an editor working on low-budget horror films. Their big opportunity came when they met Sam Raimi, a young man determined like themselves to break into the industry, which he soon did with *The Evil Dead*, which was made on a shoestring budget but, after a Cannes screening that drew the approval of the novelist Stephen King, won a commercial release. *Evil Dead* was a surprise hit, grossing more than $1 million in its first week of limited national exhibition. Raimi showed Joel and Ethan that they could break into writing and directing if they had the right kind of project (a genre piece with assured commercial appeal) and if they could arrange sufficient financing. The brothers decided to do a kind of contemporary film noir, based less on their viewing of classic films than on their reading of crime fiction, particularly the novels of James M. Cain. Joel and Ethan wrote the script for what would become *Blood Simple*, working side by side, during the weekends of 1980. Unlike Raimi, who was happy to use unknown actors in the featured roles, the Coens managed to assemble an impressive cast of (mostly young) professionals, including the character actor M. Emmet Walsh in the role of the crooked detective, who is also the film's philosophizing narrator. Interesting performances were turned in by the supporting players, including John Getz, Frances McDormand (who would marry Joel not long afterward), and Dan Hedaya. The Coens were lucky in their choice of the cinematographer Barry Sonnenfeld, whom Joel had met in New York. Sonnenfeld had also gone to NYU, but in the Graduate Institute of Film and Television. He had made some documentaries before signing on for a small fee to make the film's two-minute trailer, which was to be the brothers' vehicle for raising money for the actual production (including making personal appeals to members of the Jewish community in their home town). They raised just enough to cover the costs of production.

In order to make the most of their limited budget, they spent many hours on preproduction tasks, including the design of elaborate storyboards. The twentysomething Coens supervised the shooting, which was done in and around Austin, Texas. Out of money, they handled postproduction duties themselves (including the film's spectacularly successful editing and even some reshoots). *Blood Simple*'s success with audiences and critics at film festivals (which I discuss at length later) led to a commercial distribution contract in 1985 with Circle Films, a small company trying to make a place in the independent market. Ben Barenholtz, Circle's chief executive, was optimistic about the Coens' prospects for further success, and so he signed them to a three-picture deal. Budgets would be small, suiting the kind of profit earned by *Blood Simple* (the film made about $3 million, substantial money for two neophytes, but a pittance measured against huge amounts budgeted for the average blockbuster).

Their next production, featuring two rising Hollywood stars, Nicolas Cage and Holly Hunter, offered a complete change of pace. This new focus made the point, which has been borne out by the rest of the Coens' career, that the brothers are not interested in developing some comfortable generic niche to exploit. *Raising Arizona* is a wacky comedy about a career criminal who marries (or imagines he marries—the whole film is perhaps a dream) a prison guard and attempts to go straight. Hi (Cage), ironically enough, finds that the demands of marriage, in particular the imperative to procreate and start a nuclear family, lead him back into crime, this time abetted by his wife, Ed (Hunter). Because the couple proves infertile, Ed urges Hi to kidnap a baby, one of a celebrated set of quintuplets. But their domestic equilibrium, newly established, soon disintegrates as two of Hi's prisoner buddies conspire to return the child for the reward money; all concerned barely escape destruction at the hands of a vicious Hell's Angel bounty hunter. In the manner of zany comedies, *Raising Arizona* offers a number of impressive set-piece chase sequences (such as Hi's theft of diapers from a supermarket and his subsequent madcap pursuit by the police).

Like *Blood Simple*, it is a highly stylized film, but with a very different regime. The Coens abandoned the Expressionist noir effects of their debut production for the fast-paced action and rapid changes of perspective associated with cartoon stylization, particularly Chuck Jones's *Roadrunner* series, a deep influence on the film that they have acknowledged. With its expanded cast, sprinkling of name actors, and more elaborate production values, *Raising Arizona* was much more expensive to make than the Coens' first film. Circle provided the brothers with $3 million, or about half of the estimated budget. The remaining $3 million was advanced by Twentieth Century Fox, and this was an investment that came with no strings attached (in short, the Coens retained creative control over the film). *Raising Arizona* was modestly successful, generating about $22 million in box office, and received mostly praiseworthy reviews. That the film became part of a short-lived but highly popular series of films addressing issues of family life, including Ron Howard's blockbuster *Parenthood* (1989), showed that the Coens had hit a popular vein with the right kind of product. As far as art-house patrons and studio executives were concerned, *Raising Arizona* did nothing but solidify the reputation of the writing-directing team.

In making *Miller's Crossing*, the Coens were thus able to dispose of an even higher budget, which was still small, however, by Hollywood standards of that time: $10 million, with Fox once again partnering with Circle on the financing. In choosing the classic gangster film as their generic base, the Coens once again found themselves as part of a Hollywood trend of sorts. The end of the 1980s saw the successful release of two widely acclaimed entries in the gangster genre: Francis Coppola's *The Godfather III* and Martin Scorsese's *Goodfellas* (both 1990).

Whereas Coppola and Scorsese offered serious updatings of the rise and fall of a charismatic criminal, with an emphasis on compelling characters and chillingly violent action sequences, the Coens gave the form the postmodern treatment. Their film is at times self-consciously ironic, even dismissive toward its conventions. As Terence Rafferty, writing for the *New Yorker*, put it, "This is not so much a gangster movie as an extended, elaborate allusion to one."[3] For many filmgoers, a central problem with *Miller's Crossing* was not just the complexity of the story, but the often-obscure way in which it was told. The relationships among the varied members of an Irish mob (obviously modeled on the O'Bannion gang that warred with the Capones in Prohibition-era Chicago) are not clearly set forth at the beginning. The resulting twists and turns of a narrative that hinges on loyalty and betrayal are thus very hard to follow. In part, these difficulties are to be traced to the Coens' general reliance on a Dashiell Hammett novel, *Red Harvest,* that was never brought to the screen, presumably because it not only contains much cold-blooded violence, but also features no sympathetic main character who might mitigate a sense of crushing fatality and pointlessness. *Miller's Crossing* is a smart, witty, and often engaging film, but in the end it proved too confusing and remote even for art-house audiences. Though the main character, played by Gabriel Byrne, is a good bad guy in the mold of Humphrey Bogart's roles in the classic noir films *The Maltese Falcon* and *The Big Sleep,* his motives are never explained clearly enough to make him the emotional center of the narrative. Reviews were often quite laudatory, though some journalists, in an era of political correctness, were offended by the film's often-coarse deployment of ethnic stereotypes. In any case, the paying customers stayed away.

As will be explained in more detail further below, the script for *Barton Fink* was born in the course of the troubles that the Coens had with finishing the screenplay for *Miller's Crossing* (whether this was writer's block or simply a matter of straightening out the plot entanglements depends on which interview might be more accurate on the subject). While their first three productions use the conventions of the standard Hollywood entertainment film as a structure to exploit and modify, *Barton Fink* distinctly departs from this method of working. Firmly in the modernist vein, this production draws a portrait of the (film) artist, in particular the discontents a well-known writer has with writing both for the Broadway stage and for Hollywood. The film is set in 1941, and according to the Coens, their inspiration was Otto Friedrich's famous *City of Nets: A Portrait of Hollywood in the 1940s.* While Friedrich's book certainly provided some important background (particularly in its bitter portrait of studio executives), *Barton Fink*'s sources are in truth more literary, including the experiences of the writers Nathanael West and Clifford Odets with Hollywood, as well as what these famous chroniclers of the age say in their works about the inauthenticity and dangers of what came to be known as the culture industry.

If *Miller's Crossing* offered spectators difficulties of presentation (Who did what, and why?), *Barton Fink* presented them with difficulties of interpretation. Are Barton's horrific experiences in the film's gothic hotel real? If so, what is in the box given him by a serial killer? Though the film is undoubtedly much more artistically successful than its immediate predecessor, once again the Coens seem to have overestimated the taste of the art-house faithful for a difficult, however rewarding, cinematic experience. Fox's investment of $9 million in the project translated into only $5 million at the box office, with European ticket sales (perhaps predictably) much brisker than those in the United States. Except for those unalterably opposed to the Coens' style and thematic interests (notably, Jim Hoberman of the *Village Voice*), reviewers were generally favorable to the film, which went on to win the Palme d'Or at Cannes for best film, along with two other awards. A strong cast of Coen regulars (chiefly John Turturro, Jon Polito, and Steve Buscemi) was given excellent support by Michael Lerner and Judy Davis, both of whose performances received prestigious awards that year.

Despite its lack of financial success, *Barton Fink* brought the Coens to the notice of the Hollywood producer Joel Silver, who became convinced that they could achieve a breakthrough to substantial profitability (if that is what the brothers really wanted, of which there is some doubt) were their next production "packaged" more effectively. The Coens had written *The Hudsucker Proxy* some years before but then abandoned the project because it would require the building of elaborate sets to create the impression of a completely constructed fictional world. Silver encouraged them to revive the project, which was eventually funded at about $25 million, though some sources suggest that the film cost much more, perhaps as much as $40 million. *The Hudsucker*

Proxy would also be a more mainstream film in terms of casting, with stars Paul Newman, Tim Robbins, and Jennifer Jason Leigh in the featured roles. Newman's agreement to participate made it possible for Silver to raise the requisite funds from Warner Brothers and Polygram.

The Hudsucker Proxy is a witty, inventive meditation on the Horatio Alger myth, with a special nod to the comedies of Frank Capra, Preston Sturges, and Howard Hawks, and to Hollywood Golden Age film in general. Yet it never found an audience, generating not even $3 million in domestic box office. As in the case of *Barton Fink,* the film was more appreciated abroad, especially in Europe. Reviewers praised the film's complex references to America's cinematic past and its engagement with the foundational myths of American culture, but they generally echoed David Ansen's view that the reuse of earlier films had become more entrapping than liberating: "Here they seem as much imprisoned by old movies as inspired."[4] But it seems that it was the reviewers who could more properly be thought of as "imprisoned," by their unshakable conviction that movies always needed to be entertaining in some conventional sense. More than anything else, perhaps, the Coens' experience with *The Hudsucker Proxy* demonstrated that, unlike other independent filmmakers such as Steven Soderbergh and David Cronenberg, they were not suited, and might never be, to conceiving big-budget films aimed at a mass audience.

The Coens proved they had learned this lesson with the release of their next film, a return to small-budget filmmaking of a more "realist," simply stylized kind. Set in Minnesota, *Fargo* also draws, if somewhat obliquely, on the Coens' experience with their home state, which gives the film an authentic feel. Ironically, it was made for only $6 million and featured no stars in the cast, but it did more than four times that amount in box office, in the process proving much more appealing to average moviegoers than the brothers' two previous releases. A masterpiece of naturalist stylization, with its carefully crafted location shooting providing unforgettable images of a snowbound Minnesota, *Fargo* tells the story, ostensibly based on real events, of a feckless car salesman who finds himself, for reasons never explained, in enormous debt and arranges for two local thugs to kidnap his wife. The plan to use the ransom money thereby extorted from a cantankerous father-in-law goes completely wrong, with consequences both humorous and horrifying. *Fargo* is a triumph of ensemble acting, with the actors in the Coens' "stock company" turning in their best collective performance. As the unruffled pregnant police detective who solves the case without ever knowing what it really is, Frances McDormand was particularly effective and won a well-deserved Academy Award. Joel and Ethan also won for best original screenplay, and the film garnered three other well-deserved nominations. Among many foreign awards, the Coens received the best-director prize at Cannes for their efforts.

The Big Lebowski, unfortunately, did not capitalize on this success. Once again, the Coens tried to work on a somewhat larger scale and budget, with a name actor in the featured role (Jeff Bridges). The $15 million budget permitted them to create a kind of picaresque narrative, replete with dream sequences staged like Busby Berkeley musical numbers. A kind of comic send-up of Raymond Chandler's *The Big Sleep,* the Coens' film traces the adventures of the aptly named "Dude," a seedy "player" in the Los Angeles demi-monde, who, much like the Philip Marlowe character in Robert Altman's anti-Chandleresque Chandler adaptation *The Long Goodbye,* is sent out on a strange quest after he is mistaken for someone else. Naturally, the quest comes to nothing, while his many musings about its true nature and significance lead nowhere. Along the way, Dude and his two buddies (played to good effect by John Goodman and Steve Buscemi) meet up with many unusual characters. Notable among these is a loud-mouthed feminist interested in "vaginal art," a viciously racist Hispanic bowling buddy who is also a pedophile, and a comically promiscuous trophy wife. While filled with wildly comic sequences and many quite smart self-referential moments (the film constitutes a kind of portfolio of Coen brothers motifs), *The Big Lebowski* seemed to many of their admirers an exercise in postmodern pointlessness, with its wacky mixture of genres and huge inventory of quotations both literary and cinematic not adding up to much. Reviews were mixed, and the film was mildly profitable, though it added little to the reputation of the writing/directing duo.

Though it is one of their most richly textured films, *O Brother, Where Art Thou?* proved a much more commercial effort, their most profitable film to date, in fact, earning more than $45 million in domestic box office alone against production costs of about $26 million. As they had in *The Big Lebowski,* the Coens cast a name actor in the featured role, with their stock company (John Turturro, John Goodman, and Holly Hunter in particular) adding strong support. George Clooney proved a lucky choice to play Ulysses McGill, a con man who engineers an escape from a Deep South prison with two pals by luring them with the prospect of recovering buried treasure. The plot turns out to be a misdirection, as McGill is actually interested only in preventing his estranged wife from remarrying. The Coens borrow motifs from Homer, with Goodman especially impressive as a latter-day Cyclops turned Bible salesman, while the film's title, and its chain-gang narrative, are loosely based on parts of the Preston Sturges film *Sullivan's Travels*. Location shooting in Mississippi under the expert direction of the cinematographer Roger Deakins made *O Brother* a luscious visual experience, while its sound track of bluegrass songs provided the wacky tale with the appropriate musical background (and the film's backers with an additional source of profit that actually topped the box office take). The Academy nominated the brothers for best screenplay, while Deakins earned yet another nomination for his camera work.

The Coens, however, did not have as much luck with *The Man Who Wasn't There*, even though it is arguably their best film. This neo-noir resurrection of James M. Cain, with its recognition of both Albert Camus in particular and existentialism in general, was a smaller production, made on a budget of only $20 million. With box office of only about $14 million, it has as of this writing yet to turn a profit. Even the usual detractors of the Coens found much to like about the film, which has a slow and meditative pace that runs against noir conventions, but audiences were likely turned off by the complicated plotting (Cain rewritten in the style of Raymond Chandler with a nod to Cornell Woolrich), the many cultural references (including a long disquisition on the Heisenberg Uncertainty Principle), and the generally unsympathetic characters, including a bravura turn from Billy Bob Thornton as a catatonic barber with plans for self-improvement that go horrifyingly awry. With a soundtrack featuring mostly classical music, the film lacked yet another of the elements that had made for the broad popular appeal of *O Brother*. Once again Roger Deakins did a superb job (shooting a black-and-white film noir in color while inventing a new spin on noir visual style); he received another Academy Award nomination for his work on *The Man Who Wasn't There*.

What does the future hold for Joel and Ethan Coen, who, despite an uneven record at the box office, have become fixtures in the generally profitable independent sector of contemporary Hollywood filmmaking? Another big-budget production is in the works, scheduled for a 2004 release, and it promises to be a big hit: a remake of the classic 1950s Ealing comedy *The Ladykillers*. According to reports, the story's location will be shifted from London to the American South, with Tom Hanks taking the part of the criminal mastermind played so effectively by Alec Guinness in the original. The Coens also did the original story for Terry Zwigoff's *Bad Santa,* released in late November 2003 to mixed reviews. Starring Billy Bob Thornton as a genial con man (a Santa Claus who finds his marks at shopping malls), the film is a kind of picaresque comedy romp in the vein of *O Brother,* but in a darkly comic vein not for the sentimental or faint-hearted. Another directorial/writing project, titled *Intolerable Cruelty,* was released in late 2003. Starring George Clooney, Billy Bob Thornton, and Catherine Zeta-Jones, it is a dark comedy like *The Ladykillers,* with a plot tracing the revenge taken by an attractive gold digger on a divorce lawyer, whom she marries. Another interesting meditation in the screwball comedy tradition, *Intolerable Cruelty* deals with love and romance, not a characteristic Coen brothers theme. Whatever else might be said, the brothers from Minnesota are certainly not running out of ideas.

Notes

1. Timothy Corrigan, *A Cinema without Walls: Movies and Culture after Vietnam* (New Brunswick, N.J.: Rutgers University Press, 1991), 103. Subsequent references will be noted in the text.

2. The best of these is undoubtedly James Mottram, *The Coen Brothers: The Life of the Mind* (Dulles, Va.: Brassey, 2000). Mottram's analysis at times parallels my own.

3. Terence Rafferty, "In Brief," *New Yorker,* October 15, 1990, 32.

4. David Ansen, "A Blast of Hollywood Bile," *Newsweek,* March 14, 1994, 63.

1. A Different Meaning for the Same Old Song: *Blood Simple*

> *I feel all dead inside. I'm backed up in a dark*
> *corner and I don't know who's hitting me.*
>
> —Detective Brad Galt, in *The Dark*
> *Corner* (Henry Hathaway, 1946)

At the New York Film Festival in 1984, the biggest hit with audiences was *Blood Simple,* and it was no rarefied art house production like so many festival winners of the decade, most notably David Lynch's *Eraserhead,* Jim Jarmusch's *Stranger than Paradise,* and Todd Haynes's *Poison. Blood Simple* was the first feature effort for an unknown writing-directing team of brothers from Minnesota, and it was a true independent, having been made on a very limited budget with no studio financing or distribution guarantee. Even so, the film struck many in New York as much more commercial than the usual, rough-edged independent entry. *Blood Simple* displays a surprisingly professional polish. And it hardly respects the central elements of cinematic modernism most often reverently featured in festival entries. *Blood Simple* eschews the self-conscious exploration of unusual character or weighty theme. It does not, in the name of anti-pleasure, deconstruct Hollywood conventions such as linear narrative, plausible plotting, and continuity editing. With their sights set firmly on careers in the industry, the young

Minnesotans had opted instead for the more visceral appeals of the classic studio thriller.

A Commercial/Independent Film

Based on the Coen brothers' original screenplay, *Blood Simple* nonetheless draws heavily on the well-worn conventions of noir film and classic American crime fiction, especially the novels of James M. Cain (though the title comes from a phrase in Dashiell Hammett's *Red Harvest*). In effect, the film that wowed viewers was nothing less, and quite a bit more, than a finely crafted genre exercise.

Doubtless, the Coens had taken this studio-era type in a different direction, especially in terms of theme and setting, as the film's striking beginning makes apparent. *Blood Simple* opens not with a dismal view of the archetypal threatening city, but with a montage of bleak landscapes. A low angle shot captures a highway stretching into the distance, empty save for a shredded tire prominent in the foreground. An expansive vista of ugly yellow prairie betrays no sign of human presence except for the oil wells, slowly pumping, that penetrate it at irregular intervals. A drive-in movie theater sits baking in the sun, no picture flashing across its blank screen. Suddenly, a drawling and not too friendly voice fixes the meaning of these inhospitable images. "The world is full of complainers," the man mutters with world weariness, imparting what seems to be his philosophy of life, "but the fact is that nothing comes with a guarantee." The speaker's intent, however, is not just to offer backhanded praise to the free enterprise system and the American dream (as contrasted with Russia, where people earn only "fifty cent a day," as he observes later in the film). He is also eager to explain the individualist ethos that dominates life in Texas, where "you're on your own."

The narrative that follows illustrates the complex connections between these two truths. The relentless pursuit of self-interest motors the plot, even as intention has little to do with outcome. No matter how well conceived, the characters' plans are derailed by mischance and play out to the fatal bad luck of both this seedy opportunist and most of his fellows—who are hardly his moral superiors. Ironically, at film's end the only survivor in this world ruled by the principle of red tooth and claw is the woman whose weakness and dissatisfaction set the story into motion. She saves herself against all odds, but this is more a matter of random good fortune than of either sangfroid or intelligence (though she displays more of these qualities than do the men in the story). The man who loves her cannot protect her, despite his best efforts, all of which prove misguided. When she most needs him, he lies dead at her feet (shot in the back by an unseen assailant, fittingly enough). Isolation is thus shown to result from misunderstanding, mischance, and mistrust. At least in the world the film conjures into existence, isolation in fact seems to be an inalterable condition of human experience. And thus, as the narrator remarks, there truly is no point in complaining. No authority figures appear who might listen, and in any case, the law is entirely absent. Even the innocent never think to appeal to it.

What is most certain is uncertainty itself, the fact that "something can always go wrong," as the narrator wryly observes, scorning those without the guts to face the worst. His own plans are clever, perhaps ingenious, but they too run afoul of the unforeseen. In the end, however, he is undone by obsessive thoughts of insecurity, which, of course, are hardly unjustified. Imagining the worst but misreading the threat he actually faces, he ironically brings on his own death, killed by the woman he tries to murder, who thinks he is someone else. But, dying, he knows better than to voice dissatisfaction at the outcome, even though this irony of her misunderstanding prompts a bitter laugh. This story differs in many details from Cain's novel *Double Indemnity*, which seems to have been the Coens' main inspiration. But the screenwriters were obviously inspired by the self-destructive fatality of Cain's conclusion, where the adulterous and husband-murdering couple, having boarded a boat to Mexico, contemplate suicide by throwing themselves into the shark-infested waters. In *Blood Simple*, too, death is the end toward which the desire of every character seems to lead. Like the bewildered and rightly paranoid protagonist in that most typical film noir, *The Dark Corner*, the characters in *Blood Simple* find themselves trapped in an unfathomable universe of deadly violence.

Like Cain's *The Postman Always Rings Twice*, *Blood Simple* opens with a romance born of necessity, dissatisfaction, and opportunity. A man and a woman explore the possibilities of a relationship, their barely visible heads framed in the darkness against the rain-swept windshield of a car speeding off toward distant lights. Ray (John Getz) is driving Abby

(Frances McDormand), the wife of his boss, Marty, a local bar owner, to Houston, some miles distant from the small town where they live. She has determined, if vaguely and impulsively, to begin a new life apart from her husband. The two discover they are being trailed by a man who later turns out to be a private detective—and the film's narrator. Marty (Dan Hedaya) had hired Visser (M. Emmet Walsh) to follow his wife because this is not the first time she has left him. Abby says to Ray, "I just think I'm making a mistake," but, instead of returning to her husband, she decides to spend the night with Ray in a nearby motel, perhaps fearful that their pursuer intends them some harm. Ray, after all, had confessed to "always liking" her, and this seems reason enough for a sexual escapade. But this roadside refuge provides the new couple with no protection from the detective's curiosity as he manages to photograph them making love. He then informs Marty, whose phone call finds Ray *in flagrante delicto*. Why begin an affair in the presence of the detective hired to follow her? Perhaps Abby intends the detective to discover them, thinking his report will wound Marty. Perhaps she feels the need of a male protector now that she knows Marty won't let her be. We never learn; like many of the crucial turnings in this narrative, her motive remains a mystery.

In any event, Visser does bring incriminating photographs to a sullen Marty, who hadn't asked for them. The husband's unpleasant shiftiness contrasts interestingly with Visser's faux joviality and unashamed self-possession. None of the characters in *Blood Simple* is particularly sympathetic. The encounter with the smirking detective, who obviously relished observing the illicit couple's night of lovemaking, is yet another blow to the husband's pride, which has even more to suffer. The lovers return to town, and Ray confronts Marty, who tells him that Abby is in the habit of running off with other men, which is why he had her followed. Abby decides to move in with Ray, but Marty surprises her at his apartment one morning. The husband's attempted abduction fails, however, when Abby manages, with two swift and emasculating gestures, to, first, break his index finger and, then, kick him brutally in the groin. Marty vomits and slinks away before Ray, wakened by the noise, can confront him.

Unable to repossess Abby by force, Marty determines to destroy both her and Ray, hiring Visser for the job. But the detective, though tempted by the money he is offered, admits to some misgivings. What is to prevent Marty from going "simple" on him once blood is spilled? And why should he trust Marty not to betray him? It turns out later that Visser's suspicions are correct, but by then it no longer matters. Wary, Visser accepts the job and orders Marty to spend a few days at the coast in order to set up an alibi. Relishing the erstwhile lovers' imminent destruction, Marty suggests that the two may be disposed of in the huge furnace used for burning waste that sits behind his bar. The detective, however, has a different plan in mind. Once again, he takes photographs of a sleeping Ray and Abby, but this time he doctors the images to make it appear the couple has been shot dead. When Marty returns from his fishing trip, Visser goes to his office at the bar to show him proof of a job completed and collect his fee. He asks for the photograph back before quite suddenly shooting Marty with Abby's pistol, which he had earlier stolen. Apparently, he hopes to implicate her in the crime, from which only he will then profit. He leaves the gun on the office floor. This scheme will work, however, only if he has come away with the photograph and has left no trace of his presence. It turns out that he fails on both counts. Something, indeed, can always go wrong, as Marty might now agree with him.

Nothing, however, is quite what it seems. Before Marty can be discovered, Ray calls at his office, kicking Abby's gun with his foot (it fires, leaving only one of its three cartridges undischarged). Seeing Marty shot and apparently dead in his chair, Ray concludes that Abby must have killed him. He determines to clean up the crime scene so that her involvement will not be suspected, mopping the blood up with a satin jacket that only spreads it across the floor, and then loading the body into his car so that he can bury it in the desert. And so he does, but not before making a shocking discovery. Though obviously mortally wounded, Marty is not yet dead, and Ray proves unable to finish him off with a blow from his shovel. Instead, he buries the shrieking man alive. Horrified at his experience but understanding it as the inarguable proof of his deepening love for Abby, Ray calls her from a nearby gas station but finds no words to describe what he has done.

Later, when they are together, he manages: "I took care of everything." But Abby doesn't know what he is talking about. She asks him what happened. But he says that's not important, thinking Abby is simply asking for details. The selfless act Ray thought would cement their relationship begins through this misunderstanding to tear them apart, feeding suspicions about her promiscuity planted earlier in his mind by Marty. The phone rings; Abby picks it up. No voice can be heard. Abby thinks it must be Marty, as she tells Ray. Puzzled by what he believes must be a lie, Ray concludes that some other man is phoning Abby, as Marty had warned him would happen. The caller, in fact, is the now panicked detective, who has made two disturbing discoveries: that the envelope he thought had contained the photograph does not (Marty had hidden it in the safe, intending to use it against Visser); and that a cigarette lighter sporting his initials was left behind at the scene of the crime.

Visser breaks into Ray's apartment, rifles through Abby's tote bag, but does not find what he is looking for (the lighter? the photograph? some other clue to what is now happening?). Meanwhile, Ray's strange behavior has aroused Abby's suspicions; she goes to Mary's office, sees bloodstains on the floor, and finds a hammer, wrapped in a towel, that had apparently been used unsuccessfully to open Marty's safe. It was Visser who in fact made the attempt, thinking to recover his photograph. Abby concludes that Ray has killed Marty after she learns from another of Marty's employees that her husband had reported a good deal of money missing from the safe. He blamed Ray. This was to be Marty's explanation for the money he used to pay Visser. Ray, in turn, is convinced that Abby has betrayed him with someone else, and he makes preparations to leave town. Before he does so, however, he goes to the office once more, opens Marty's safe, and discovers the incriminating photograph, giving no indication that he understands what it means. He then goes to see Abby (to reconcile with her? to warn her of danger? to ask about the photograph?). What is the meaning of that glimpse of himself ostensibly lying dead? It must be that Ray has just seen what the future, the immediate future in fact, holds in store.

Walking into Abby's apartment that night, he warns her that the room has no curtains. He asks her to turn out the light, but she refuses (once again not understanding his meaning), and the detective, who had taken an apartment across the street, suddenly shoots Ray dead with a hunting rifle. What Visser intends is never made clear. Does he think that Ray and Abby have figured out his scheme to murder Marty and implicate them? Does he believe that if Ray and Abby are killed this will somehow shift any suspicion that the photograph and lighter might arouse if discovered? Has he concluded that Marty, whose body is gone when he returns to force open the safe, has survived long enough to engineer some plot against him, enlisting the help of Ray and Abby? Is he simply eager to retrieve the photograph and lighter, thinking that the lovers have somehow acquired them? Whatever his motive, Visser, with no little irony, finds himself attempting to do exactly what Marty had commissioned. But the job, which no longer requires simply shooting helpless sleepers, proves beyond him.

After Ray is killed, Abby shatters the ceiling lamp so that she cannot be shot in the same way, finally convinced of the wisdom of Ray's warning. Trapped, she awaits her attacker. As Visser reaches for her, she pulls a window down on his hand and impales it with a hunting knife. But Visser frees himself and comes looking for her. Abby finds her pistol, returned earlier to her by Ray, with one cartridge remaining (though she doesn't know the gun is almost empty). She then shoots Visser through the door before he can attack her. Hearing him grunt and the body fall, she defiantly shouts: "I ain't afraid of you, Marty." This final misunderstanding elicits a bitter laugh from the dying detective, who answers: "If I see him, ma'am, I'll sure give him the message."

Blood Simple was not the first film in the decade to draw on noir traditions in general, and the fiction of James M. Cain in particular, to construct a neo-noir "melodrama of mischance," to use Foster Hirsch's appropriate term for this subgenre, which emerged in the early 1980s to a popularity it still enjoys.[1] The film is traditional in many ways, not the least of which is its finely crafted narrative, with an Aristotelian inevitability linking events that are alternately motivated by the characters' sharp reading of others and the grossest forms of miscalculation. Yet *Blood Simple* also seems to reflect "the postmodern sensibility," an aesthetic that was emerging to prominence in the middle years of the decade. This was most obvious at the time, perhaps, in its resurrection of a classic Hollywood genre. One of the central elements of cinematic postmodernism is that such films take, as their object of representation, not the "real" or the "contemporary social scene," but the history of the cinema or other cultural forms. Postmodern films are often *about* other films. In their renovation of noir film and fiction, the Coens were anticipated by noirish productions of the Hollywood Renaissance in the

Abby (Frances McDormand) waits in the dark to
confront her unknown assailant in *Blood Simple*.
(Courtesy of the Academy of Motion Picture Arts
and Sciences)

early seventies, particularly Arthur Penn's *Night Moves* (1975) and Roman Polanski's *Chinatown* (1974). But the 1980s film that firmly established the popularity of what soon became known as neo-noir film was Lawrence Kasdan's *Body Heat* (1981), which was released while the Coens were finishing their own script.

Both films offer versions of the murderous violence, motivated by lust, greed, and mistrust, that is a central feature of Cain's most notorious novels. Like the Coens, Kasdan transplants his noir tale from its customary dark city setting. His lovers conspire and betray in an overheated Florida resort town. Interestingly, however, it was *Blood Simple*, with its use of the Southwestern desert as a setting, and not *Body Heat*, that would inspire a series of sincerely complimentary imitations: *The Hot Spot* (Dennis Hopper, 1990), *Red Rock West* (John Dahl, 1992), and *U-Turn* (Oliver Stone, 1997). All these films follow *Blood Simple* in relocating Cain's archetypal story of conscienceless violence to the spare inhospitality and anomie of the southwestern desert, with its small, hardly prosperous towns. Such settings are to be found in the crime fiction of Jim Thompson, an obvious literary influence the Coens somewhat disingenuously deny. The current revival of interest in Thompson's novels, such as *Pop. 1280*, also transferred to the screen in the 1980s, as the sensational French film noir *Coup de Torchon* (1981), may have something to do with the popularity of *Blood Simple*. In any event, few independent films achieve commercial and critical success *and* also find themselves admired enough within the industry to inspire a series of virtual remakes.

It is not hard to see why this happened. *Blood Simple* features a complex yet tightly woven and excitingly resolved narrative of marital infidelity, betrayal, frustrated affection, and brutal murder. Its intricate ballet of clashing motives and violent movement is driven not only by the recklessly destructive pursuit of illicit desire (Cain's principal theme), but also by the impenetrable mystery that is posed by the presence and intentions of other people. Abby has an affair with Ray out of desperation and loneliness, not, like Phyllis in *Double Indemnity*, because she intends to use an amoral insurance agent to get rid of her husband and claim his insurance benefits for herself alone, an end game that obliges her to get rid of this new lover. In *Blood Simple*, by way of contrast, the plotting and double plotting result in misunderstandings with dreadful and deeply ironic consequences, and these are motivated as often by good intentions as by *mauvaise foi*. In the end, there is little to choose, morally speaking, between violence coolly calculated and violence that is the accidental result of ghoulish farce, between, that is, Ray's gruesome silencing of Marty (in order to save Abby) and Visser's shooting of Ray (where self-preservation is the motive). The film's rough justice spares only Abby, who has no innocent blood on her hands, even though she is guilty of the betrayal and humiliation of Marty. The resolution is deeply ironic, a proof of the propositions about human life the detective had advanced at the film's beginning. Visser tries to kill Abby because he thinks she is trying to pin Marty's murder on him (she doesn't even know Marty is dead), and Abby shoots him in self-defense, mistaking him for her husband. Only Visser, dying, knows enough to recognize the absurdity of his situation, which is certainly worth a laugh, misidentity being, after all, one of comedy's most universal motifs.

These complexly intertwined themes—the unpredictability of human experience and the failed communications that render impossible any meaningful relations with others—are the contribution of the Coens to 1980s neo-noir. Even more original is the connection they make between violence and farce as forms of failure, which becomes the basis of their particular brand of black comedy, so pervasive a feature in their subsequent films. This rich, complex mix of motifs and tonalities is anticipated somewhat by Cain's narratives, where the adulterous couples successfully dispose of inconvenient husbands, then survive flawed legal proceedings that mock the justice system, only to have their own relationships destroyed by growing mutual distrust. In Cain's novels, however, the focus is on illicit sexuality and the machinations of a femme fatale, while the tone is resolutely serious, never darkly comic.

There is nothing in either novel that remotely resembles the final encounter between Ray and Marty, where the Coens follow the lead of Alfred Hitchcock, another director with a deep interest in the macabre and black humor. In his *Torn Curtain* (1966), a snooping East German agent proves spectacularly difficult to kill. In a sequence that borders on slapstick, his would-be dispatchers have to run through a variety of methods before finally finding one that works. Ray's experience is even more a series of misadventures, from his foolish decision to mop up blood with a satin jacket to his reticence about finishing Marty off with a shovel—but then, amazingly, deciding to bury the man alive. Like Hitchcock, the Coens emphasize suspenseful effects as Ray is in danger throughout, constantly risking discovery, while a reviving Marty even tries to shoot him at one point.

Thus, very much as in *Torn Curtain*, the sequence oscillates between riveting drama and the grimmest kind of humor, ending with a tableau (Ray stomping on the grave that contains a screaming man) straight out of a horror film. For such complex effects, it seems that the Coens also drew on the noir-shaded comedies of Preston Sturges (a deep influence on their entire body of work), particularly *Unfaithfully Yours* (1948). In that film, a jealous symphony conductor determines to kill the beautiful wife he mistakenly thinks has betrayed him, but he finds his preparations for an elaborate scheme frustrated by a series of misadventures, including his own clumsiness. The difference between the two films, however, is that in Sturges's dark vision of human possibility, frailty and good fortune prevent violence from ever being done. In *Blood Simple,* the body and blood are real, as is the suffering of a man suffocated by the dirt shoveled into his mouth. With the Coens, the very worst does happen, but even so it can be shown to have its funny side; black humor finds its source in the wreckage that can result from human imperfection.

The Coens alter Cain's sexual politics as well. Though a cheating wife, Abby is no manipulative woman, plotting to turn the men in her life into money. Marty is interested strictly in revenge, and so it is Visser who provides the narrative with its initial strange turn, as he tries to "earn" Marty's money and yet ensure his own safety by eliminating the husband and implicating Abby. Thus he can profit from a crime no one can hold him responsible for, in the manner of *Double Indemnity*'s scheming adulterers, he is eager to preserve appearances. In any event, such an emphasis on uncertainty and mystery proves typical of the stories the Coens choose to tell. In what we might, roughly speaking, call their comic and tragic forms, these two themes can be traced across the entire body of their film work.

Blood Simple also displays a technical excellence surprising for a debut film. It was expertly edited by the Coens themselves, with several sequences, including the memorable and pyrotechnic finale, featuring well-handled cross-cutting patterns as well as striking graphic matches. The action proceeds at a measured but relentless pace, as the narrative focus alternates among several characters, none of whom ever knows as much as the viewer, who is regularly provided the safe haven of dramatic irony. When suspense is appropriate, identification is enhanced by point-of-view editing in the Hitchcockian fashion, but more often the spectator is invited to view this black comedy of errors from an ironic distance. Such an unsympathetic approach to their characters became a hallmark of Coen films. Jon Lewis goes too far, perhaps, when he complains that "all their films are about stupid people."[2] This is, of course, an exaggeration—not all Coen characters are stupid, only most. It is true enough, however, that the Coens, in their cynicism and, perhaps, misanthropy, do often violate the canons of political correctness, but this is a charge to which satirists from Juvenal to Jonathan Swift to Joseph Heller must always plead guilty. In any case, we should not underestimate how interesting stupid people can be, especially when they exemplify important trends within American culture. *Blood Simple's* narrator, we should not forget, introduces a drama firmly rooted in a central feature of the American character, the imperative of self-determination.

Striking visual effects (some achieved with a technical innovation the brothers termed the shakycam, a camera supported on a board carried by two operators) are complemented by a bravura use of subjective sound in the fashion pioneered by Walter Murch in his "sound montages" for Francis Coppola's *The Conversation* and *Apocalypse Now* (there are shameless borrowings from the latter film). The spare mise-en-scène, making room only for symbolic detail in the Expressionist manner, cannily reflects the psychology and moral nature of the protagonists. Consider the final encounter between Marty and Visser. The sequence opens with a closeup of the fish Marty caught at the coast while establishing his alibi; they lie on his desk as a kind of offering that is never acknowledged or appreciated. As the financial arrangements of Visser's "murder for hire" are concluded, the fish serve as a correlative of the two lovers, supposedly murdered, and the two conspirators, locked in a deadly and mutually disagreeable embrace. After Marty is shot, the fish remain on the desk, rotting, to appear in the subsequent scenes in the office, a reminder of the killing of Marty by Visser and, unknown to him, Ray. The scoring is a striking blend of popular songs with an original, haunting piano melody from the music director, Carter Burwell. It offers an ironic, bittersweet comment on familiar genre conventions and, along with Barry Sonnenfeld's muted color cinematography, lends the film a distinct *stimmung*, or tonality, that nicely accords with film noir's stylistic roots in German Expressionism.

A Symptomatic Critical Response

It was not just the festivalgoers in New York who thought the film a minor masterpiece. *Blood Simple* also found eager admirers at a number of festivals that year, including Cannes, where foreign distribution deals were readily negotiated and signed as the brothers formed a company to handle this part of their burgeoning business. Meanwhile, in the United States, Circle Releasing (which already had arranged to handle other neophyte independents, like David Lynch) not only agreed to distribute the film, but also offered the brothers a deal they could hardly refuse. Circle would provide financing and distribution for their next two productions, over which they would have more or less complete artistic control, including script selection and the determination of the final cut. In January 1985, *Blood Simple* opened in selected American art houses, with quite surprising box office success, though not on a scale of later independent blockbusters like *The Blair Witch Project*. Wider release soon followed, as did a cable TV run, an unusual achievement for a production that had begun life as a mini-budget independent.

Perhaps even more significant, at the end of the year, the Coens' debut effort found itself on several top-ten lists, including that of the prestigious *Washington Post*. It was not the most substantial success, critical and popular, achieved by the first film of an independent director in the decade. That honor must go to Steven Soderbergh's *Sex, Lies, and Videotape*, released in 1989. But *Blood Simple* was a striking and memorable debut nonetheless. Critical opinion, however, was far from unanimous in its assessment of what the Coens had accomplished, which seemed to detractors an unwarranted and cynical commercialization and to enthusiasts a highly effective popularization of independent filmmaking. Reaction to the film is worth looking at in some detail. Reviews by Elliot Stein, Richard Corliss, and David Ansen, in fact, anticipated (perhaps even established) the terms of the debate over the value of their work that continues today.

In his commentary on *Blood Simple*, published as part of a larger evaluation of the various offerings at the New York festival, Elliot Stein suggests that the film was quite different, in both positive and negative ways, from the other independent films exhibited.[3] Most of these films, Stein maintains, conformed more closely to high-culture, modernist notions of what an independent film should be. Conventionally, independent filmmakers practice outside the mainstream, commercial institutions of studio production, in order to create films that are "artistic" in ways that the Hollywood feature film, with its necessary appeal to mass desires and tastes, cannot. Independent filmmaking, which is often explicitly autobiographical, foregrounds the idiosyncrasies of individual authorship. The films are usually "difficult," with narratives that are hard to follow or even bewildering, stylizations pushed to excess, and nearly impenetrable themes.

Independent film, at least stereotypically, thus contrasts markedly with the standard Hollywood product, which emphasizes spectacle (action, stars), easily followed narratives that are straightforwardly resolved, and transparent genre conventions. Such aesthetic differences, however, were certainly not evident in the case of *Blood Simple*, as Stein reports. In fact, audiences "cheered themselves hoarse" because this film was "considerably less rarefied" than those they had previously sat through. Tellingly, Stein characterizes these viewers as "dutiful," suggesting that more visceral pleasures were not something they normally expected to experience at such a festival. The other festival entries "moved like glue." They did not feature the suspenseful realism of *Blood Simple*, which had the effect of a "tonic" on the hitherto understimulated audience.

And yet, Stein condemns *Blood Simple* on the grounds of inauthenticity, finding it a cynical bid for promotion to more commercial forms of filmmaking. Thus, though slick and appealing, the film was not true art. It was hardly expressive of its authors' outlook and obsessions but rather an insignificant narrative that is "really about nothing so much as Coen's avidity to earn points on his first big studio project." The result is thus a "callous banality" that has been cobbled together from genre conventions gleaned from "Prof. Lawrence Kasdan's Film Noir 101 course." Even worse, the Coens have dressed up the emptiness of their story with stylistic excesses that are irrelevant and pointless. Stein fulminates about these at some length: "Amplified chunks of face are shoved up close to our dumbstruck gaze, prosaic household objects are given the fisheye and magically attain ominous connotations that don't mean anything in particular. . . . Most of this vacant virtuosity is what the American screen can't get enough, and emphatically doesn't need." With its quite calculated "commercial" trajectory, the film cannot truly be considered either "independent" or "artistic."

What can hardly be reconciled easily with Stein's evaluation, however, is that the film achieved an overwhelming success with an audience assembled for the purpose of viewing not commercial but rather independent films. And he identifies, I think, just those features that might have accounted for this enthusiastic reception among a self-selecting enthusiast elite. The most important of these is the conscious quotation/reuse of generic conventions from the classic American cinema. *Blood Simple* is what has traditionally been termed a crime thriller, but more crucial is its specific indebtedness to film noir, which is both a "type" of studio-era film and an important element in critical discourse about Hollywood practice. Also significant is the film's visual excess, by which I mean that its visual design is motivated not only by story, genre, or mise-en-scène. The film's bravura stylization is, as Stein suggests, the outward sign of self-consciousness, an advertisement of the authors' presence. Significantly, it is the one form of cinematic modernism that the Coens chose to exploit.

This aspect of the film is rather ambiguous, and Stein's comments are only one way in which it can be evaluated. It could be seen not as "showing off" but as the reflex of the Coens' desire to bestow distinctiveness on familiar materials handled on a very low budget (even the shakycam is a very low tech device). It could also be seen as the filmmakers' forswearing of self-effacing, illusionistic narration. Such rejection, in its most radical form, is a plea for pleasure in its own right, a sly wink to the viewer that this film recognizes that it is a film. In fact, it is easy to demonstrate that everything Stein condemns in *Blood Simple* could be valued differently, shaping a more favorable view of what the Coens had accomplished as *engagé,* sophisticated, and above any simple pandering to presumably vulgar popular tastes. Stein's reaction, of course, is itself not without contradictions. At first he describes *Blood Simple* as a film with interesting and affecting differences, but then he condemns what is most distinctive about it as a "vacant virtuosity."

His hesitation, I suggest, shows how carefully the film negotiates between notions of the commercial, on the one hand, and "independent artistry," on the other. The result is that it fits neatly in neither category. *Blood Simple* is best described as a commercial/independent film, a particular form of postmodern cinema that complexly intersects and deconstructs the contrast between high culture and mass culture. Like the nine releases that have followed it, *Blood Simple* was calculated to appeal to the young, hip, "knowing" spectator whose tastes, like those of the Coens themselves, run the gamut from popular cinema and television to the art films of honored European auteurs. It finds its content in the first and its penchant for technical virtuosity in the latter. We may imagine that the audiences who raved over the film at New York and the other festivals that year found such a combination intriguing.

Joel and Ethan Coen have forged a successful career for nearly two decades making commercial/independent films of this kind, thus fueling a continuing debate over the value of their oeuvre, for they cannot be assimilated easily either to standard commercial filmmaking or to contemporary art cinema. Are their hybrid productions exercises in a "vacant virtuosity" further compromised by the filmmakers' cynical, perhaps even misogynistic and politically incorrect view of their characters, most of whom, no doubt, are mentally underpowered and morally challenged? Interestingly, or regrettably, according to your point of view, the Coens' characters are usually regional and ethnic stereotypes, whose predictable quirks are not treated gently. If they abjure political correctness, the Coens are, however, committed to a kind of rough equity. Though they are Jewish themselves, their list of targets pointedly does not exclude Jewish ones, and for this the Coens have been roundly criticized by the humor police.

Have these talented brothers, obviously wise in the ways of the cinema, achieved something notable? If so, is their achievement to offer in more accessible and conventional form, shaped by a distinctive artistic vision, the stylistic, thematic, and narrative complexity hitherto associated mainly with art-house offerings? Are these films to be appreciated because of their cynical, often blackly humorous commentary on what they portray as the everyday, even commonplace violence of contemporary American culture? In his survey of contemporary American independent production, Geoff Andrew declares the brothers who came from Minnesota, were signed up by Hollywood, and live in New York to be "among the most exciting, adventurous, and original film-makers working in the American cinema." Their strength, as my account of *Blood Simple* should at least suggest, is "a tendency to structure the films around repetitions, paradoxes, symmetries and doubles, so that each movie may be seen as a series of imaginatively executed variations upon the same theme." In Andrew's view, their oeuvre betrays a "consistent philosophy of human experience."[4] It seems there is much truth in this. I would add only that many of the themes in their films, like the noir traditions on which they draw, find a resonance with central ideas of existentialism (particularly, the encounter with the absurd and the leap into faith). The sections that follow will emphasize how deeply their films engage with such issues, offering a riposte to those critics who think their films to be much ado about nothing. Undeniably, however, no other body of work produced in the New Hollywood era has been met with such a divergent reception from audiences and critics alike.

Thus Elliot Stein's ambivalent response to *Blood Simple* is not idiosyncratic but symptomatic. Read within the traditional framework of conventions, values, and expectations called into play by the concept of "independent film," the Coens' debut film is likely to be judged unsuccessful. For the Coens have selected from the menu of modernist/postmodernist techniques available to them only those that can easily be accommodated to the tastes of a broader, commercial audience. The film's narrative and narration, for example, only appear to offer difficulties of interpretation. Though some mysteries remain in regard to the characters' motivations, the complex plot at least gives the appearance of tying everything together quite neatly in the end. And though the Coens often eschew some of the principles of traditional Hollywood continuity, such as the use of establishing shots, the film's narration always supplies enough information to orient the viewer without more than momentary confusion. The film's visual and aural stylizations, though often flamboyant, primarily serve to create a mood of unfamiliarity and mystery that complements the main themes of the narrative.

Operating with many of the same assumptions about cinematic value as Stein, Richard Corliss evaluates *Blood Simple* quite differently. The film would have been "the same old song" had the Coen brothers not managed to "subvert" the conventions of film noir and thereby "revitalize" them. This subversion, he implies, is accomplished largely through the stylization that, in the modernist fashion, flaunts its presence and virtuosity; the camera here is "worlds hipper than anyone on screen" and is therefore able to create "elegant riddles of space and time," which it then "solves with an originality that hits the viewer like a rabbit punch." Interestingly, Corliss calls attention to the ways in which the film's plot diverges from generically conventional patterns, concluding that film noir is here "stripped down to its basics . . . then customized with camera style."[5]

The sound track features the Four Tops 1960s release "It's the Same Old Song," which is then reprised quite self-consciously over the closing credits, underscoring the filmmakers' "knowing" reuse of cultural materials. Corliss's mention of subversion is an argument for the film's value in terms of modernist practice. If this text is repetitive, generic, and conventional, then to be valuable it must rework and transform these inherited elements into something different and unexpected. And such transformation is what Corliss thinks that the Coens have accomplished, with what he calls a "whirligig wit." But for this reviewer the film offers something more: an enjoyable viewing experience in the emotional rather than intellectual sense of commercial Hollywood, for "it infiltrates the central nervous system even as it opens the cultist's sharp eye." *Blood Simple* thus proffers a double pleasure: a realist story that engages the average viewer's interest in what will happen next and a commentary, elegantly cynical, that pleases the "cultist" eager for intellectual arousal.

Though much more positive in the final analysis, Corliss, like Stein, betrays a certain ambivalence about the film: "*Blood Simple* has plenty of flash—the kind of cinema virtuosity that can be over praised precisely because it is so difficult to describe. Just as easily, the movie can be underrated as a film school exercise." The word "flash" signifies the empty manipulations of Hollywood spectacle more than the provocative stylizations of modernist practice, while the term "film school exercise" indexes the critic's uncertainty about both the talent and the vision of university-trained directors. Corliss might be referring to one of many well-known visual *tours*, perhaps the forward tracking camera shot that, scanning a late-night saloon, moves up and over a patron sprawled unconscious on the bar.

Some reviewers, however, took little notice of such self-reflexive moments and simply praised *Blood Simple* for its superior entertainment qualities. David Ansen, for example, termed it a "maliciously entertaining murder story," poised, with effective ambivalence, between two genres: "It's at once a bated-breath thriller and a comedy as black as they come. Its humor, however, emerges only because the actors never let on that there is anything remotely preposterous about the wild melodrama in which they are enmeshed."[6] Ignoring the extent to which stylistic commentary produces this comic effect, Ansen instead attributes it to both "a brilliant, fiendishly complex plot" and an astute use of dramatic irony—"only we know who's murdering whom and why, and that's part of the joke." Ansen's review is intriguing because he evaluates *Blood Simple* strictly according to the standards of the effective commercial film. There's exciting action, "narrative precision," some sophisticated humor, good acting from a largely unknown cast, and "clean, eerily spare cinematography." For Ansen, the Coens are an "off-Hollywood" team, by which I suppose he means that, lacking proper financial support, they were forced to make what is essentially a commercial film for less money than the studios do. The notion of independent filmmaker in the traditional, "artistic" sense doesn't figure in this review at all.

The divergent response to *Blood Simple,* and to the nine films they have since released, *can* be traced, as I have said, to what some have identified as the Coens' "postmodern sensibility," a central feature of which is said to be the transgression of the boundary between high and low culture. If the mixture of hitherto distinct art forms is a central feature of the postmodernist aesthetic, then something along the lines of the generically ambivalent commercial/independent film is what one would expect. Here is a film that, with its existentialist themes, reconfigures film noir's preoccupation with misogyny and sexual transgression, providing the genre with a different form of seriousness. And yet the Coens also emphasize bloodcurdling spectacle (a man buried alive, a white-gloved hand impaled by a hunting knife). These effects seem designed for more popular appeal, invoking the era's most profitable "low" genre, the horror film. The brothers' interesting engagement with postmodernism will be considered more fully further below. Yet it is not only an aesthetic choice that defines the ambivalent position of the Coens within the contemporary film industry. No doubt, they are more "in" than "of" Hollywood, consistently disdainful of any expectations that they play the role of "serious" established director and writer.

But, it should be emphasized, they are not the only contemporary filmmakers who have found themselves drawn to commercial/independent practice. To be sure, however, they are the most consistent practitioners of the form. Consider the career of Steven Soderbergh. He has likewise achieved some notable success with commercial/independent films, not only the famous *Sex, Lies, and Videotape* (1989), but also, more recently, *The Limey* (1999), which perpetuates, yet redefines, noir conventions in the manner of *Blood Simple*. Unlike that of the Coens, however, Soderbergh's oeuvre also includes traditional art films of different types. His *Kafka* (1991) is a kind of postmodernist biopic, a strange mixture of accurate historical reconstruction (Soderbergh's Franz is quite accurately drawn, as is the Prague of the writer's youth) and fabulous fiction, with Kafka stumbling into strange, macabre adventures of persecution and obsession that, one is meant to suppose, might have then led him to write *The Castle* and *The Trial*. *Gray's Anatomy* (1997), in stark contrast, is a kind of documentary, a filmed record of a long monologue, sometimes dramatized, delivered by the American raconteur Spalding Gray, who took as his main theme his sufferings from, and unusual attempts at healing, a rare eye disease. But, rather surprisingly for many of his admirers, Soderbergh has also devoted much time and energy to resolutely mainstream star vehicles: *Erin Brockovich* (2000), *Ocean's Eleven* (2001), and *Solaris* (2002). Or consider David Lynch, whose career has veered from surrealist art film in the tradition of Buñuel and Cocteau (*Eraserhead,* 1976) to a quite mainstream Hollywood period piece (*The Elephant Man,* 1980) and even a prime-time TV series, a kind of postmodern mystery drama (*Twin Peaks,* 1989–91). Despite obvious divergences in style and theme, Lynch's most notable release, *Blue Velvet* (1986), is a commercial/independent crime film similar in many ways to both *The Limey* and *Blood Simple*. Like several of the Hollywood Renaissance filmmakers, a number of the independent directors of the contemporary cinema share an interest in film noir.

Compared with the works of their most noted contemporaries, however, what differentiates the oeuvre of the Coen brothers from that of Lynch or Soderbergh is its consistency. They have made no star vehicles as such and have resisted, *The Hudsucker Proxy* excepted, the temptation to make bigger-budget productions with name actors that would of necessity therefore be less personal and over which they could exercise less control. Significantly, *The Man Who Wasn't There* also resurrects and revitalizes noir film and fiction conventions. Though quite distinct stylistically, it is a film that evidences the same themes and "personality" as *Blood Simple*. Commercial/independent filmmaking has been a striking feature of the Hollywood scene since the 1980s, with a substantial number of well-known practitioners. A short list of notables would include Spike Lee, Susan Seidelman, George Romero, Alan Rudolph, Quentin Tarantino, Henry Jaglom, and Jim Jarmusch. Because the Coen brothers are, in a very loose sense, part of a movement, understanding their accomplishment requires some broader consideration of American filmmaking, especially of the independent variety, during the last two decades. A brief exploration of that history has the added advantage of shedding more light on the evaluative controversies that continue to surround their work.

Notes

1. Foster Hirsch, *Detours and Lost Highways: A Map of Neo-Noir* (New York: Limelight, 1999), devotes a chapter to "melodramas of mischance," 211–50.

2. Jon Lewis, "The Coen Brothers" in *Fifty Contemporary Filmmakers,* ed. Yvonne Tasker (New York: Routledge, 2002), 112.

3. Elliot Stein, *Film Comment* 20 (November–December 1984): 67. All subsequent quotations are from this same page.

4. Geoff Andrew, *Stranger Than Paradise: Maverick Film-Makers in Recent American Cinema* (New York: Limelight, 1999), 165.

5. Richard Corliss, *Time,* January 28, 1985, 304. Subsequent quotations from Corliss's article are from the same page.

6. David Ansen, *Newsweek,* January 21, 1985, 71. Subsequent quotations from Ansen's article are from the same page.

2. The Coen Brothers: Postmodern Filmmakers

Hollywood is a generic cinema, which is not quite the same as saying that it is a cinema of genres.

—Richard Maltby

The 1980s, some film historians suggest, was a decade of artistic regression for Hollywood, a disappointing coda to the industry's surprising revival from incipient cultural obsolescence and financial collapse during the 1970s. This decline from what has been widely thought a new beginning or "renaissance" of Hollywood as a central cultural institution was, so the standard argument runs, occasioned by economic changes within the film industry. The most notable of these was the accelerating commitment on the part of major studios to a policy of globalization that was most profitably advanced by lowest-common-denominator blockbuster filmmaking. In such films, spectacle and action took precedence over the complexities of character, theme, or style. But the different industry that emerged during the 1980s was not to be explained solely by an altered business plan. Also important was a profound ideological shift within American society, which had taken a pronounced turn toward the right-wing position espoused by Ronald Reagan, whose landslide election in 1980 to the presidency of the United States solidified this widespread change of political sentiment.

Hollywood in the 1980s and 1990s

Whatever the causes, the beginning of the new decade saw a retreat, which many supposed was quite thoroughgoing, from the thematically and stylistically rich filmmaking of the Hollywood Renaissance, roughly datable from the *succès de scandale* that greeted Arthur Penn's iconoclastic *Bonnie and Clyde* in 1967 to the mixed reaction accorded Francis Coppola's extravagant epic *Apocalypse Now* in 1979. While for the most part studio-financed and -distributed productions, such films were independent in the sense that they offered critical reflections not only on American society but on the traditions of Hollywood filmmaking, even as they adopted much of the countercultural spirit and many of the striking stylizations of the European art cinema, with a special nod to the writers/directors of the French New Wave.

With some oversimplification that will require nuance below, the change from one decade to the next can be traced in the dominant characters of the two eras' films and the quite distinct journeys of self in which they are caught up. The archetypal protagonists of 1970s renaissance cinema are alienated outsiders whose attempts to find some moral center or authentic way of living characteristically fail, the result of their own weakness (moral, physical, or psychological) and of the flawed institutions of American culture: Travis Bickle in *Taxi Driver* (1976), Joe Buck and Ratso Rizzo in *Midnight Cowboy* (1969), Harry Caul in *The Conversation* (1974), Lenny Bruce in *Lenny* (1974), all the characters in any Robert Altman film.[1] But these questing, unsatisfied loners achieve an at least symbolic revenge and deliverance in the mainstream films of the following decade. In productions whose project seems in part a cultural revisionism, such antiheroes are displaced by the decade's Rockies and Rambos, who, though also suffering from either an inchoate dissatisfaction with life or a disillusionment with the state of American society, do not end up as marginalized outsiders. Changing social values helped shape a different kind of narrative in which such characters might find redemption.

The stories that mainstream cinema came to tell in the 1980s are in many ways throwbacks to classic Hollywood. They often find their moral center in a Horatio Algerism that valorizes hard work, endurance, and resolution, tracing a reformatory passage to psychic and civic wholeness that reenacts the foundational American myth of self-fashioning. We might say that the lonely protagonist of renaissance cinema suddenly finds his energies and anger directed toward an unexpected and righteous transformation, as he becomes an unconquerable defender of American values. Elevated to near mythic status, he finds himself charged with the vindication and rectification of national weakness. At first opposing him are the callous, impermeable institutions of American society, exemplified by the corrupt world of big-time boxing and the petty intolerance of small-town life, with its indifference toward the sufferings of strangers. The temporary defeat of these institutions in the original *Rocky* (1976) and *First Blood* (1982) offers their protagonists but a partial restoration of integrity, which is nothing less than the incomplete satisfaction of not losing.

But later entries in these two "franchises" bring these characters full transcendence. Urgent national need summons the aging palooka (in *Rocky IV*, 1985) and the former war hero (in *Rambo First Blood Part II*, also 1985) to abandon their obscurity and irrelevance. Rocky and Rambo embark upon rigorous programs of self-reclamation that fortify them for apocalyptic struggles against the Soviet Union and its allies, who prove cunning, powerful, but finally vulnerable foes. Both characters are played by a heavily muscled Sylvester Stallone, who became the very image of the reclaimed national self that was invoked by Reagan. From this point of view, Rocky and Rambo are "remasculinized" versions of their less traditionally male (that is weaker, more voluble and more sensitive) counterparts in 1970s cinema, as the cultural critic Susan Jeffords has observed.[2] Their mute inexpressiveness speaks volumes, epitomizing the black/white moral simplifications of a renewed cold war. Presided over on the national stage by an actor from the classic studio era, this struggle seemed to require Americans and America to be represented as powerful, resolute, and united. Such films exulted in the righteous violence so prominent in many of the classic studio productions of the chief executive's Hollywood career (e.g., *Santa Fe Trail, International Squadron,* and *Desperate Journey*).

In contrast, the feckless and unsatisfied protagonists of Coen brothers films inhabit an America where, as Visser says, everyone is "on their own." In their more serious narratives, the schemes of such characters for self-improvement, for some salvation from troubles familial, financial, or psychological, come to nothing as something inevitably "always goes wrong." If in spite of failure and mischance they do achieve transcendence (most do not), it is not because their experience is somehow archetypal, a reenactment of that "regeneration through violence" Richard Slotkin has identified as a central national myth.[3] Visser's attempt to transform Marty's rage into safe profit comes to nothing. Mischance defeats him at every turn, in the end denying him even the right to his own identity when he is shot down as "the wrong man." Yet with a bitter laugh and an acknowledgement, perhaps, of his own damnation Visser manages to surmount, if not master, this unexpected turn of events. In partial contrast, the loner protagonists in the Coens' more comic films sometimes win through to a kind of happy ending, whose completeness is undermined in some fashion. They become reconciled to dissatisfaction. Capable, at best, only of ironized victories, the protagonists in Coen brothers films are perhaps best seen as the "others" of the Rambos and Rockies of the decade. Productions like *Blood Simple* offer a return, albeit in a more cynical vein and in a more marginalized area of the industry, to the questioning of cultural certainties that gave so much intellectual force and enduring value to the principal films of the Hollywood Renaissance.

The demise of that movement as a mainstream form of filmmaking has been thought mostly to be the result of large-scale economic and cultural changes, which found their joint reflex in those blockbuster productions whose avoidance of sophistication both thematic and stylistic brought them widespread acceptance in the international marketplace. But villains have also been identified within the ranks of those Hollywood directors, who, during the period, began to think of themselves more as artists or auteurs than as craftsmen. The perhaps indulgent commitment of unprecedented control over all aspects of production to this generation of self-conceived American auteurs doubtless led to the making of films that would have been inconceivable within the more rigidly controlled system of financing and distribution, on the one hand, and storytelling conventions, on the other, that had prevailed throughout the 1950s and 1960s.

The Godfather (1972), *M.A.S.H* (1970), *Taxi Driver* (1976), and *A Clockwork Orange* (1971), to name only a few of the period's notable productions, benefited from a new openness to the penetrating exploration of social themes in the manner of European filmmaking, whose intellectual complexity and stylistic flourish were much admired and imitated by an emerging generation of directors: Arthur Penn, Martin Scorsese, Francis Coppola, Stanley Kubrick, Hal Ashby, and Robert Altman chief among them. The path to directorial self-expression that they followed had been blazed by the unexpected success not only of *Bonnie and Clyde* (1967), but also of *Easy Rider* (1969) and *The Graduate* (1967), all three more or less small-scale productions whose box office popularity contrasted markedly with the disappointing earnings of the period's blockbuster productions.

At the end of the decade, however, this investment in independently minded directors seemed more folly than wisdom, as Coppola's *Apocalypse Now* (1979) and Michael Cimino's *Heaven's Gate* (1980) proved to be disastrously runaway projects. While Coppola's film, despite seemingly interminable shooting delays and monstrous budget overruns, probably turned a small profit and did garner much critical attention and praise, *Heaven's Gate* was an unmitigated disaster. The projected budget of $7.5 million swelled, under Cimino's doubtful stewardship, to more than $35 million, but the film took in only $1.3 million in its first week of exhibition; it could not be saved by further tinkering and a subsequent release. Both films had been financed by United Artists, which found itself ruined by this joint debacle; it was soon sold by its parent company, Transamerica, to MGM.

The auteurs of the 1970s, no doubt, in some sense overreached. United Artists' demise was replicated soon afterward by the bankruptcy of Coppola's Zoetrope Studios, which was to have provided an alternative to the conventional restrictions of mainstream studio production. Coppola's ambitious project received a deathblow from the director's commercially miscalculated *One from the Heart* (1982), where once again production expenses did not suit the "small" film's potential for earning. These failures are often contrasted with the success that greeted the films of another cadre of young directors, whose most important representatives were Steven Spielberg and George Lucas. They developed what has proved a more predictably popular and profitable model for filmmaking success, which in its strict adherence to classic conventions and conservative politics provided the model for the Rambo and Rocky series. *Raiders of the Lost Ark* (1981) and *Star Wars* (1977) eschewed the cultural engagement and stylistic preciosity of films like *Taxi Driver* and *Nashville* (1975), choosing as their models not the classics of the European art cinema but the film serials of the classic studio era.

Such was their popularity with an audience susceptible to the infantilizing appeal of nonstop action, two-dimensional characters, and heart-thumping spectacle that these two films were easily transformed into franchises whose sequels proved extraordinarily successful during the 1980s and after. If *Star Wars* and *Raiders of the Lost Ark* can be said to engage in politics, it is that they evoke both the antifascism of the World War II era (thematized most directly in the case of the Spielberg film, whose villains are Nazis bent on cultural theft) and the anticommunism of its immediate aftermath. Significantly, President Reagan drew quite self-consciously upon the totalitarian villains of the *Star Wars* cycle for the metaphor of the "evil empire" that he used to characterize a similarly expansionist and confrontational Soviet Union.

It is certainly true that many of the Renaissance directors did not fare well in the 1980s because of changed economic and cultural conditions. So dominant in the previous decade, Coppola became a director for hire, many of whose films met with no or limited commercial success. Robert Altman found it impossible to acquire major studio financing for any of his projects and was reduced for a time to making low-budget filmed theater. The careers of Hal Ashby and Arthur Penn declined. And yet the commitment to blockbuster filmmaking and the franchising that is hugely profitable in ancillary markets (toys, theme parks, computer games) did not eliminate other forms of filmmaking, including the development of commercial/independent productions (a result in part of the expanding influence of film school training and film festivals). It is here that something of the Hollywood Renaissance found renewed voice and energy. The Coens may be seen as an important part of that collective initiative.

Independent Filmmaking in Contemporary Hollywood

The case has often been made, in fact, that the 1980s was a period that offered independent directors unparalleled access to commercial exhibition.[4] In part, this was a reflex of an expanding "delivery system" for film. The decade saw an increase in theatrical screens, as the mall multiplex replaced the single-screen downtown cinema, while ancillary markets grew substantially because video and cable television provided additional forms of release. The result was something of a content shortage that the major studios, their money tied up in limited slates of blockbuster and moderate-budget productions, could not easily satisfy on their own. In this context, which was receptive to an infusion of money, talent, and energy from outside, what seems great wisdom is the decision of the Coens to make small-budget films of an easily identifiable kind over which, because of their track record for consistency within the industry, they proved able to retain almost complete control. The Coens have been able to achieve on a smaller scale the independence from studio interference that Francis Coppola had wanted on a much grander one. Independent filmmakers like them offered distributors both the talent and productive capacity that could be exploited with minimal commitment. Hence they could be left to make films on their own terms.

At the end of the decade, the attractiveness of independently made films to the major players in the industry was nowhere more obvious than in the feeding frenzy that greeted the successful exhibition of *Sex, Lies, and Videotape* at the 1989 Sundance Festival. Nine distributors bid for rights to an admittedly unfinished production with a temporary soundtrack. The director, Steven Soderbergh, eventually signed with the then fledgling company Miramax, and a film that had been made—including prints and advertising costs—for only $1.2 million grossed in excess of $100 million in worldwide distribution. Greg Merritt suggests that *Sex, Lies, and Videotape* "proved to be the perfect movie to expand the art-house audience of cineastes into a broader base of literate adults."[5] To many, the film seemed a "polished, upscale conversation piece," following the path blazed by, among other indie hits of the decade, the Coens' *Blood Simple*.

The boom in independent production, however, predates Soderbergh's spectacular success with his debut film. In the early years of the decade, for the reasons just mentioned, there was a huge increase in independent releases, judging simply by films that received an MPAA rating (these figures do not include the many productions, especially in the horror genre, that went straight to video release, so the actual number is substantially higher). There were 206 rated indies released in 1983, already a huge number in comparison with that of most years in the preceding decade, but this figure had swollen to 316 by 1988, more than a 50 percent increase in only five years. By the 1990s, a number of the distribution companies specializing in independent films had gone under, including Circle, which had been crucial in handling the early films of the Coens. But independent filmmaking, like the brothers themselves, has continued to prosper as now firmly established companies (like Working Title, which has distributed some of the Coens' more recent films) took control over the marketplace.

The career of the Coens developed in this congenial industrial context. But these favorable circumstances explain only in part why they have continued to find financing even though, of their ten releases to date, only *Fargo* and *O Brother Where, Art Thou?* have enjoyed more than modest box office success (*Fargo* grossed in the neighborhood of $25 million, and *O Brother* a little less than twice that, but this is still a far cry from the much more substantial take of *Sex, Lies, and Videotape* and the similarly huge profits of the micro-budget 1998 release *The Blair Witch Project*). The success of the Coens has much to do with the content of their films, not just their limited budgets. At the beginning of the 1980s, the art-house market was dominated by two types of domestic productions: traditional art cinema on the genteel European model, especially worshipful, serious adaptations of esteemed literary classics (an area in which the writing-directing team of Merchant-Ivory long held sway); and edgier productions in the modernist-postmodernist vein that often engaged interestingly with popular, as opposed to literary, culture. Along with directors such as David Lynch, Quentin Tarantino, Spike Lee, and Jim Jarmusch who have also maintained a cynical distance from Hollywood even while making commercially financed and distributed films, Joel and Ethan Coen helped ensure the predominance of this second kind of art cinema. Like the films of Lynch and Tarantino in particular, the Coens' works manifest a recognizable and idiosyncratic style (in the largest sense of the term) and thus issue a consistent, if not always very broad, appeal to niches within the film-going audience. To put it another way, the Coens are most definitely a name brand of note on the contemporary scene.

But does this kind of filmmaking have any real value? My view, shared by many others, is that their films are interesting and worthy because they continue (on a smaller scale and with a cynicism and distanced tone that are part and parcel of the postmodernist sensibility) the critique of American society and its national cinema begun during the Hollywood Renaissance. A number of prominent critics find fault with this judgment, offering a quite different interpretation of the history I have traced in this section.

Most notable, perhaps, is the schema developed some years ago by Pauline Kael to describe the evolution of serious American cinema since the 1970s.[6] Kael's view is that the emergence to prominence of independent cinema figures as nothing less than a regrettable fall from grace. She finds no significant connection between independent filmmakers such as the Coens and those who emerged to success in the 1970s, such as Martin Scorsese and Robert Altman. During the Hollywood Renaissance, the "third-generation auteurs," to use Kael's term, pioneered the adoption of art cinema techniques and filmmaking principles from the European art cinema of the 1940s and 1950s. Their project, which met with a great deal of success, was inaugurating a critical reexamination of classical Hollywood, its genres and their underlying cultural mythology. In the process, this generation created a politically engaged form of American cinematic modernism, in the tradition of directors and theorists such as Jean-Luc Godard and Bertolt Brecht. These achievements were short-lived, however, being first undermined and then displaced by the reversion to traditional Hollywood filmmaking led by the film school–trained movie brats of the next wave.

In Kael's view, Spielberg and Lucas took a step backward, if with reverence and faux seriousness, to the most simple-minded of classic forms, the despised genres of outer space and wartime adventure serials. Theirs was a cinema of entertainment, not enlightenment. It is thus not a changed politics that characterizes this group of filmmakers, but a different conception of the cinema's function. This wave succeeded mainly (if not exclusively, for Spielberg at least also tried his hand at art film in such productions as *Empire of the Sun*) in infantilizing the mainstream American audience. To this end, they promoted a meaningless cinema of affect that featured figures (easily turned into marketable toys) drawn from cartoons, comic books, juvenile fiction, and the earth's biological past. As Jim Hoberman, echoing Kael's analysis, has observed, the "spiritual father" of this wave of filmmakers is not Godard but Walt Disney, who was "the first to saturate America systematically with cultural trademarks, to fabricate a world that was better than nature (even as he denatured one childhood 'classic' after another)."[7]

Kael, however, reserves her greatest scorn for the current generation of independent filmmakers, including the Coens, for whose work she, like Hoberman, shows a special dislike. Kael does not doubt the love of these enthusiasts for films, especially those from Hollywood, and she does find impressive their encyclopedic knowledge, which is the reflex both of formative years saturated in moving images and of college film courses. She complains, however, that the films of these directors are all flash and no substance. Such productions, morally speaking, are even worse than infantilizing entertainment. They are merely pointless deconstructions or hybridizations of familiar generic categories, art objects that become, in Hoberman's phrase, "lost in a hall of mirrors." They offer no engagement with the "real" or with "history," but simply make a string of allusions that entertain the knowledgeable, if intellectually shallow, aficionados of film in the younger generation. This is the hallmark of postmodernism, and, to quote Hoberman once again, it is merely "a form of Trivial Pursuit, used to connote the past or provide a sense of pseudo-historical depth."[8]

The advent of postmodernism provoked the dismay of many cultural critics, notably Fredric Jameson, whose nostalgia for the "solidity" of modernism much influenced the judgments of Kael and Hoberman. But such dismissal of its significance is hardly universal. As we shall see, negative judgments of postmodern artists like the Coens have not gone unchallenged by those who appreciate the creative reworking of received forms. A film like *Blood Simple* is, as the filmmakers' knowing musical commentary suggests, "the same old song," but it does have a "different meaning." We now turn to a consideration of how within the postmodern aesthetic of the Coens such a "different meaning" can in fact be achieved.

Film Noir's Useful Duplicity

The Hollywood phenomenon known as film noir (as well as its literary counterpart, and often source, the American *roman noir*) provides a useful starting point for an examination of how Coen brothers films characteristically engage with the films of classic Hollywood, which, as they have often stated, they consider their cinematic inheritance. The Coens' self-conscious insertion within the continuing history of this most discussed of studio types, however, is no merely playful recycling of established forms. In fact, their oeuvre betrays a serious fascination with the film noir (and with the vision of American life it communicates), and this fascination forges a substantial link between the Coens and the filmmakers of the Hollywood Renaissance, giving the lie to the discontinuous pattern of degeneration Pauline Kael says characterizes the history of the American cinema in the last three decades. Despite obvious differences, films like Martin Scorsese's *Taxi Driver,* Arthur Penn's *Night Moves* (1975), and Francis Coppola's *The Godfather* bear comparison with *Blood Simple, Miller's Crossing, Fargo,* and *The Man Who Wasn't There.* All belong to the diverse and now more than three-decades-long movement usually termed neo-noir.

Properly understanding this aspect of the Coens' accomplishment can perhaps best begin with the recognition that what we call film noir actually plays two distinct if complementary roles within cinema culture. The films themselves often thematize betrayal and double-dealing, even as they ironically juxtapose different social milieux and moral visions. And the genre (now an uneasy mix of two periods of production, classic and neo) is itself fundamentally duplicitous, a counterpoising of popular texts and art film values, unstably suspended between the "low" and the "high." Film noir figures, first, as the unnamed (at the time in America) collective site of certain textual features and contextual forces within 1940s and 1950s cinema; and, second, as the critically formed category of reading/appreciation of that body of film that took definitive shape in France during the middle 1950s and was introduced to American journalistic and academic film criticism in the late 1960s by Andrew Sarris, who also, and this is not without significance, was largely responsible for popularizing what he called "the auteur theory" in the Anglo-American critical world. Within film scholarship, these two aspects of film noir—that is, roughly speaking, the films themselves and their later critical classification and evaluation—are often collapsed. But we must separate them here.

On the one hand, film noir circulates in cinema culture as an unidentified set of conventional Hollywood elements most often talked about in terms of genres (e.g., the "hard-boiled" detective film, the thriller, the crime romance). As such, this set of elements can be used to establish a generic contract with contemporary film viewers in general and aficionados of classic Hollywood cinema in particular. In fact, many viewers, including those eager only for entertainment, find themselves very much attuned, if largely unconsciously, to conventions such as these because of the continual recirculation of classic Hollywood films on television and video. This notion of film noir, an aspect of popular discourse about and consciousness of film genres, can be used to set up a text's readability. In other words, an invocation of this tradition can ease the understanding, and thus increase the enjoyment, of a film that might otherwise present difficulties or impediments in terms of narrative, style, or theme. Throughout the New Hollywood period (from the 1970s renaissance to the films that Pauline Kael terms the "third wave"), genres derived from the studio era have been used in this way. It is easy to identify their appeal, for they offer post-studio filmmakers a readymade set of coordinates for texts that can then respectfully repeat, cannibalize, transform, or subvert those conventions in some fashion, thus utilizing the "already said" to say something new. Such a preoccupation with genericity, of course, is even, perhaps most especially, true for the "infantilizing" blockbusters of the 1970s and 1980s. Spielberg's *Raiders of the Lost Ark,* for example, can be enjoyed on the level of spectacle and nonstop action, but also in reference to the norms of 1940s war adventure serials, which, with self-conscious irony, it often amusingly subverts in the process of recycling them.

In its other, critical sense, film noir is a much more complex phenomenon, an element of "taste" that affects filmic practice only in a *post facto* fashion. Originally a description of some French Poetic Realist films of the 1930s, the category was later invoked by postwar French journalists as a criterion of value to guide the appreciation of the American cinema. Here was a means of distinguishing certain "artistic" productions of 1940s Hollywood from the commercial nonart usually churned out by the studios. As such, film noir was a critical formulation not dissimilar to the *politique des auteurs,* another criterion of "taste" that valorized certain Hollywood films. It is hardly coincidental that a number of the French New Wave critics/directors who, so to speak, put the *politique des auteurs* in practice (most notably, François Truffaut and Jean-Luc Godard) also evidenced a fascination with noir, in its literary as well as cinematic forms. We may, without exaggeration, say that they thus inaugurated, if only implicitly, a *politique des genres.*

For these French students of American cinema, film noir, perhaps inevitably, became associated with modernist practice, and this revisionism was taken up by French-influenced American directors such as Martin Scorsese and Arthur Penn. For these filmmakers from both sides of the Atlantic, classic film noir constituted a body of texts that offered stylistic resistance to the norms of studio realism. Here were films that refused the patness of institutional optimism but foregrounded instead the dark underside of American life. As Jane Root has explained, noir films, like the noir novels and stories upon which they were based, were sometimes read in an intellectual way, as embodying image and themes that were vaguely consonant with then fashionable existentialism.[9] Along with the auteur theory, the concept of film noir has dominated critical work on the films of the 1940s and 1950s during much of the New Hollywood era. This trend is connected closely with the valorization of the oppositional or subversive text within film criticism—and, of course, within independent filmmaking as well.

As a critical category, film noir retains some connection with the films whose features gave rise to it, but, at the same time, the concept has acquired a life of its own. As I have suggested, what dominates the actual texts of the movement is a concern with sexuality and gender roles, with misogyny and the righteous violence against women that it generates. The gloominess or despair of their collective mise-en-scène reflects only superficially, if at all, an existential uncertainty about the form and values of human life. Only with some analytical violence can these Hollywood films be said to stage either the determining role of a Sartrean bad faith or the liberating possibilities of a Camusian self-fashioning. Instead, the classic film noir typically thematizes an uneasiness with male weakness and female perfidy, as well as a skepticism about the promise of the American dream of psychic wholeness, fulfilled desire, and attainable affluence. Albert Camus's *The Stranger* is a meditation on the salvatory meaninglessness of existence (the inevitability of death and the absence of transcendent values are the source of human freedom). As Camus once suggested, his renowned philosophical novel may have been inspired by his reading of Cain's *The Postman Always Rings Twice*. But, that said, Camus's ethical preoccupations find little or no resonance in the grim naturalism of noir fiction and film.

In any event, what matters more is that the concept of film noir has become associated not only with certain antirealist aspects of modernism (including stylistic excess and narrative complexity), but also with what might be called a popular existentialism. This means that two types of connection to film noir are available to the contemporary filmmaker, and these have been utilized not only by the Coens, but by David Lynch, Steven Soderbergh, and other directors of New Hollywood. On the one hand, the actual conventions of dark cinema from the 1940s and 1950s can be revived and reproduced in a relatively faithful manner (as in *L.A. Confidential* [Curtis Hanson, 1997]). On the other hand, the critical notion of film noir itself may dominate the process of textual re-creation, as in *Blue Velvet* (David Lynch, 1986), which explores, in a startlingly original fashion, the grim world of sexual obsession and criminality concealed within the banal everyday.

Blood Simple negotiates between these two options, offering both the expected repetition of a time-honored film type (here is yet another version of Cain's familiar story) as well as its revitalization in line with the *post facto* critical formulation "film noir." As such, the film has obvious entertainment value yet also flaunts its postmodernist revision of a classic genre. Such doubleness is an appeal to both the ordinary spectator's desire for stimulation and the cultist's discerning eye, as Richard Corliss puts it. As with other New Hollywood productions, the conventions of the classic studio film were modified by an infusion of spectacle, including what is known as "adult situations" (though the film's sexual themes are muted) and a healthy dose of bone-chilling violence that sometimes provokes the terror and disgust associated with the horror film. In both instances, however, this spectacle is carefully linked to effects of both suspense and surprise, and it is also motivated thematically, functioning as an expressive heightening of the sense of incomplete knowledge that envelopes the two characters at these turning points in the narrative. *Blood Simple*'s violence, then, can be read as something more than exploitation.

Because it can be consumed on two different levels, film noir has proved an astute choice of genre for the Coens to use for launching their career. Elitist yet popular, the noir narrative offers the perfect vehicle for commercial/independent filmmaking, especially since the Coens' idiosyncratic revitalization of a classic genre demonstrates their awareness of cinema history and their responsiveness to those opportunities for expression that such history makes available to those in the know. This "hipness" no doubt has always appealed to their fans, but not all critics find it valuable. Emanuel Levy, for example, suggests that it is the very "knowingness" of the Coens' engagement with traditional Hollywood forms that makes their films empty, because virtuoso, exercises: "The shallowness of most of their work is a result of their creating sealed universes that have few references outside the world of cinema. The Coens believe that linking form and content is irrelevant, that brilliant style will somehow lure viewers into uncritical acceptance of their schemes. Filled with artifice, their films are both unique and derivative."[10]

Curiously, Levy allows that their work is not "devoid of serious themes or ideas," particularly since the films often limn the moral dangers posed by "unbridled individualism." But the obvious point, which Levy and detractors of the Coens often miss, is that these ideas and themes are developed in the context of cinematic re-creation, of the fabrication of derivative "sealed universes" quite distinct from one another. Some recognition of their unconventional reality seems to be expressed by Levy's observation that Coen brothers films are "both unique and derivative." Such an artistic method should not be discounted simply because it eschews a realist preoccupation with "the world" (meaning whatever is thought to exist outside textuality, if that is possible) for an engagement with the bewildering "array," as some theorists term it, of forms and representations that confront the artist, and everyone else, in postmodernity, where nothing is truly past, not even the Hollywood films of a half century ago. After all, "the world" has become in large measure "the array," as the films of Ethan and Joel Coen often make us acknowledge.

A Postmodern Authorial Absence?

The Coens once made the following declaration about their filmmaking practice:

> JOEL: I don't think there's a thread, at least a conscious thread, anyway, between the different stories we're telling.
> ETHAN: It's what you call style in retrospect only. At the point of actually making the movie, it's just about making individual choices. . . . if there's some consistency to it, they say, "Well, that's their style."[11]

With its confession of a lack of interest in shaping a signature style or building a unified body of work, this dismissal of authorial intent reads like a page from the autobiography of Roger Corman, master of the low-budget exploitation film. If true (and that is always a question raised by anything the Coen brothers say in interviews), such statements offer an interesting comment on the opportunity for more or less unfettered self-expression they have enjoyed since their breakthrough into commercial production with *Blood Simple*. For how many other contemporary American filmmakers, exploiting the space between commercial and independent production to avoid being absorbed into global genre filmmaking, have been able to exercise nearly complete control over writing, directing, and producing, shaping their films right down to the final cut, without the extreme financial limitations normally encountered by Corman? What is more, like Ingmar Bergman, Yasujiro Ozu, Federico Fellini, Orson Welles, and, more recently, Woody Allen, the Coens have also enjoyed the considerable advantage of working with what amounts to a stock company of first-rate creative personnel. This talented group includes cinematographers Barry Sonnenfeld and Roger Deakins, production designers Jane Musky and Dennis Gassner, music director Carter Burwell, as well as actors Frances McDormand, John Goodman, John Turturro, Jon Polito, and Steve Buscemi.

But like Roger Corman (to extend the comparison just a bit more), the Coens have carved out a market niche while fashioning a mode of filmmaking that permits them to exploit it successfully. No doubt, the Coens have sought and made an effort to retain the artistic control that flows from such a favorable regulation of the conditions of production.

Their first venture into bigger-budget filmmaking met with commercial failure. And this was, at least in part, because *The Hudsucker Proxy* was made in collaboration with a Hollywood moneyman, Joel Silver, working for Warner Brothers and Polygram. Silver required the brothers (to name just one compromise) to give the featured roles to well-known stars: Paul Newman, Tim Robbins, and Jennifer Jason Leigh. Such casting was, arguably, not very effective, because the narrative had not been designed to accommodate the star personas involved. After this financial debacle, the Coens immediately returned to small-budget filmmaking and their earlier formula for success, including depending exclusively on their stock company of actors. This decision was ratified by the acclaim and popularity accorded to *Fargo,* their next release.

Surveying the results of a practice so conceived, we can see that the plan of the Coens to make commercial/independent films has now been carried out with admirable consistency and productivity for almost two decades. Even *The Hudsucker Proxy,* budget and star player considerations aside, is by no means an ordinary Hollywood product; it too offers a sealed fictional universe quirkily derived from Hollywood models, in this case the films of Preston Sturges and Frank Capra (this aspect of the film will be discussed more fully below). Such consistency can be understood only as the reflex of determination, energy, and strength of purpose—as shaped by a clear understanding of the limited market for the kind of films they make. It is surprising, perhaps, that their ten productions to date do not constitute an oeuvre in the neo-romantic sense of the *politique des auteurs* and that the Coens have felt (or at least confess to feeling) no desire to create any continuity from one film to the next.

Inevitably, and in spite of avowed intentions, of course, their films manifest similarities of various kinds. We might say that they are either comedies in the tradition of Frank Capra and Preston Sturges or crime dramas that are noir in some sense, with the influences here, interestingly enough, being primarily literary rather than cinematic. James Cain, Dashiell Hammett, Raymond Chandler, and Jim Thompson are the authors most often mentioned by other critics, while *Barton Fink* offers a complex meditation on Clifford Odets and Nathanael West. Yet it seems to me that the Coens' films have a wider intertextual reach. *Fargo's* black comedy of misunderstanding owes more than a little to the neon noir fiction of Elmore Leonard and Raymond Carver, while the dark themes of *The Man Who Wasn't There* deliberately recall, in addition to Cain, that subvariety of the roman noir popularized by Cornell Woollrich, Patricia Highsmith, and David Goodis. It must be admitted, however, that any absolute distinction between crime drama and comedy is problematic. Despite its unblinking dramatization of gruesome murder and conscienceless violence, *Fargo* gives equal emphasis to black humor, risible ethnic stereotypes, and, occasionally, even a kind of slapstick. In contrast, *The Big Lebowski*'s comic send-up of Raymond Chandler's *The Big Sleep* is undercut by a violence and mayhem that are hardly funny.

We might also say that Coen brothers films are, once again broadly speaking, uninvested in realism either as a style or as a protocol to guide the choice of subject matter—by which I mean that the Coens do not engage deeply with "reality" or "history," apart from the representations to be found in film or fiction. Thus they bear little comparison to their contemporaries such as Spike Lee and John Sayles who are more committed to the political analysis, in the social realist vein, of American culture rather than to the exploration of its cinematic and literary heritage. *Raising Arizona, Blood Simple, The Man Who Wasn't There,* and *Fargo* are exceptions to this rule, but only partial ones, as we shall see. Another point of commonality, as the Coens themselves have frequently pointed out, is that all their films are thoroughly and most often ostentatiously stylized—and with strikingly contrasting regimes of visual design, camera movement, sound effects, and even editing patterns. Another way of grouping the films would be to distinguish among those that are genre exercises in some sense, which is by far the bigger category (*Blood Simple; Fargo; Miller's Crossing; The Man Who Wasn't There; The Hudsucker Proxy; O Brother, Where Art Thou?; The Big Lebowski;* and *Intolerable Cruelty*) and those that are not (*Raising Arizona* and *Barton Fink*). This distinction, however, might not be particularly meaningful since all these films, no matter whether they have strong genre affiliations, feed off other texts, literary, cinematic, and cultural.

As I have already suggested, the films the Coens have made thus far also find unity in common themes, the twin impossibilities of human experience: coming to any meaningful understanding of others and mastering a brute reality ruled by the principle of seemingly diabolical mischance. These noirish themes are realized either in a somewhat positive or, most often, in a rather negative fashion. Thus, the typical Coenian narrative focuses either on pathetic losers whose attempts to make a "big score" of some kind spectacularly misfire or on those of more virtue or purer heart who in their cunning or simplicity persevere to transcendence of some kind. Some of their films, most notably *Fargo* and *Barton Fink,* are structured around the conflict between these two types; an upholder of virtue encounters an inept villain, whose half-baked schemes unleash a destructive storm of unforeseen consequences that lead to his defeat.

But what characterizes these films as a body is not only their thematic unity. As many critics have pointed out, this oeuvre manifests a consistent authorial tone, an unsympathetic, cynical, and derisive attitude toward the characters and their desires for success or release. Like many films of the Hollywood Renaissance, *Blood Simple* and most of the works the Coens have made since tell the stories of those who have either failed to realize the American dream or cannot represent institutions that command respect and regulate desire. When, more rarely, the protagonists of their films are in some sense successful, it is because they prove able to resist the attempts of the rich and the powerful to control them. Once again, this is a theme anticipated by Renaissance filmmakers such as Hal Ashby (*Harold and Maude* [1971], *Being There* [1979]) and Robert Altman (*M.A.S.H.* [1970] and *The Long Goodbye* [1973]).

A thoroughgoing mistrust of conventional pieties permeates all Coen brothers films. The Coens' scarcely disguised authorial attitude not only connects them to the Hollywood Renaissance directors (differentiating them from the movie brats). More interesting, perhaps, it reflects the depth of the Coens' fascination with film noir, which furnishes them with a perspective that can be traced across an otherwise disparate oeuvre, across their summoning into existence a series of distinct, seemingly disconnected fictional worlds. It is difficult, in fact, to underestimate the influence of film noir on their work. For if their "lighter" films such as *The Hudsucker Proxy* and *The Big Lebowski* show the deep influence of classic Hollywood's most noted directors of comedy, we should remember that, among other of their films, Preston Sturges's *Unfaithfully Yours* (1948) and Capra's *It's a Wonderful Life* (1946) barely contain the noir themes and representations they call into being, only with difficulty winning through in each case to problematic happy endings, as will be discussed further in chapter 6. If the stories that Capra and Sturges tell are finally comic, they come perilously close to ending with the worst kind of disaster: either humiliating exposure to public ridicule or the self-confessed moral failure of suicide. These are alternatives considered as ways out by the protagonists in Capra's *Mr. Smith Goes to Washington* (1939) and Sturges's *The Miracle of Morgan's Creek* (1943), among other examples—and the Coens characteristically put the theme of suicide at the very center of their homage to Capra and Sturges, *The Hudsucker Proxy*.

It thus proves easy to locate different kinds of commonality in the films. And yet the authorial decision to emphasize surface difference has in the end something of an anti-authorial effect. The Coens' commitment to discontinuity, and their persistent refusal to accept, with conventional seriousness, the role of Hollywood auteurs, deconstructs the sense in which authority achieves a textual presence through obvious forms of repetition and sameness. And such discontinuity also contests any simple notion of a univocal "personality" whose *quidditas* can be traced across a series of recapitulated fictional worlds (Faulkner's Yoknapatawpha County, Hitchcock's modern city, Capra's American small towns). This is to say that the Coenian oeuvre occults, if only to some degree, the marks of the author in what is best seen as a postmodernist gesture. But, it might be objected to this postmodern reading of their project, such a deliberate absence of the author's self from the work is not unprecedented during the classic studio era.

The best example from an older Hollywood is undoubtedly John Huston, who also sought, and in the end achieved, substantial control over his films. Like the Coens, Huston did most of his best work on small pictures, at least one of which (*The Red Badge of Courage*) suffered the same kind of mutilation at the hands of its producers as did Welles's *The Magnificent Ambersons*. And yet Huston was no Hitchcock or Hawks, from whose work a univocal worldview can easily be extracted. Nor did his films manifest a more or less consistent approach to mise-en-scène or style, broadly considered. Some contemporary scholars (Gaylyn Studlar in particular) would mount some challenge to Robin Wood's assessment of Huston's career, but my point here is that it is surprisingly similar to what many have said about that of the Coens: "It seems significant that attempts to trace a consistent pattern in Huston's work should lead one chiefly to an awareness of absences."[12]

One might object, of course, that Huston's personality was complex, his intellectual and artistic interests too diverse to be reflected in a "consistent pattern." After all, just to take a brief biographical approach, he was what used to be called a man's man, who also fancied himself a card-carrying member of the intelligentsia. Huston (much like Hawks) showed enthusiasm for the popular adventure tale with its ritualized male behavior. He adapted not only Dashiell Hammett and B. Traven for the screen, but also Rudyard Kipling. Yet (and here the contrast with Hawks could not be more telling) Huston also felt a deep attraction to high-culture fiction (Herman Melville, Flannery O'Connor, and Stephen Crane certainly make for a trio of literary heavyweights). Thus, somewhat remarkably, Huston oversaw the best screen adaptations of, on the one hand, W. R. Burnett (*The Asphalt Jungle*) and, on the other, James Joyce (*The Dead*). But even if we grant that the variety of Huston's films responds to the diversity of his interests, the standard auteurist judgment is that he never developed a transtextual visual style. Instead, Huston conceived a stylistic plan for each film that responded to the material being adapted.

How different, and yet how similar, has been the practice of the Coens, whose material is original with them, with the ad hoc stylizations therefore best considered as central elements of the creative process. Thus the Coens can hardly be considered mere craftsmen, even if to some degree they have no interest in continuity. In contrast, the infamous *Cahiers du cinéma* category of the *metteur en scène* (a scene stager, not an artist) was often invoked to characterize Huston, though today his reputation is certainly more substantial. Let us, in any event, follow this auteurist argument to its conventional conclusion. The authorial absence in Huston's work can finally be accounted for by both intention (the desire to mount literary adaptations) and the conditions of production under which the director thereby operated (working with another's story materials). In contrast, there is nothing in the conditions of production to dictate that an essential feature of the Coens' films should be one of difference rather than resemblance. Of course, there are other contemporary independent filmmakers whose work shows considerable diversity. It would be hard, for instance, to imagine three films more different from one another than Steven Soderbergh's *Sex, Lies, and Videotape*, *Kafka*, and *Ocean's Eleven*. And yet this is the reflection of Soderbergh's decision to work not only on independent films for the art-house niche market, but also on big-budget productions that permit much less in the way of directorial control over both subject and approach. There are yet others among the Coens' contemporaries who have chosen consistency, colonizing a genre in the Hitchcockian fashion in order to offer a concentrated and quite personalized vision. For example, David Cronenberg's films explore the complexities of male identity through the conventions of the horror genre, even as they give varied shape thereby to his misogynistic, sadomasochistic fascination with gendering, polymorphous sexuality, and the reproductive organs.

Certainly, the boldly announced preoccupation of the Coens with authorial impersonality (Huston would never have confessed to that) in part suits a different historical moment in which the concept of the bourgeois "individual" has been exposed by some as a mystification. In the Coens' films, one underlying principle may be seen to be a calculated dissemination or dispersal that is not, in the end, so far from the Hustonian project of adaptation.[13] We must remember that the subjects of these films are never "the real" but rather other texts and genres. In a sense, then, all Coen films are adaptations of other texts, from which are confected diegetic worlds or, perhaps better, ontological modes that usually engage complex intertexts. In other words, an aspect of Coen films is that they contain networks of allusions to other works both literary and cinematic. To offer but one brief example, the first image of Abby and Ray (two unilluminated heads looking through the windshield toward a nighttime highway shimmering under the glare of headlights) is a direct borrowing from Robert Siodmak's *The Killers* (1946), a classic film noir. Such an artistic practice, often termed *bricolage,* or scavenging, is typically postmodern, that is, if anything postmodern can be characterized as typical.

Among other chroniclers of the postmodern, Dick Hebdige has suggested that this aesthetic privileges the reworking of received materials. And thus, through the formal invocation of "parody, simulation, pastiche, and allegory," an author is no longer needed as an "originary power," but becomes simply the force required to "rework the antecedent."[14] Postmodernism, then, would be as much concerned with what the art object comes to be (that is, its relation to the "already said"), as with what it might mean, especially in terms of expressing the author's ideas or personality. In his widely quoted *Postmodernist Fiction,* Brian McHale similarly proposes that, while "the dominant of modernism is epistemological," with characters and readers launched on a search to discover "the truth," that of postmodernism is "ontological." In other words, the postmodern artist abandons "the intractable problem of attaining to reliable knowledge of *our* world" and, instead, improvises a "possible world," one that is, implicitly, entirely under the artist's control.[15] But, so McHale continues, this improvisation, this fictionalization, feeds on other representations, not on the "real" itself. The postmodernist's characteristic mode is pastiche, the so-called flat parody famously first identified by Fredric Jameson as one of the most distinguishing features of the aesthetic.

Let us consider for a moment Jameson's original formulation of postmodernist pastiche, published in 1984: "Pastiche is, like parody, the imitation of a peculiar mask, speech in a dead language . . . without any of parody's ulterior motives, amputated of the satiric impulse, devoid of laughter . . . blank parody, a statue with blind eyeballs."[16]

As famous as Jameson's description of postmodernism's preoccupation with textuality is his negative judgment of such practice, especially in its extreme form, the nostalgia film (his example is *Body Heat*): "The producers of culture have nowhere to turn but to the past: the imitation of dead styles, speeches through all the masks and voices stored up in the imaginary museum of a now global culture."[17]

Thus postmodern art has "emerged as an elaborated symptom of the waning of our own historicity, of our lived possibility of experiencing history in some active way."[18] Even in the postmodernist genre that seems most eager to make contact with history, the novels and films Linda Hutcheon appropriately terms "historiographic metafiction," there is no engagement with the real, at least according to Jameson. In works like E. L. Doctorow's *Ragtime* that seem to engage with important aspects of the past, Jameson observes that "those 'official subjects' float above the text but cannot be integrated into our reading of the sentences."[19]

What is most interesting, perhaps, about the postmodernist debate that so preoccupied theorists during the late eighties and early nineties is that such bleak accounts as those of Jameson and, from quite a different angle, Terry Eagleton, were called into question by scholars like Hutcheon, who promoted a more positive view of postmodernism's engagement with politics, broadly defined. For her, the parody so obvious in the dominant aesthetic of this period is hardly flat; it is, *contra*

Jameson, no "statue with blank eyeballs." Instead, Hutcheon, like Roland Barthes, celebrates the end of mimesis, or the notion that art imitates the real, seeing this as the historical moment when the political in art becomes dominant: "And this is where the self-reflexive, parodic art of the postmodern comes in, underlining in its ironic way the realization that all cultural forms of representation—literary, visual, aural—in high art or the mass media are ideologically grounded, that they cannot avoid involvement with social and political relations and apparatuses."[20]

Such objections aside, there is no doubt, however, that the blank parody of pastiche figures as an element, perhaps the most important one, of postmodernism. Hutcheon can point to a number of cinematic counterexamples, films such as Woody Allen's *Zelig* (1983) where pastiche is shaped by a political or culturalist rhetoric. These progressive productions, offering what Robert Stam calls "subversive pleasure," are more the exceptions than the rule.[21] Perhaps this is inevitable at a historical juncture when culture is inundated with a textual flow so reified and so ostensibly "present" that all connections with the moment and context of original consumption are either readily effaced or ignored, if they can be identified at all. Television and, to a lesser degree, the cinema would be the imaginary museums of such an era—but only if there were still museums in the older sense of places of honor where the unusable but undiscardable past can be preserved from the instrumental needs of the everyday in such a fashion that difference in "period" should be underlined, not obscured. In postmodernity, instead, as many have observed, the past is always available to the present, can always be reconstituted as stylistic flourish or witticism or intertextual reference. After all, instrumentalization in the postindustrial stage of capitalism, as Jameson has stated elsewhere, means that "a thing of whatever type has been reduced to a means for its own consumption."[22]

In any case, we can easily grant Jameson his symptomatic reading of *Body Heat*, which undoubtedly typifies a new artistic sensibility in its collapsing of the difference between the texts of the past and those of the present. But that does not mean that all texts of the postmodern era can signify only their lack of engagement with the contemporary in some sense, can only purvey an aggressive flattening of the past. Traditional realism continues to enjoy a significant popularity in contemporary Hollywood, alongside other regimes of representation, including both the European-influenced modernism that is a direct bequest of the 1970s renaissance and also the cartoonish fantasy of films such as *Spider-Man*, which are derived mainly from comic books and juvenile fiction.

A major point to be made about the films of Joel and Ethan Coen is that they are undoubtedly postmodern yet engage in a dialogue with genre and with classic studio films that does not slight the political and the cultural. The films of the Coen brothers, I hope to show throughout this book, are among the exceptions to the general regime of pastiche in genre filmmaking. A desire to speak through and beyond the significant texts of the past can be seen, first, in their engagement with film noir and the roman noir, which together constitute the countercultural movement of greatest strength, reach, and endurance of the twentieth century and beyond, stretching, as it does, from Dashiell Hammett, through the great European émigré auteurs like Lang, Wilder, and Siodmak, through the novelists Richard Condon, Chester Himes, and Patricia Highsmith in the fifties, down to the reemergence of film noir in the seventies and eighties as well as the revivification of the roman noir with the fiction of Elmore Leonard, Raymond Carver, and others during the last two decades. And, second, I would point to the Coens' eagerness in their comedies to engage specifically with the work of Preston Sturges and Frank Capra, studio-era directors who, with cynicism and uncertainty, explored the conventional pieties of American culture. As we will see later, the reconstitution and reconfiguration of material drawn from Sturges and Capra in *The Hudsucker Proxy* and *O Brother, Where Art Thou?* eschews the slick, shallow invocation of the cinematic past in films like *Body Heat*. Much the same can even be said of *The Man Who Wasn't There*, which, because it aims not simply to invoke but to recreate film noir, could be mistaken for a nostalgia film. And yet the Coens find a different meaning for this version of the same old song as well.

Notes

The epigraph is from Richard Maltby, *Hollywood Cinema*, 2d ed. (Oxford: Basil Blackwell, 2003), 74.

1. Of the several useful works on the so-called Hollywood Renaissance of the 1970s, by far the most perspicacious is Robert Kolker's *A Cinema of Loneliness: Penn, Kubrick, Scorsese, Spielberg, Altman*, 2d ed. (Oxford: Oxford University Press, 1988).

2. See Susan Jeffords, *The Remasculinization of America* (Bloomington: Indiana University Press, 1989).

3. See Richard Slotkin, *Regeneration through Violence: The Mythology of the American Frontier, 1600–1860* (Middletown, Conn.: Wesleyan University Press, 1973).

4. The following discussion is indebted, especially in regard to facts and figures, to Stephen Prince's comprehensive history of the decade, *A New Pot of Gold: Hollywood under the Electronic Rainbow, 1980–1989* (Los Angeles: University of California Press, 2000).

5. Gregg Merritt, *Celluloid Mavericks: A History of American Independent Film* (New York: Thunder's Mouth Press, 2000), 351.

6. Pauline Kael, "The Current Cinema," *New Yorker,* February 24, 1985, 81–83.

7. Jim Hoberman, *Vulgar Modernism: Writing on Movies and Other Media* (Philadelphia: Temple University Press, 1991), 7.

8. Ibid.

9. Jane Root, "Film Noir," in *The Cinema Book,* ed. Pam Cook (New York: Pantheon Books, 1985), 93–97.

10. Emanuel Levy, *A Cinema of Outsiders* (New York: New York University Press, 1999), 223.

11. Quoted in Ronald Bergan, *The Coen Brothers* (New York: Thunder's Mouth, 2000), 29.

12. Quoted in Cook, *Cinema Book,* 130.

13. Interestingly, Huston's films also parallel those of the Coens in their frequent foregrounding of the failure that comes at the end of extraordinary adventures. Like *Fargo,* in which the "loot" for which so much blood has been spilled is buried irrecoverably in the snow-covered prairie, so *The Treasure of the Sierra Madre* ends with the gold that has cost so many lives simply blowing away in the wind.

14. Dick Hebdige, *Hiding in the Light: On Images and Things* (New York: Routledge, 1988), 191.

15. Brian McHale, *Postmodernist Fiction* (New York: Routledge, 1989), 10.

16. Fredric Jameson, "Postmodernism, or the Cultural Logic of Late Capitalism," *New Left Review* 146 (1984): 65.

17. Ibid.

18. Ibid., 68.

19. Ibid., 69.

20. Linda Hutcheon, *The Politics of Postmodernism* (New York: Routledge, 1989), 3.

21. See Robert Stam, *Subversive Pleasures: Bakhtin, Cultural Criticism and Film* (Baltimore: Johns Hopkins University Press, 1989).

22. Fredric Jameson, "Reification and Utopia in Mass Culture," in *Signatures of the Visible* (New York: Routledge, 1992), 11.

3. Uncertainty Principle:
The Man Who Wasn't There

The act of accepting meaninglessness is itself a
meaningful act. It is an act of faith.

—Paul Tillich

The view of Fredric Jameson and others that New Hollywood's obsession with genericity gives rise only to the blank parody of pastiche over-
simplifies industry offerings in the postmodern era. At the same time,
with a nostalgia for the high modernist past, it ignores the impact of
changing cultural conditions on film production and reception. Jameson and company certainly raise an indisputable point. But a closer look
at the genre films produced in contemporary Hollywood reveals a much
more interesting diversity than Jameson's global analysis suggests. Jim
Collins, for example, calls attention to the fact that contemporary Hollywood production emphasizes two distinct kinds of genre films that
hardly fit into the category of "blank parody," even though they draw
heavily on classic studio traditions. On the one hand, genre hybrids such
as *Back to the Future III* (1990) play their knowingness of forms like the
western and the science fiction film for laughs, exploiting a "dissonance"
produced by the unpredictable yoking together of disparate, irreconcil-
able elements. Such pastiche is structured around a bizarre eclecticism

of ideas and values. This is the effect that Collins describes as "John Ford meets Jules Verne and H. G. Wells," exemplified by the sequence in the film when Marty and Doc find themselves transported back not to the Old West, but to the Old West of Hollywood film.[1] At one point, their DeLorean "time machine" is hauled across Monument Valley like a buckboard, an incongruous invocation of many Ford movies, most notably *Stagecoach* (1939).

On the other hand, "new sincere" explorations of classic genres, like *Dances with Wolves* (1990), aim at recovering some kind of "missing harmony," some transcendent significance that the celebrated exemplars of the genre allude to but never either fully express or properly configure. Thus the western can be reshaped through an engagement with "real" American history, thereby revealing the meaning that, for either ideological or institutional reasons, has hitherto been confined to its margins. This approach emphasizes the conflict between nature and civilization, the underlying myth that animates the genre. In the post–studio era, the focus of the western can be diverted from the righteous violence reluctantly employed by the good/bad hero in the service of restoring communal order and his own honor. The new western can occupy itself instead with the struggle for control over the land between native peoples, who, no longer demonized as Indians, emerge as representatives of a natural, self-sustaining, and peaceful society. Opposed to them are the rapacious white settlers bent on extracting wealth from the land through its mindless destruction.

Blood Simple is hardly an example of this "new sincerity." The film's relationship to classic film noir is somewhat ambivalent, only in part an extended homage to time-honored literary and cinematic conventions, especially in terms of stereotypical characters (the private detective, the rich man betrayed by an unfaithful wife). With its color cinematography, contemporary rural setting, and spectacular violence, *Blood Simple* not only has a different look. It engages with a divergent set of cultural meanings (especially the transitory nature of relationships in contemporary society), providing a new context for understanding the noir narrative of betrayal, jealousy, greed, and murder. The coupling that develops between Ray and Abby, for example, plays out in reference to post-sexual-revolution values, in particular, the acceptance of casual coupling as a not terribly immoral act. Thus Abby, despite Marty's jealous ranting and Ray's mistrust, is no femme fatale in the tradition of classic noir. She does not manipulate sexual desire in the service of her own urge for independence, destroying all who are attracted to her. In fact, Abby's dissatisfaction with Marty and use of Ray as a protector only provide the initial movement for a succession of events that are largely determined by a character from outside the romantic triangle. It is the detective's greedy desire for the money Marty offers him, as well as his eagerness to protect himself from betrayal, that takes the noir story of sexual malfeasance inherited from Cain in a different direction.

Like most of the films of the noir revival of the 1980s, *Blood Simple* updates classic conventions but does not attempt to identify the "truth" of the genre by giving expression to what it should have said but never could. But this is exactly what *The Man Who Wasn't There* does with Cain's two similar stories of sexual mischief and murderous plotting, *Double Indemnity* and, especially, *The Postman Always Rings Twice*. These tales unfold in the early years of the Depression and reflect that era of social breakdown and economic scarcity. The original Hollywood versions of the novels (Billy Wilder's *Double Indemnity* [1944] and Tay Garnett's *The Postman Always Rings Twice* [1946]) are set in a vaguely contemporary America, but neither film attempts to make any connection to deeper currents within the culture, including and especially the profound changes being brought about by the war.

The Man Who Wasn't There, in contrast, offers a deeply particularized context, closely linking the noir narrative to the era that shaped it and thus making present the cultural history hitherto mostly absent in the genre. *The Man Who Wasn't There* is set in 1949, as the revelation that the Russians now possess the atomic bomb began to mark profoundly what in retrospect seems truly "the age of doubt," as the historian William Graebner terms it.[2] This was a time strongly colored by "the anxiety of the lonely, fragmented individual" (2), of which the Coens' protagonist is a striking representative. Unlike Cain's scheming adulterers, who are trapped by limited economic horizons and oppressive institutions, especially marriage and social class, all the characters in the Coens' film suffer from a vaguer but perhaps deadlier malaise, the deep feeling of the age that, as described in Graebner's apt account, "like life itself, values seemed to come and go, without pattern or reason" (19–20). This anomie produces a strong sense of disconnection, even absence, to which they react in various ways, seeking either to "make it big" in the tradition of the American dream or to withdraw from the struggle by numbing themselves with alcohol and music. They settle in the end for neither success nor escape, but for death, which haunts and frustrates all their aspirations, yet paradoxically offers as well the opportunity for transcendence. They are thus typical of an era when one could ignore only with difficulty the absolute contingency of existence, for a nuclear annihilation might descend upon them at any time without warning, or so it was widely thought.

The film's main character, frustrated in his plans to make it big, comes to see life as a series of sudden, inexplicable, and irretrievable losses, his thoughts haunted by the memory of the thousands of "Nips vaporized at Nagasaki." Another is convinced that she and her husband were briefly abducted by aliens, an incident they then report to the "proper authorities," only to be persecuted, she thinks, by the government, which for reasons unknown is reluctant to admit the truth—all this an evocation of the mass paranoia that resulted in the great UFO panic, beginning in 1949 and extending throughout the next decade. Printed (but not filmed) in black and white and with a meticulously authentic art design, *The Man Who Wasn't There* thus offers itself as a rich period piece, as a "new sincere" version of film noir in which Cain's explorations of lust and its discontents yield a meaning that is perhaps closer to the "truth" of film noir, with a deeply ironic representation of the uncertainty of human life. Here the notion, first put by the Coens in the mouth of Visser in *Blood Simple*, that "something can always go wrong" is traced back to its cinematic and cultural origins, which are examined but also "authenticated," if not without a certain amount of irony.

Thus the film eschews much of the visual style associated with film noir, which, updated and marked by technical innovation, creates such an atmosphere of dread and anxiety in *Blood Simple*. With that film, the Coens helped renew a tradition to be followed by later entrants in the neo-noir cycle, such as *U-Turn* or *Lost Highway*. In contrast, *The Man Who Wasn't There* features few striking chiaroscuro effects or deglamorized low-key lighting setups, no unbalanced compositions marked by slaked angles, no disorienting disruptions of continuity editing, and no unmotivated camera movements designed to unsettle. Instead, the later film proceeds at a stately pace, never frantic or frenzied, that matches the simplicity of the Beethoven piano sonatas and American hymns that dominate its sound track. The music, in fact, offers a pointed contrast to the *weltschmerzig* symphonic scores of the European émigré composers like Max Steiner and Dmitri Tiomkin whose work suffuses classic film noir with a sense of desperate romanticism. The most striking stylistic flourish in the film is provided by a moving, sometimes restless camera that, breaking free from the characters, shows spectators, conceived as visitors to another time and place, what they need to understand about this resurrected world. As viewers, we strongly sense the presence of a detached but diligent observer, who occasionally with wry humor discovers the characters' limitations.

And yet the overall impression created in the film is not *just* that they are ignorant, lazy, venal, unsophisticated, and gullible, though, undeniably, they are all of these things. The focus of *The Man Who Wasn't There* is not, as in classic film noir, the identification of, and then a bare escape from, the threat to orders both sexual and cultural posed by an underworld of temptation and rapacious criminality. *The Man Who Wasn't There,* surprisingly enough, is about the hope for spiritual growth, the leap of faith made possible by the embrace of meaninglessness. The film thus finds its closest analogues not in the pulp novels and genre films of the period, but in the serious writing favored by intellectuals in the early 1950s, from Camus's *The Stranger* and *The Rebel* to Saul Bellow's *The Dangling Man* to Colin Wilson's *The Outsider,* and Jean-Paul Sartre's *Being and Nothingness.* Also relevant here are the theological writings of Reinhold Niebuhr and Paul Tillich, as well as the popular moral appeals of Billy Graham and Norman Vincent Peale that were the most obvious signs of the religious revivalism that swept postwar America to become an important and enduring element on the national political scene.[3]

Like *The Postman Always Rings Twice, The Man Who Wasn't There* occupies itself with the working middle class, tracing the effects of a get-rich-quick scheme gone wrong. This modest plan for self-improvement seems innocuous enough at the outset, but in the end it poses a threat to the social order that the legal system, shown to be a province dominated by cunning shysters, can neither anatomize nor regulate. Dissatisfied with his life as a barber working for his brother-in-law in Santa Rosa, California, Ed Crane (Billy Bob Thornton) decides to become the partner of an entrepreneur who comes by the shop one day. This fast-talking guy touts the as yet untapped potential of a new method for doing laundry: dry cleaning. All that the entrepreneur needs to get started in his first store, soon to be expanded into a national chain, is a partner with money and vision. But how is Ed to get the large stake, ten thousand dollars, a sum that is completely beyond his resources? He knows that his wife, Doris (Frances McDormand), is having an affair with her boss, Big Dave (James Gandolfini), who manages the local department store. Dave, Ed reasons, probably has some access, legal or otherwise, to a good deal of money, and he may be willing to pay up to protect his marriage—and his livelihood too, for his wife's family owns the store and Dave serves at their pleasure. Ed sends Dave an anonymous letter threatening to reveal the affair with Doris if he does not hand over the money. And, against all odds, this strange scheme succeeds. When Ed gets the money, he immediately hands it over to his erstwhile partner, who gives every indication of being a crook, even though Ed doesn't realize it. No plans are made for how the partners will proceed; Ed goes back to waiting for what life will next bring. What it brings is retribution of a strange sort. Dave discovers that Ed is the blackmailer, lures him to his office at midnight, and there attempts to murder him. But Ed, caught in a deadly bear hug, manages to stab his attacker in the neck. Dave expires in a pool of blood, and Ed leaves the store without being seen. He rejoins Doris at home, where she is still sound asleep in an alcoholic daze. Ed has been found out, confronted, and forced to take even more desperate action. Yet he goes home to get a good night's sleep before starting another day at the barbershop. Nothing, it seems, can shake him from his soul-numbing routine.

There, Ed once again avoids, with his inscrutable passivity, any recognition that he is more than he seems. When two policemen come in, Ed thinks he is about to be confronted with what he has done. But they have been dispatched to tell him that Doris has been arrested for Dave's murder; he barely reacts to the news. Thus Doris finds herself in jail for a crime she has not committed, and, thanks to the workings of mischance, misunderstanding, and her husband's silence, she has little hope for release. Doris cannot establish her innocence, being guilty of another crime, "cooking" the books of her lover's business so that he'd have money to pay off the blackmailer. But she did not kill her boss (their affair

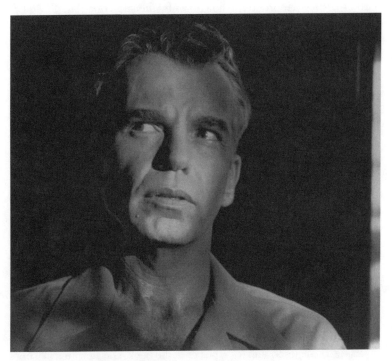

The Coens' neo-noir mystery *The Man Who
Wasn't There* features Billy Bob Thornton as the
anti-hero Ed Crane. (Courtesy of the Academy of
Motion Picture Arts and Sciences)

has not been discovered) because, as the police have reconstructed the
sequence of events, he found out she was embezzling from the firm and
so threatened her with exposure. This official version of events is incorrect, even though it does adequately account for what the police know.
The truth is that Big Dave asked her to steal the money so that he could
pay off some blackmailer, whose identity Doris has never learned.

But the legal system, though officially committed with its forensic
proceedings to the discovery of the truth, is really concerned only with
credibility, the issue at the thematic center of the film. Doris's fate hangs
upon what the jurors and judge can be made to believe. Her hotshot
lawyer, Freddy Riedenschneider (Tony Shalhoub), complains that this
explanation for financial impropriety, however truthful, will prove to be

of no use to the defense since Doris can provide no corroboration. The two men who might testify on her behalf cannot: Dave is dead and is not able to reveal the identity of the blackmailer, who thus remains unknown and unavailable. Ed proves willing, if not eager, to save Doris, and as the couple strategizes with Riedenschneider one day the distraught husband suddenly blurts out: "I killed Big Dave." Ironically enough, Doris and her lawyer, however, interpret his statement as a ploy, not as an admission of actual guilt. Perhaps they have misjudged too harshly his incapacities.

In any event, like Doris's alibi, Ed's confession proves useless to the defense because Ed has not told the whole truth. Killing Dave becomes in Crane's laconic retelling a crime of passion, his motive the jealousy he feels after discovering Doris's affair with Big Dave. Does he withhold the whole story so that Doris will be found guilty? Is he reticent about admitting his reasons for blackmailing Big Dave, only one of which is anger at his seduction of Doris? We never learn. What is significant, however, is that this version of events can no more be proven than Doris's. Despairing of a way to get Doris off (and thus preserve his considerable reputation), Riedenschneider can imagine no other defense that might induce "reasonable doubt" in the jury. He resolves not to give up, though he cannot see any hope. Then the private detective they have hired makes a discovery that, the lawyer exults, will spring Doris for sure. He summons his client and her husband to another meeting.

Before revealing what has given him cause for hope, Riedenschneider explores the philosophical implications of the legal concept of reasonable doubt. There's "a guy in Germany," Riedenschneider says, who maintains that when you want to understand something scientifically, you have to look at it, but "your looking changes it." Applied to human affairs, this means that you can't truly know "the reality of what happened" as you explore actions and motivations. Thus the lawyer places his concern about alibis and workable defenses within a broader context of ideas through these meditations on the Heisenberg Uncertainty Principle (which is never named as such). For it no longer seems the case that lawyers like Riedenschneider are simply being cynical when they ignore getting at the "truth" of the case as they search for an explanation that will work rhetorically, as it were, to convince jurors that they in fact *do not know* what happened.

Viewed from the perspective of universal and inescapable uncertainty, reasonable doubt is no more than the admission that provisional certainty (a certainty subject to only minimal doubt) is always a mirage. In the courtroom, the provisional certainty needed to convict is undermined by the demonstration that there is a plausible alternative, some other way of construing the facts. This plausible alternative, however, does not require absolute and detailed proof; it does not require, in fact, provisional certainty. It must point only toward the improbability of knowing for sure. Thus Riedenschneider's profession, as he explains, occupies itself with the serial demonstration of a central epistemological axiom, of whose ineluctability he must persuade jurors. As he puts it, "there is no what happened," and the ironic correlative of this postulate is that "the more you look, the less you know." Thus an inescapable paradox rules human affairs: the "only fact," the only certainty, is uncertainty. Not only does uncertainty undermine the all too human search after determinate knowledge. It also reveals an unknowability that deepens as the desire to know and thereby master experience grows stronger.

The lawyer understands, in a partial and self-serving way, some of the larger implications of Heisenberg's theorizing (whose ultimate point, of course, is quite the opposite of what he maintains, it being to identify a provisional form of certainty, the relative probabilities in the tracking of the position and momentum of subatomic particles). But Riedenschneider deceives himself that the uncertainty principle offers him mastery over Doris's plight. And this is because he falls victim to another paradox, his own certainty about uncertainty, the mistaken conviction that the chain of "unknowing" must end somewhere in unshakable predictability, that there are no more surprises in store. He had earlier despaired about finding a workable defense, rejecting those proposed by Doris and Ed because they could not be grounded in a series of credible claims. But now he is confident that his detective has uncovered something about Big Dave for which a credible claim can be advanced, and that something will produce reasonable doubt in the minds of the jurors.

Big Dave, it appears, was not what he seemed to be. With authentically gory stories about his experiences during the New Guinea campaign in World War II, he had convinced everyone, including Doris and his wife, that he was a war hero, who, in Riedenschneider's memorable description, "practically liberated the Pacific all by himself, with a knife in one hand, a gun in the other, and twenty yards of Jap guts between his teeth." But Big Dave actually spent the war serving as a clerk in a San Diego naval station, never shipping overseas or seeing more action than a bar fight broken up by the Shore Patrol. As Riedenschneider explains to a dumbfounded Doris and Ed, Dave's fabrications provide the blackmailer Doris says had approached her lover with an exploitable weakness. Big Dave would have been easy prey to anyone learning the truth of his service record, which would not have been hard to do. And, as Riedenschneider points out, the fact that Big Dave had lied to the very people sitting on the jury means that they would be more likely to see such a blackmailer as a real possibility. Thus, he exults, the jurors will feel reasonable doubt about the state's version of Dave's death. Riedenschneider is *certain* about it.

And yet, we should not forget that "the more you look, the less you see." Big Dave's continual self-revelation, his incessant bragging, actually concealed unexpected secrets. But the exposure of these lies offers only a slim point of certainty with regard to him. And, most important, that Dave has been unmasked does not mean that either Doris or Ed is now knowable. Riedenschneider, as it turns out, hasn't even learned all there is to know about Dave. But knowledge, even the immediate kind that flows from one's own experience, is of dubious value. This point is made in an earlier scene, which occurs just after Doris's arrest. Dave's widow, Ann, pays Ed a nighttime visit to exculpate Doris by telling him the real explanation for Dave's murder (but, because it would never be believed, it cannot be used to save her). One summer, while vacationing in Oregon, she and Dave were abducted by aliens, with Dave taken into their spacecraft, there to undergo things that afterward he would never talk about. In any event, this experience had marked a turning point in their marital life, or so Ann believes—Dave never "touched me again," she tells Ed. Dave and Ann made a report to the government about their experience, and Ann is convinced that Dave was murdered by government agents who were eager to "limit knowledge" about extraterrestrial life. The conclusion that Ann not surprisingly draws from her experience is that "knowledge is sometimes a curse."

This Oedipean theme finds a resonance in Riedenschneider's shattering experience at Doris's trial. The knowledge he thought would assure his client's deliverance actually drives her to suicide, making any question of legal proceedings irrelevant. Riedenschneider never takes the trouble to determine if Doris and Dave were actually having an affair, even though Ed's "confession" offers his jealousy about their relationship as his motive, which Doris never disputes. Thus the revelation about Big Dave's past has an effect on Doris that Riedenschneider in no way foresees. Doris's attraction to her lover, as Ed had earlier surmised, was based on, first, the he-man image he presented to the world (so much of a contrast to slightly built, unassuming, and depressive Ed, who proved unfit for war service because of his fallen arches); and, second, the promise Dave offered her of a deliverance from economic marginality and sexual boredom. Dave was going to expand his department store operation by building an "annex" where Doris would be the comptroller. The blackmailer deprived them of this hope by taking the money Dave needed for the new enterprise and put them in jeopardy by forcing Doris to betray her profession ("my books were always perfect"). Then Dave himself is killed, with the deeply ironic result that Doris, who had sacrificed herself to save him, stands accused of his murder.

All this Doris suffers stoically, even acknowledging that their transgressions might require retribution of some kind ("we knew we'd have to pay," she tells Ed after her arrest). But the revelation that Dave's "bigness" was, in the final analysis, only a mirage proves too much for her to bear. As Riedenschneider leaves the conference room, already celebrating the triumph he will win in court the next day, Doris can only manage a bitter laugh, like the dying Visser in *Blood Simple*. Dave, she tells Ed, fighting back the tears, was, after all, only a "big dope," and this, of course, also means that she was a fool to have believed in him. There is another reason Doris no longer wants to live, a secret she carries to the grave. Ed will find it out, but only unwillingly, from the medical examiner who performs the autopsy on her. He thought Ed "should know," but, having told him, he wishes he had held his peace. Doris, it turns out, was pregnant, and it must have been Dave's child since, as Ed tells the examiner, "my wife and I had not performed the sex act for many years." This developing life might have augured a new beginning for the illicit couple, who had been childless and unhappy in their marriages, but with Dave dead the pregnancy must have brought Doris only further shame and chagrin. The court convenes the next morning, only to be summarily dismissed when the news comes from the jail that Doris had hung herself the night before, using the sash from the dress Ed brought for her court appearance. Shocked, Riedenschneider still fails to understand, thinking that Doris had despaired of his ability to get her off. Because he does not even consider the truth of Ed's revelation that Doris and Dave were having an affair, Riedenschneider never thinks that "getting off" might no longer matter to her once she learned the truth about him. Sometimes knowledge is indeed a curse, as Doris discovers.

The Man Who Wasn't There thus offers a series of interconnected variations on the uncertainty principle ("there is no what happened") and its twin, though opposed, correlatives, unknowability ("the more you look, the less you know") and the discontents of knowing ("sometimes knowledge is a curse"). What animates the characters' experience with uncertainty and knowing is a kind of Sartrean nausea, a vague, numbing dissatisfaction with the absurdity of things that gives rise to an inchoate dissatisfaction and, finally, a desperate desire for change. Doris, Ed, and Big Dave all regret their too easily granted acquiescence to mediocrity and ordinariness. The illicit couple hopes their entrepreneurial urge will provide them more of the good life. This plan, however, is desperately flawed because their love affair must remain secret if their business scheme is to succeed. For even after gaining a measure of independence, Dave will not be able to forgo Ann's good graces. Nirdlinger's, main store and annex, will still belong to her family, and if Dave leaves Ann, he will lose what he has worked for. In fact, it is this vulnerability that makes him easy to blackmail. Ed has chosen no more wisely. The man to whom he has handed over the money whose cost is so much blood and misery is running a scam so transparent that anyone but the eminently gullible Ed would have seen through it.

Despite their differences, Ed and Dave share much in common. Also married to a woman he no longer cares about, Ed, too, owes his livelihood to his wife's family. He is the film's narrator, and his first words reflect his dissatisfaction: "Yeah, I worked in a barber shop, but I never considered myself a barber." Ed has made no choice to spend his life in this way. He simply "stumbled" into what he now thinks is a kind of invisibility. Who notices the barber? He is, in effect, a man who isn't there. And Ed has learned to embrace this disengagement, this refusal to connect, which also characterizes his relationship with Doris. Cutting hair, he has learned, requires no interest and only minimal attention, once you learn the "moves," the limited repertoire of haircut styles that he numbly catalogues.

In his depressive self-containment, soothed and sustained only by chain-smoking, Ed offers a stark contrast to his irrepressibly talkative partner, his brother-in-law Frank. Now sole proprietor of the business he inherited from his father, who worked for thirty years to own it "free and clear," as Ed says, Frank has no other ambition but to "cut the hair and chew the fat," as he enjoys the freedom from want and worry that a modicum of material success affords. Frank, in fact, is like most people. He accepts existence on the terms offered to him and seems destined to pass a life much like that of his father, who died of a heart attack in the middle of completing a "junior flattop" for one of the many young boys who seem to be the shop's main customers.

Ed's silence indexes his refusal to accept what life has brought him. His lack of interest in "chewing the fat" is the outward sign of dissatisfaction, not acquiescence. This impassivity, like his taciturnity, flows from endurance and inner suffering. Ed quietly agonizes over what life has brought, as he describes his possessions, in apparent descending order of importance: a house, an in-sink disposal, and, almost forgotten, his wife, Doris, whose sole interests seem to be discount nylons, makeup, and midweek bingo. At home the night after learning of the dry-cleaning "opportunity," Doris, immersed in a tub of soapy water, summons him into the bathroom and asks him to shave her legs. Like cutting hair, the job strikes Ed as disgusting, a descent into human contact he would rather not endure; dry cleaning, as Ed imagines it, is thus not only a better method of laundry ("less shrinkage," as the entrepreneur tells him), but also a Platonic transcendence of the material. Must he continue to suffer working at the barbershop? Must he endure Doris's affair with Big Dave, which he strongly suspects? A start in the dry-cleaning business seems to promise a way out or, perhaps better, a way beyond.

Ed's plan, however, has set a chain of events in motion that he has not foreseen and cannot control. Like all of the Coens' would-be schemers, he finds himself unable to solve the mysteries of other people or to contest successfully the most general rule of human experience—that something always goes wrong. This is the fact of "contingency" with which the postwar era was so obsessed, a sense in which, William Graebner observes, "virtually everything, one's employment, one's values, one's very life, seemed dependent on the vagaries of chance" (19). Ed does not know that the "entrepreneur" had earlier approached Dave for the same sum. Receiving the blackmail threat, Dave draws an incorrect conclusion from the facts he knows, thinking that his disgruntled would-be partner has now turned to threats to get from him what he could not obtain by persuasion. Confronting his supposed tormenter, however, Dave then learns the truth, that Ed is the blackmailer. His plan to solve the problem by murdering Ed goes wrong in turn, resulting ultimately in his death and Doris's, as well as in Ed's, at least temporary, vindication. The innocent suffer along with the guilty. Doris's brother must mortgage the barbershop his father worked thirty years to own in order to pay for Riedenschneider, who, it turns out, never makes an appearance on Doris's behalf because his very success with controlling uncertainty has had the unforeseen consequence of driving her to suicide. Her brother lives in a world ruled by common sense (that is, the predictability and limited repertoire of human motives). And so he is devastated by Doris's death, which is simply beyond his ken, and slips into an alcoholic withdrawal from human contact.

Yet the habit of the daily routine, though interrupted by the most unusual and unforeseeable events, proves impossible to break. Ed tries his best to improve his lot, but even in the smallest ways this proves impossible. He continues working in the shop after hiring the most taciturn partner his interviewing can locate. Yet the man, it turns out, talks incessantly once hired. With Doris gone, he begins to dream of another kind of deliverance, a platonic friendship with Birdy (Scarlett Johansson), the pretty but seemingly innocent seventeen-year-old daughter of a family friend. She plays Beethoven sonatas on the piano, and the music offers Ed a peacefulness he has never found elsewhere. Convinced that she has exceptional talent, even though she is obviously no more than merely competent, he determines to help Birdy launch a career as a concert performer. He arranges for her to audition for an impresario in San Francisco, who deflates Ed's expectations with the truth.

This scheme, too, comes to nothing. As they drive home, Ed learns that Birdy really isn't very interested in playing the piano for a career. It seems she really wants to be a veterinarian. She appreciates Ed's friendship, however, and attempts to perform oral sex on him to show her gratitude. He is shocked and dismayed as the material intrudes once again upon his dream of transcendence. Ed is forced perhaps to acknowledge that his interest in Birdy had, all along, been sexual rather than vaguely paternal. The scene, in fact, seems intended to recall not only the famous car crash in *The Postman Always Rings Twice* that delivers Frank to delayed justice, but a similarly surprising moment of automobile romance in Vladimir Nabokov's *Lolita,* with Birdy playing the role of the precocious nymphet who takes the lead with her older, shyer "admirer." Ed crashes the car. He awakens in a hospital to learn that he has been charged not with sexual transgression, but with the murder of the dry-cleaning entrepreneur, whose body and car have been found in a lake. Big Dave murdered the man after learning the truth about Ed, but Ed is charged and convicted with the crime after the papers attesting to their partnership are found in the man's briefcase. Once again, Riedenschneider is summoned to aid in the defense, but as before, he cannot demonstrate his expertise, this time because a mistrial exhausts Ed's funds and leaves him to the tender mercies, if extraordinary incompetence, of the local trial lawyer. Like Frank in *The Postman Always Rings Twice,* Ed is not executed for the crime he has committed, and yet justice is mysteriously still served. Much like the body of the unfortunate entrepreneur, the past is only belatedly and provisionally laid to rest. A part of the unpredictability that rules over all human affairs in Ed's world, the past suddenly, as if in response to some unknowable design, emerges to call him to account.

Again like Frank Chambers, Ed is not only the main character of the story, he is its narrator, his voice-over commentary a continuing presence as this bizarre sequence of events unfolds. At the film's end, Ed offers an explanation for this uncharacteristic desire to talk about himself and his experiences. While he awaits execution in prison, a crime magazine offers him a good deal of money to write up this bizarre chain of events. Since he is being paid by the word, he feels encouraged to tell more of it than, perhaps, he otherwise would have chosen to do. The film is thus to be understood retrospectively as a visualization of his story as, in effect, an extended flashback even though there is no present "frame." That the narrator is located in a present looking back at his experiences, however, becomes obvious from the first sequence, where typical shots of Ed's life are overlaid with a commentary in the past tense. Thus what we see is earlier in time from the words that fix its meaning, that reveal an inner significance the images alone cannot communicate, for only with the passage of time has this been revealed or clarified.

Flashbacks, of course, are a common feature in 1940s Hollywood productions and are particularly prominent in the film noir of the period. In the many films like *Double Indemnity,* the story begins near its inevitably unhappy end, with an unredeemable protagonist seeking to explain the disasters that have befallen him even as he is forced to acknowledge that he cannot escape the destruction they portend. The spectator is thus encouraged to attend more to the how of his story, not the what, a rhetorical aim that William Graebner puts into a wider social context of the period. The 1940s were an "age of doubt" when Americans were generally, as Graebner puts it, "fearful and distrustful of the past . . . the repository of the most frightening memories" (52). With the past falling like a shadow over events as they are related, the rejection of strict linearity in 1940s films meant the exploration not "of an open-ended present, replete with possibilities and options, but of closure, impasse, and limits" (54). Graebner suggests that two questions were posed by stories that probed the past from the viewpoint of an entrapping present: "The first was the existential question: how would a person react when confronted with a condition of virtual hopelessness? The second . . . how had such a condition been generated?" (54).

Classic film noir, to simplify somewhat, addresses itself to the second of these questions, sketching the chain of events that lead to impasse and closure. For example, in *D.O.A.* (1950), a poisoned man seeks out his killer, and the story he tells the police before expiring offers an explanation for his murder and the investigation that led to the discovery of the killer. Like some of the philosophers and theologians of the period, the Coens, in contrast, address themselves to the first. How do people react to the realization that life is nothing more than "virtual hopelessness"? In *The Man Who Wasn't There,* everything goes wrong, in perfect accord with the ironic poetic justice that is the operative principle of Cain's universe, where the postman of destiny always makes a second visit, rectifying the unearned good fortune delivered on his first. Uncertainty, however, does not manifest itself only in the unpredictability of the future, which may obey laws beyond human ken, making a mockery of the expectation that anyone can escape the consequences of wrongdoing. As the Coens reconfigure the seeming arbitrariness that marks human affairs, uncertainty is less a reminder of a retribution long overdue that must be "delivered" than a force that shapes all attempts to understand both the present and the past.

Uncertainty thus points to the even larger unknowability that haunts human relationships, thwarting all plans to escape the ordinariness of everyday life, with its petty compromises, pointless routines, and spiritual emptiness. Learning the truth about Big Dave prompts Doris's suicide. Shaken from the anaesthetizing effects of an invariant routine by the revelation of a deep uncertainty in human affairs, her brother can find relief only in the bottle, while Big Dave reacts to the frustration of his schemes with a murderous anger that does nothing but destroy him. Thinking that Ed is the cause of their misery, both men ask him the same bitter question he cannot, or will not, answer: "What kind of man are you?" The film, however, offers its own response. Ed is a kind of everyman, whose persistence in a life of "quiet desperation" is irregularly interrupted by unpredictable turnings that respond to but also exceed his dissatisfaction. Because it is the principle that accounts for an enveloping meaninglessness, uncertainty unexpectedly offers the film's anomic loser the comfort of transcendence. Ed discovers the self-possession that derives from having an end appointed to his life, as he finds himself "pulling away from the maze." "Seeing it whole," he admits, "gives you some peace."

Much like Camus's "stranger," another average man trapped by routine and punished for what is seen to be unconventionality and a crime never intended, Ed faces with equanimity his execution for a murder he never committed. In this impending absence, he at last experiences complete presence, or at least he is able to imagine doing so. Now he does not "regret being the barber." He is thus no longer "the man who wasn't there," whose silence was a refusal of intimacy and commitment. Ed hopes instead to find a place where "maybe the things I don't understand will be clearer." There he can at last tell Doris what "they don't have words for here." As Paul Tillich argued in *The Power of Being* (1952), one of the most influential spiritual meditations of the period, "the embrace of meaninglessness is a meaningful act." Only in this way, so Tillich argues, can a "New Being" emerge from a process of "*re*-conciliation, *re*-union, and *re*-surrection."[4]

The film, however, hardly catches the serious intensity of either Tillich's desperate hope for a new spirituality or the reformist spirit of Norman Vincent Peale's aptly titled *Guide to Confident Living* (1948), a popular book to which many uncertain Americans at the end of the decade turned for direction in a world that seemed to have lost its moral compass. Although *The Man Who Wasn't There*, true to the emerging aesthetic of "new sincerity," resurrects the structure of feeling of the late 1940s, the Coens do not take Ed's musings on spiritual transcendence *au grand sérieux*. His hopes for such a transformation, in fact, take shape as somewhat cartoonish fantasy. The anticipated last moments of Ed's life "play" out in an execution chamber whose abstract, minimalist design comes right from a German Expressionism as Walt Disney might reimagine it. Ed's hope, in other words, is thoroughly ironized as unrealizable, the Coens' comment, perhaps, on the religious revivalism that swept a postwar America very desirous of teleological certainties and dramatically increased church membership. Ed's is the vain dream of a dissatisfied, conflicted age that sought deliverance from the "thereness" of its historical moment, which, as the Coens suggest, was dominated by the unforgettable threat of nuclear annihilation, unsatisfiable needs for belonging, and restless demands for self-improvement.

Notes

The epigraph is from Paul Tillich, *The Power of Being* (New Haven: Yale University Press, 1952), 144.

1. Jim Collins, "Genericity in the Nineties: Eclectic Irony and the New Sincerity," in Jim Collins, Hilary Radner, and Ava Preacher Collins, *Film Theory Goes to the Movies* (New York: Routledge, 1993), 243.

2. William Graebner, *The Age of Doubt: American Thought and Culture in the 1940s* (Boston: Twayne, 1991). Subsequent references will be noted in the text.

3. For a full discussion of these developments, see Mark Silk, *Spiritual Politics: Religion and America Since World War II* (New York: Simon and Schuster, 1988), 23–86.

4. Tillich, *Power of Being,* 147.

4. The Exotic Everyday: *Fargo*

> *We get into the habit of living before acquiring the habit of
> thinking. In that race that hastens us toward death,
> the body maintains its irreparable lead.*
>
> —Albert Camus

Like their counterparts in *The Man Who Wasn't There* and *Blood Simple,* the criminal characters in *Fargo* are derailed by uncertainty, which immerses them in a deadly cloud of unknowing. Yet none of these films imagines a strictly deterministic universe, whose inhabitants are crushed by both random mischance and the unreliability of what knowledge they manage to attain. If their plans fail, and they always do, it is as much the result of their bungling, irresolution, or venality. Such a conception of human life can be tragic, and both *Blood Simple* and *The Man Who Wasn't There* at least suggest the tragic dimensions of human failure. The revelation of horrifying realities brings anxiety, even alienation. Awareness of the worst, it seems, can destroy the will to live, as the withdrawal of Doris's brother into alcoholic self-destruction exemplifies. But, so the Coens suggest, disaster can also be mastered. What emerges in these films are two ways characters can rise above their circumstances. The fact of failure and unavoidable accident can be accepted with bravado (consider Visser's bitter amusement at how death finds him); or it can prompt the leap into faith (as in Ed's desperate hope for new words to tell the one he's lost what no words before ever could).

As *Fargo* demonstrates, however, a narrative dominated by confusion and failure offers yet a third possibility, a darkly comic commentary on human frailty. In their versions of classic Hollywood screwball comedy (particularly *The Hudsucker Proxy* and *O Brother, Where Art Thou?*), the Coens explore the deepest tradition of the comic experience, its celebration of a disgraceful death avoided against all odds. *Fargo*, in partial contrast, does not shrink from the representation of annihilation in its most horrible forms. But the film does dramatize how ignorance or incomprehension (its close relative) provides a numbing retreat from such truths, exposing a startling incongruity between revelation and reaction that is bitterly humorous. Seeing the worst, we may be pushed back from the abyss by the "habit of life," bewildered by what we see, returning unchanged to the existence we have always led.

Such is the instinctive reaction of *Fargo*'s chief representative of normality to the horrifying tangle of crime and misadventure she must unknot. Marge Gunderson (Frances McDormand) is a policewoman, the chief detective for a rural Minnesota department, who one frozen morning is suddenly faced with an unaccustomed challenge: three people have been murdered, their bodies strewn along several miles of snowswept highway. Marge is a woman in what is traditionally a man's profession, one that requires the resolution (in the simplest melodramatic terms) of wrongdoing in the public sphere. Into that world, whose horrifying disorders, as the story shows, have all been caused by hysterical men gone wrong, the detective imports the common sense of the traditional domestic realm: a trust in the prescriptive value of moral absolutes, a practical appraisal of advantage and loss, and a proper appreciation of simple pleasures.

Fargo is a self-consciously odd, off-center film, even within the Coenian oeuvre, and its idiosyncrasy is in large part a displacement of familiar categories, not the least of which is that the detective has the attributes of both the traditional wife and the new working woman. Occupying a place of unquestioned authority (Marge is never shown answering to anyone or taking advice from any man), she must, and does, remain composed when faced with the results of horrifying violence. She uses logic and common sense to contain the emotional instability of men, villains and victims alike. And she does so with the wisdom of the hearth and family life, whose very image she is. For this detective is no old-maidish Miss Marple or hard-edged Charlie's Angel on a steep career trajectory. Marge is homely in the best sense of the word, glowing with an obvious pregnancy. As the investigation proceeds, Marge suffers from the normal consequences of her condition, an insatiable appetite and morning sickness. But she does not let such problems sidetrack her. Despite a wave of nausea, she examines, and with professionally appropriate detachment, the frozen body of a young woman so that she can analyze the gunshot that killed her.

Lacking complexities of motive and dark surprises (the film's characters pursue self-interest nakedly—even their betrayals are straightforward), *Fargo*'s plot is easily summarized. Like Ed Crane (and his many predecessors in noir fiction and film), Jerry Lundegaard (William H. Macy) is driven to crime because he is inept and a failure. He holds a respectable position in society (if selling cars is ever respectable), but only through the good graces of his wife's family. Jerry runs a car dealership for his rich businessman father-in-law, Wade Gustafson (Harve Presnell), and when we first see him, he desperately needs a huge sum of money to preserve the illusion he has created of respectability and success. How he has gotten into this fix is never revealed.

Until this point, it turns out, Jerry has staved off ruin by fraudulently raising loan money from GMAC, the General Motors "bank," providing an inventory of nonexistent vehicles as collateral, but company auditors are getting wise to the deception and plan to call in the loan, more than $300,000. Jerry has attempted to raise the money by persuading Wade to make an investment in the building of a parking lot. Jerry intends to turn the investment, at least temporarily, to his own purposes, but Wade is loath to hand over money to a man for whom he quite obviously feels only contempt. So, again like Ed Crane, Jerry determines upon blackmail, with his well-heeled father-in-law the target. There's only one thing he can use to extract money from Wade, and that's his daughter, Jerry's wife, Jean (Kristin Rudrud). So Jerry does what seems obvious to a man of limited intelligence and vision. Consulting an ex-con who works as a mechanic at his dealership, he hires two out-of-state thugs unknown to him, Carl (Steve Buscemi) and Gaear (Peter Stormare). Without any apparent second thoughts, he trusts them to kidnap his wife and hold her without injury until Wade pays the money, making sure that the transaction never comes to the notice of the police.

But things go wrong from the start (naturally enough, this is yet another version of the Coens' customary fictional world). The pair attacks Jean in broad daylight at her home. She bites Gaear, which distracts him from the task at hand, launching him on a search for soothing "unguent." Jean tries to hide from the pair, and Carl can't even manage to corral a frightened woman on his own. To her misfortune, however, she has picked the shower in the bathroom, where the pained Gaear makes his way to rummage through the medicine cabinet. Bolting suddenly from her hiding place after Gaear spots her, Jean gets tangled up in the curtain, which wraps around her. She spins helplessly, tripping, then falls down the stairs and knocks herself unconscious. Meanwhile, Jerry tries desperately to call off the kidnappers because Wade is showing some interest in an investment opportunity Jerry has found. This success, of course, comes to nothing. The meeting between the two men to discuss the deal takes place while the kidnapping is going on. And Jerry's one chance to impress his father-in-law with his business acumen is ruined by misunderstanding and crossed purposes. Wade thinks Jerry is looking for a finder's fee, while Jerry, whose financial needs cannot be satisfied by a few thousand dollars, is planning for Wade simply to turn a million dollars over to him. Perhaps he imagines his father-in-law to be as bad a businessman as he is himself. Wade, of course, simply laughs off the suggestion ("Jerry, for God's sake, I'm not a bank"). Like his wife, Jerry is tangled up and knocked unconscious, at least metaphorically speaking, by his own frantic and ill-considered energies.

Things go no better for the ostensible criminals. As they speed away on a country road, with Jean whimpering in the back seat, toward the remote lake cabin where they plan to keep her, Gaear and Carl are stopped by a state trooper. Carl then remembers he had forgotten to affix the license plates he had stolen for the purpose. Telling Gaear "I'll handle this," Carl tries ineffectually to bribe the trooper, who, refusing, then orders him out of the car. But as the officer looks into the car to see what's making the noise in the back seat, Gaear quickly grabs his head and shoots him dead. Horrified, Carl tries to move the body off the road, but a car, coming in the opposite direction, slows down, and the couple inside get a full view of the grisly scene. They speed away, and Gaear chases after them. Their car flips, and Gaear then shoots them both. Three people are dead, a worse crime committed for no profit to cover one commissioned and paid for. The police are not informed about Jean's kidnapping (Jerry tells Wade they will kill Jean if they do so). It is only by killing the trooper and the two passersby that the kidnappers come to the notice of law enforcement. In fact, Marge solves this crime only to discover its connection to others she had not suspected.

A straight cut, with no exterior establishing shot, moves the action from the side of the road to an interior dominated by artist's supplies: paints, a canvas, sketches of ducks, and some decoys. The camera lingers over these enigmatic objects, then locates, with a panning movement, a sleeping couple: Marge and her husband, Norm (John Carroll Lynch). The editing suggests the permeability of the two settings, with the exterior affording quick and easy access to an interior. There is a "rhyme" later in the film when a shot showing the kidnappers holed up in a cabin watching a public-television documentary on insects is immediately followed by one of Marge and Norm in bed, their set tuned to the same channel. At this point, the threatening crime scene (where sudden death, unpredictable and to them motiveless, suddenly overtakes three people who are simply in the wrong place at the wrong time) is juxtaposed with a vulnerable home, easily entered by the prying camera, its inhabitants asleep and as yet unaware of what has happened. Marge is glimpsed first in her bed, as a wife, not as a policewoman, which she becomes only when, after being awakened by a phone call, she dons her uniform. This scene of married life is touchingly affectionate. Norm gets up to fix his ravenous wife some breakfast and then, when her cruiser won't start, cheerfully gives her a jump-start.

Once out of the house, however, Marge requires no other assistance. Surveying the three bodies, she quickly, and correctly, figures out what must have happened. But she is concerned only about the who, not the why. Confronted with a scene of mayhem, the likes of which she had never before encountered, Marge is not only completely unflappable. She also never wonders what could have led to the commission of such horrible crimes that have, in no obvious way, been committed for profit. Partly, her lack of response resonates with the ethnic stereotypes the Coens play for laughs in this film. *Fargo* is populated by Americans of

Scandinavian descent who are politely placid, either never showing their feelings or never feeling anything to show. Thus in one scene, a car buyer who is being played for a sucker by Jerry has to reach a point of near apoplexy before he can blurt out, to his wife's evident disapproval, "Mr. Lundegaard, you're a liar, a fucking liar." Significantly, the only characters in the film who lose their tempers or act impulsively are male. Among *Fargo*'s calm and compliant women, however, Marge seems exceptionally self-contained, never displaying any interest in probing the threatening otherness she encounters. Fortunately, Marge doesn't need to understand why these people were murdered in order to identify the malefactors. The only clue the killers have left is the trooper's logbook, which registers the last car he stopped, a tan Cierra, as DLR. Marge's deputy thinks these are the first three letters of their license plate. Marge knows better, gently reproving him. DLR must stand for "dealer," the mark that soon enough will link Gaear and Carl to Jerry. It is all the clue she will need to begin an irresistible inquiry that leads to their identification and capture.

Meanwhile, Jerry meets with Wade and his financial adviser, Stan (Larry Brandenburg), to talk about the arrangements that the "kidnappers" have ostensibly conveyed to Jerry. As in their previous business deal, Jerry and Wade struggle for control, with Wade insisting, first, on calling the police (Jerry convinces him that this may cause Jean's death) and, second, negotiating the ransom price downward. But Jerry finds an at least temporary ally in Stan. Though Wade angrily stalks off, it is agreed that a million dollars in cash will be raised, then handed over to Jerry to deliver to the kidnappers. For the most part, this scene, in its antic dramatization of male frenzy and rivalry, simply offers a humorous contrast to Marge's cool, rapid handling of the initial phases of the investigation. There is one additional element, however, that gives it a more complex tone. As the trio departs to go their separate ways, Stan asks how Scotty, Jerry's son, is bearing the absence of his mother. Jerry is completely taken by surprise, his face revealing how he had never before considered that his plan might actually cause pain to anyone he cares about. This spasm of empathy, however, passes quickly and changes nothing. Jerry remains focused on getting the money, even as Wade stays committed to what Stan calls "horse trading" for Jean's life. Scotty, as the next scene reveals, is concerned that something will go wrong and that his mother will die as a result. Jerry tells Scotty, who is not persuaded, that "Grandad and I are making sure that this gets handled right."

And yet these male authorities, if for different reasons, prove completely unable to protect the woman they care about. In fact, neither one gets the chance once Jerry sets into motion a plan that is almost immediately dominated by accident and the unpredictable willfulness of other men, who are yet another pair of bickering, self-destructive rivals. Jerry, like Marge at the very end, misreads the motives of Carl and Gaear, thinking their actions are determined by bourgeois forms of desire, moral calculus, and malfeasance. After all, white-collar crime is always nonviolent crime committed for profit. Such crime, like Jerry's scheme, often aims to raise the money needed to further an illusion of normality and prevent any loss of reputation. And so he tells Scotty what he really believes. These men only want money; they have no reason to hurt your mother. But Jerry hasn't taken into account the workings of either uncertainty or the irrational. The money, or at least most of it, will wind up buried in the wilderness, and Jean will be killed. Carl and Gaear have no reason to keep her alive (they are to get their money before releasing her), and so the latter shoots her out of simple annoyance when she won't stop whimpering.

Marge soon discovers that two men driving a tan Cierra with no tag spent the night at a local hotel, there enjoying the service of local prostitutes, who, like all the witnesses Marge interviews, are forthcoming enough but unable to describe the killers more specifically than to say that one was small and funny looking, and the other a "big fella." No matter, the trail leads first to one of Jerry's employees, Shep Proudfoot (Steve Reevis), who is serving as the go-between with Carl and Gaear, and then to Jerry himself, whom Marge, still unaware that there has been a kidnapping and not suspecting his deeper involvement in any criminal scheme, interviews briefly. Marge drives down to the Twin Cities to do so in person. Her journey there, not strictly necessary for the police business involved, also has another purpose. The previous night, Marge and Norm are in bed when a phone call wakes her. Norm doesn't stir, apparently used to his wife receiving late calls. On the line is Mike Yanagita (Steve Park), an old boyfriend from high school, who has just seen Marge on the local news discussing the triple homicide. Recognizing his voice, Marge's face brightens just as Norm's arm falls across her body, prominently displaying his wedding ring in an act of unconscious (if sanctioned) possession.

We never learn how Marge arranges to meet with Mike in a Twin Cities bar (or whether she informs Norm). This much, however, is clear. Marge certainly goes along willingly, making her way with evident excitement to a rendezvous she has planned. With Mike, Marge is at her most feminine. She wears a pretty frock, with unaccustomed makeup and her hair fixed to match. What does she want from him? Marge seems not to know herself. As she sits across from Mike, it seems clear that they were once close. Mike also thinks that Marge is interested in resuming a romantic relationship as, almost immediately, he moves across to sit next to her. But she gently rebuffs him (out of a sense of propriety? because she won't be rushed or is fearful of her own feelings?). In any case, for Marge, Mike represents more of the same. Here is yet another man, needing, like Norm, some of the power and presence Marge possesses. Mike is working for a large engineering firm, but, as he says, "it's nothing like your achievement." He tells Marge he was married to one of their schoolmates, who subsequently died of leukemia after a long struggle.

All at once, Mike breaks down and cries, confessing to a terrible loneliness and apologizing for his hysterics ("I always liked you so much"). Not knowing what else to say, Marge whispers: "That's okay." Later, she learns from a girlfriend that Mike is doing even worse than he here allows. He was never married to the schoolmate (only pestered her so much he had to be warned off by the police). Never fully reaching adulthood, Mike lives with his parents. If the rendezvous with Mike tempts Marge, in some vague way, to consider stepping outside the narrowly circumscribed boundaries of her life, she immediately abandons the idea. Considering the film's male characters (a rogues' gallery of blowhards, failures, weepy momma's boys, conscienceless killers, and feckless rebels against authority), we can hardly fault Marge's continuing commitment to normality, that is, to Norm, who is devoted to her and whose foibles are at least manageable and endearing. Norm's self-esteem may be fragile, but at least he is no psychopathic liar.

If Mike finds himself in such trouble that he can only imagine that an old girlfriend, who has "made good," somehow can save him, the other men do not fare much better. Jerry proves unable to dissuade Wade from delivering the money to the kidnappers (which, of course, will leave Jerry with no way to recover it for himself, even if the transaction is completed). Carl is staying at Shep's apartment, but his friend, discovering to his fury that the police are on his trail, returns to beat him to a pulp. Wade arms himself with a pistol and drives to a deserted parking lot, where Jerry has told him to meet with the kidnappers (actually, this is where Jerry was to meet Carl). Blundering into a situation about which he is completely misinformed, Wade approaches Carl, still bleeding from the thrashing he earlier received. Carl is puzzled why Jerry hasn't come to make the exchange. Before more than a few words can be exchanged, however, these two uncompromising and impulsive men pull out their guns. Carl kills Wade, but not before being shot in the face himself. Blood streaming from the wound, he drives off with the money, which, he discovers to his utter amazement, is exactly $920,000 more than he was to receive. Jerry arrives at the rendezvous just in time to find Wade dead—and the lot attendant too (apparently shot by Carl in a fit of anger after he didn't open the gate quickly enough). Jerry puts Wade's body

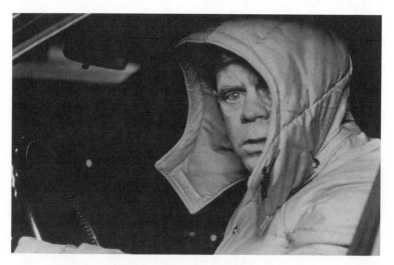

Jerry Lundegaard (William H. Macy) is bewildered by the bizarre plot he has set into motion in *Fargo*. (Courtesy of the Academy of Motion Picture Arts and Sciences)

in his trunk and returns home to an anxious Scotty, without a clue about what to do next.

In the event, the bungling and the pointless brutality that the narrative has traced so far have by no means come to an end. Carl drives back to the rendezvous with Gaear, but he stops to bury the money under the snowdrifts on a deserted field, except for the $80,000 he keeps out to split with Gaear. Though the killers have gotten what they want, they too now argue bitterly, and, thinking he has been cheated (but, ironically, without a clue as to how much he actually has been cheated), Gaear kills his erstwhile partner with an ax. Marge returns to interview Jerry, who, inexplicably, has shown up for work (perhaps he thinks that Wade's disappearance, like Jean's, can be kept from general notice). She is convinced it can be no coincidence that the criminals called someone at his dealership and are driving a car with dealer plates. Terrified that he is now a suspect, Jerry speeds off in his car. Routine police work uncovers the tan Cierra parked at a lakeside cottage. There Marge apprehends Gaear, who is occupied with disposing of the bodies. Jerry, reduced to screaming hysterics, is captured by the state police some time and one state border later. The film ends with Norm and Marge back in their bedroom discussing his career as a designer of stamps. Perhaps remembering the disintegration of Jerry's family to which she has been a partial witness, Marge says plaintively, "Heck, Norm, we're doing pretty good." Their final thoughts before falling asleep are on the baby, whose arrival is eagerly anticipated ("Two more months, Margie").

If Ann in *The Man Who Wasn't There* readily concedes the facticity of alien abduction and governmental conspiracy, even accepting the breakdown of her marriage as a plausible result of what she only surmises happened in the spaceship to Dave, Marge Gunderson reflexively contests the power of the dark truth toward which her experience leads her. That dark truth, to be sure, is nothing as spectacularly untoward as what Ann experiences. It is, instead, the exotic that everyday experience surprisingly reveals as its other side. As the closing dialogue suggests, there is no question of Marge's being shocked out of her deep-seated investment in "ordinariness," which includes, besides her job and the child on the way, a husband devoted in equal measure to her, ice fishing, and his "art." Marge does not surrender to either disillusionment or, worse, paranoia. Pessimistic interpretations of human possibility never tempt her. Nothing, as it turns out, can spoil for Marge the joy that comes from the sudden spell of more pleasant weather that arrives as she finally locates the elusive Cierra. Her surroundings can finally be more clearly glimpsed in the midst of a winter hitherto marked by an inhospitable whiteness that has made it impossible to determine, among other boundaries, where the sky ends and the earth begins.

This unrevealing blankness is the meteorological counterpart of an encompassing epistemological haze, the condition of human perception that renders impossible, at most times, any proper assessment of what is going on. Appropriately enough, the blankness dissipates somewhat only when Marge solves the crime, uncovering the very worst. She thought she was searching for the two men who had murdered, for no apparent reason, the three people in Brainerd. What she finds is something even ghastlier. But for Marge there is no irony in the juxtaposition of the day she at least considers beautiful (many might think it still stormy) and the horror she unexpectedly comes upon. Her search culminates in the sight of a careless sociopath shoving a body, handily dismembered, into a wood-chipper. In a nearby cabin, as she soon discovers, lies the body of another victim intended for the same disposal.

With a horrifying whine of protest at such an inappropriate task, the machine spews mangled flesh onto the snow-covered ground. Like some set piece from a horror film, this infernal tableau exemplifies the most elemental and disturbing truths of human experience, not only death (which is, after all, a disintegrating return to the earth) but also depravity (the annihilating instrumentalization of others, their conscienceless transformation into disposable material no more significant than the odd mulchable tree limb). Marge disables the fleeing Gaear with a merciful bullet to the thigh (it is impossible to imagine her shooting anyone dead), and while driving him back to the station house, she mentions with distaste, if not revulsion, the several corpses left in his wake. Suggesting that his motive for killing these mostly innocent people was a pointless greed (which is only partly correct), Marge scolds Gaear like some schoolmarm miffed by the misbehavior of her young charges: "There's more to life than a little bit of money, you know. . . . And here ya are, and it's a beautiful day." The man, a brutish and barely articulate primitive, has no comment. Marge and her prisoner might as well be from different planets. Though from the same community, they represent opposed, if not disconnected, ways of life. Marge's reaction to what he has done is simple bewilderment. "I just don't understand it," she admits.

The Man Who Wasn't There traces a quite different version of what can happen when the eruption of the barely imaginable shatters the pattern of everyday routine, with its predictable, manageable uncertainties (weather, the news, life's customary sorrows and joys). After Dave's death and Doris's suicide make him aware of the transitoriness that is soon to catch him up as well, Ed senses the unbridgeable gap that has opened up between him and others, who do not live in the expectation of imminent disappearance. As Ed reminisces, "I was like a ghost walking down the street." In the accompanying images, passersby take no notice of him, as they seem to move through the very space he occupies. Ordinary life will have no part of Ed (or, at least, this is his perception). The separation he feels presages his coming death (he no longer feels like one of the living). But his alienation is nothing more than the result of what he now knows, which puts him not only outside others, but also above them in a place of greater knowledge—and a different kind of suffering. As he drives through town one day, he glances at the pedestrians, who are "all going about their business," immersed in everyday concerns. But he was different because, as he recalls, "it seemed like I knew a secret—a bigger one even than what had really happened to Big Dave, something none of them knew."

And what is this secret, the knowledge only he now possesses? That death is the end of life? That anyone, even the most ordinary of hitherto law-abiding citizens, is capable of crime? That the direction of events, once set in motion by desire, can be neither predicted nor controlled? We never learn, but it is clear that experience has transported Ed to a different place, "like I had made it to the outside, somehow, and they were all still struggling, way down below." Down below, the struggle is marked by mischance and misadventure. Ed knows this—the peace he feels comes from surrendering to inevitability, to the chaos that, with no little justice, is soon to overwhelm him.

In *Fargo*, too, everything goes wrong. The passage of time brings the defeat of every expectation, exposes the flaws in every plan, revealing unsuspected viciousness, desperation, or infirmity in many a "respectable" heart. This moral bleakness is made poignant by the plight of the innocent child, Scotty, whose experience of loss helps us measure the culpability of the adults obligated to protect him. Victims and victimizers alike get caught up in the criminal scheme that sets out to harm no one, but which, when once fed by incompetence and accident and a lack of restraint, becomes a homicidal maelstrom with a life of its own. Yet uncertainty and disaster never hector Marge, who differs from Ed in that she is not called upon to suffer. Instead, alone and without other resources, she must bear witness and then restore something like order, becoming in the process the character closest to fulfilling the role of protagonist. In the circumstances, these are not inconsiderable tasks. And she accomplishes them with intelligence, energy, ingenuity, and courage, virtues that she alone among the film's characters possesses. But what she comes to know never puts her in a place of special knowledge. Marge finds the path home easy to travel, the return to routine, and to Norm's weakness, both easily managed and somehow comforting.

Marge's immunity to the way of life she encounters is, on one level, a reflection of the limited experience to be had in a small town in the American heartland. She has no capacity for ambiguity. Marge refuses, or is unable, to understand that people can commit the most horrible crimes simply because they can or because they so desire. To her, Gaear's savagery is unthinkable because of the great disparity in weighing one kind of advantage ("a little bit of money") against another (God's gift of a halcyon day). It is impossible to imagine Gaear, who seems capable of uttering only simple sentences, ever indulging in this sort of rumination. On another level, Marge, unlike Ed, remains firmly committed to the realm of the ordinary. After solving a multiple homicide on her own and apprehending the most dangerous of the criminals, she returns home to assuage the wounded ego of her husband, who feels dissatisfied with the limitations of his latest triumph. His duck design was accepted only for the three-cent issue, one of the "small stamps," as he charmingly whines.

If Marge finds comfort in life's routines, Ed feels imprisoned by them, in quiet desperation cutting the hair and chewing the fat, a pattern broken only by a weekly "indulgence" in church-sponsored bingo. He never thinks of himself as the barber or, for the most part, as Doris's husband, having drifted, without a hint of engagement, into what he does for a living and his lifelong partnership with her, both of which seem to strike him as a kind of servitude. Doris, Ed reminisces, took the lead in their lightning courtship, deciding that they knew each other well enough to marry after only a few dates. Marge, in contrast, never thinks of herself as anything but a police officer and the wife of the aptly named Norm. Ed's crime is in service of making what he hopes will be a different life for himself. It is impossible to imagine Marge ever exploring this kind of fantasy (not to say committing this kind of transgression). As her date (if that is what it is) with Mike Yanagita shows, however, Marge is not immune to being tempted by a different kind of escape from routine. The moral polarities established in a Coen brothers film are never absolute, and, although some of *Fargo*'s critics have seen her this way, Marge is hardly the film's moral center. If she does not surrender to the random and untoward, she hardly acknowledges them as such. We might say that she is willfully ignorant.

With its unflinching, but distanced and absurdist, demonstration that human beings can in fact do the worst things they can imagine to one another, *Fargo* is a comedy of the very blackest kind, a subgenre that draws its humor, as Geoff King suggests, "largely from incongruity, from mismatches between the level of investment displayed in different elements within the situation on screen; especially between the unredeemably violent and the trivial or off-hand."[1] As black comedy, *Fargo* develops with greater detail and forcefulness a theme that draws less attention in *The Man Who Wasn't There*: the realm of routinized existence (numbing or comforting, depending on your point of view) that is inhabited by ordinary people, those who are blindly running that "race which daily hastens us toward death." This is way that Albert Camus suggests most live their lives. "Weariness comes at the end of the acts of a mechanical life," he states, "but at the same time it inaugurates the impulse of consciousness."[2] For Marge, even the most extraordinary events become "the acts of a mechanical life," but the spell of this repetitive rhythm is never broken. Consciousness, at least in the sense Camus has in mind, never comes to her. Thus *Fargo* can draw humor from the juxtaposition of the "trivial" and the barely credible descent into chaos experienced by an insecure man who, like Ed Crane, tries without success to make and sustain a life for himself, despite domination by his wife's family.

The narratives in each film are ironically Oedipal, detailing failed attempts to escape what the protagonists view as castrating immobilization by a woman and belittling domination by a more powerful man. Like Ed,

Jerry tries to extort the money he needs from someone of (at least apparently) greater success and strength, who constantly puts him to shame. Significantly, in *Fargo*, Jerry's schemes are not defeated by a male authority figure (the only policeman who assists Marge is obviously incompetent, gently reproved by her for his inadequacy), but by a pregnant policewoman who easily faces him down. In fact, once confronted by Marge, Jerry and Gaear both react by taking flight. While Ed manages, if involuntarily, to escape Doris's domination, his preadolescent attachment to Birdy cannot survive a descent into sexuality. It is in struggling against her tender advances that he "crashes." Significantly, just before awaking from the resulting coma, he dreams of one day when, beleaguered by a persistent salesman hawking macadam driveways, he is rescued by Doris, who rips the man's brochure in pieces and sends him on his way. In this memory, his wife can barely conceal her disgust for Ed's weakness, for his helpless susceptibility to moronic schemes. Events, significantly enough, show that Doris is right. One day Ed's gullibility does indeed prove their joint undoing. Wade's scornful assessment of Jerry's fecklessness is also accurate. Jerry manages both to destroy himself and also to offer Wade the chance to act with fatal foolishness.

Though played by the same actress, Marge and Doris are very different kinds of women. Marge is deglamorized, a mother-to-be doing a man's job, her body most often enclosed in a bulky police parka. As Ed remembers her, Doris was most interested in perfume, makeup, and the discounted fashion items that she could buy at Nirdlinger's. Like the classic femme fatale, Doris is defined by transgressive desire and the resulting adultery. She is first shown dressed in a slip, bending over to pull on her nylons; like a snooping voyeur, the camera swoops in close, catching her in a sexy pose. But both women are called upon to exert their power over inadequate men, who are much too eager to commit themselves to impossible schemes for self-improvement. Ed escapes that surveillance, only to destroy himself and Doris. Marge cannot prevent the criminal scheme of Jerry (whom she has never met), but she easily bests him in a contest of wills. By way of contrast, Norm submits to Marge's power, allowing her to define the terms of his masculinity. Can it be an accident that Norm's "creativity" is something that he exercises at home and which the viewer sees judged only by his loving wife? Is it insignificant that Jerry and Wade (there seems to be no woman in his life) destroy themselves through something like a misguided entrepreneurship while Norm, with no obvious job but to cater to Marge's constant hunger, enjoys the comforts of a mutually affectionate companionate marriage? Hilary Radner's perceptive feminist reading of *Fargo* could certainly be extended to *The Man Who Wasn't There*. The "moral" in each case seems to be, as she puts it: "a man may escape the taint of his gender by submitting to the intelligence of woman."[3]

Marked by striking similarities and differences, the two films thus form a kind of diptych, offering, roughly speaking, comic and tragic versions of the same male failure to mature and thrive. *Fargo* shares with the Coens' "new sincere" version of film noir one of the traditional subjects of Hollywood's dark cinema: the damage human beings inflict upon one another when they act out of desperate self-interest, paying little heed to likely consequences and lacking reliable knowledge of the others upon whom they depend, at the least, to be "consistent." Like their counterparts in *The Man Who Wasn't There*, the characters in *Fargo* are constantly dumbfounded by their discovery of the dark (or darker) side of those they know. If Marge is surprised to learn that a mild-mannered car salesman has set in motion the kidnapping of his wife, Jerry is shocked to learn that the men to whom he has entrusted his wife's safety manage in their bungling to kill three innocent people. Such moments find memorable equivalents in *The Man Who Wasn't There*: Ed, emerging from his coma, thinks the policemen have come to arrest him for causing Birdy's death (but she survives the accident); Doris, caught up with Riedenschneider's enthusiastic disquisition on uncertainty, is faced with the sudden revelation of Big Dave's lies; and Ed, compelled to help Birdy make a career playing the piano sonatas he finds so soothing, discovers not only her mediocrity but that her real dream is to become a veterinarian. Such characters always miss the obvious and always fail to ask the right questions.

Fargo is a black comedy, dependent on farcical violence and regional stereotypes for its humor. Though it too deals with unpredictability, the film lacks any obvious thematizing of the "uncertainty principle" and the spiritual transcendence made possible by the embrace of meaninglessness. Yet *Fargo* is no less serious a representation of American culture and, by extension, the human condition. Black comedy is usually the vehicle for political satire or social comment, and *Fargo* proves no exception to the rule. The Coens take a cynical approach to all the characters, playing their foibles for laughs. Marge is a "new" New Hollywood woman, as Radner terms her. If she is the film's only source of "heroism," this nonetheless "depends on the triumph of the inadequate, of the less." We are disturbed, Radner suggests, by the centrality of Marge, who is "grindingly dull," a judgment that can be extended, *mutatis mutandis,* to all the other characters in the film (259). The limited comprehension of the wrongdoers matches perfectly the unsophistication of the virtuous, and the line between them is often difficult to draw. For example, Jerry's erstwhile blackmail victim, the father-in-law who thinks so little of him, shares Jerry's obsession with money. If Jerry puts his wife in danger, Wade is less concerned about risking her life than he is about the ransom he must pay, earning (quite unexpectedly, of course) only death for his troubles as he discovers, too late, his manifest powerlessness in a situation of which he actually knows next to nothing.

Representing an outraged normality, Marge discovers the ugly shape of meaninglessness, and yet she retreats from accepting that this is a part of human experience, as her inappropriate reaction to Gaear's depravity shows. The world she has come to know through this investigation is too strange, though it closely borders her own. Outrageous evil, in fact, is the underside of the law-abiding, routinized everyday. Jerry is no sociopath—the crime he commits is in service of maintaining the illusion of his success; in his insecurity and fear of failure, he is not very different from Norm. From the beginning, when she must examine a murder scene that includes a young couple and a state trooper all shot dead, Marge accepts that this other world is real enough, a place that can be mastered by the logic she uses to uncover, and with surprising speed, those responsible. Yet it does not compel her understanding, in a sense her belief (she knows what happened, but she can't *believe* it).

Such exoticness (all the more striking because of its appearance in the midst of the ordinary) perhaps challenges the spectator's credulity as well. Paradoxically, this is in large part because, with its muted color cinematography, *Fargo* develops its story with a flat realist style. The film lacks the self-conscious visual display, the striking camera movements and special effects usually a part of the Coens' approach. The stereotypes of Minnesota culture are detailed with an almost sociological accuracy, perhaps because this was a cultural landscape the brothers know well. Close attention is paid to the intricacies of the local patois and speech mannerisms (a dialect coach was hired to help members of the cast perfect their accents). However, the most obvious form of stylization in the film belongs to mise-en-scène. In the documentary tradition, this is a selection, not a distortion, of the natural. The Coens wanted a Minnesota covered with snow and a blank sky with a low wintry ceiling (no visible horizon) to create an abstract look. Confronted by a lack of snow and too many sunny days, production had to be moved out of state in order to find the right conditions for shooting the exteriors.

Surprisingly, however, the film's realist aesthetic contrasts markedly with the bizarre events of the story, whose credibility is thereby problematized. This is an intended effect, of course. In fact, *Fargo* begins with a printed text that while addressing this problem perhaps also raises it for many viewers. Purporting to tell the truth, this preface is in fact a calculated deception: "This is a true story. The events depicted in this film took place in Minnesota in 1987. At the request of the survivors, the names have been changed. Out of respect for the dead, the rest has been told exactly as it occurred." If the filmmakers' message is supposed to ease understanding and appreciation of a bizarre story, it quickly proves problematic for the spectator. The reason is simple: the chain of events that the film proceeds to relate, though replete with rarely exampled mayhem, has left no marks on the popular consciousness. How can all this be true, the viewer asks, when I have never before heard about it? Thus the truth status of *Fargo* is established as uncertain, if not undecidable. The reader's doubts provide a frame of understanding that contrasts with the ostensible affidavit that prefaces the film. The effect resembles that of the pseudofactual novel, which contains, as Lennard J. Davis states, an "overt frame" that attests to the text's truthfulness, but a "covert frame" that hints at its fictionality. Like *Fargo*, pseudo-factual fiction produces for its reader "a state of ambivalence . . . which extends through his or her experience of the novel."[4] It might be pointed out that such ambivalence, a hesitation about crediting what appears on the screen, means that the viewer must feel something of what Marge does, a sense of what, for lack of a better term, can be called "the exotic," what is, etymologically speaking, "on the outside." But the film shows that the outside is also inside, the distinction between the normal and the extraordinary being impossible to maintain. From this point of view, Marge's inability to be more than annoyed by Gaear's savagery cannot be ascribed to a kind of blindness. Her impassivity implicitly deconstructs the binary opposition of ordinary to exotic.

The film speaks no more of itself after the prefatory announcement of its relationship to "the real"; thus, it offers no answer as to whether that document is to be believed, in the face of evidence to the contrary. An answer, however, does appear in the published screenplay. As the Coens therein confess, *Fargo* "aims to be both homey and exotic, and pretends to be true."[5] Why, then, the pretense of the preface? Two answers suggest themselves. On one level, the deceptive signpost for the spectator appears to be a plea for credibility since the story the Coens have to tell violates the rule of plausibility that usually governs fictional narrative. Implicitly, then, *Fargo* will also not engage with the familiar conventions of genre, those fictional structures that naturalize character types, story patterns, and representational modes (fantasy, realism, and so forth), easing the viewer's investment of belief in the represented world. Not a generic story, therefore, in any obvious sense (though there is much that is in *Fargo* that resonates with noir, as we shall see in the next chapter), the film abounds in events that, if possible, are unconventional in crime fiction. If the story were "true," that would explain why it is not shaped in the customary fashion, why it has not been pruned of disconnections, unknowable motives, and inconsequence. Truth, so the old saw goes, is stranger than fiction, and this is because, as the Coens explain in the preface to the screenplay, "the world, however wide, has folds and wrinkles that bring distant places together in strange ways" (ix). We are reminded that Heisenberg's Uncertainty Principle was formulated to account with more predictability for the otherwise unfathomable movement of subatomic particles.

There may well be another reason for foregrounding the problematic senses in which any story can tell the truth, whether its materials find their origin in the imagination or in "reality." On a higher level, the lie meant to deceive viewers that *Fargo* is a true story reflects the difficulty in separating truth from fiction, real life from stories. Fiction, in a paradox explored since the ancient Greeks, is more readily credible than unshaped reportage because it conventionally restricts itself to the plausible, to what we expect, based on our experience and knowledge, is likely to happen. Fiction, as Aristotle maintains, can shape action in terms of generalities, according to the laws that govern human nature, and it is thus superior to history, which must confine itself to the particular, in which the operation of those laws is not so apparent.[6] Perhaps we don't expect it to be so, but the truth often proves strange, that is, hard to believe because it is not so obviously illustrative of "generalities."

The Coens draw the obvious inference from this fact: "what is closest to home can seem exotic." They are mindful that this strange tale told in *Fargo* offers a view of the culture they know best, the Minnesota that cannot be described "even to ourselves, without it seeming like the South Seas" (ix). Thus, credibility is a dubious guide at best to the distinction between fiction and reportage. The tales we tell each other are perhaps best understood as constituting a continuum, as, in their words, "having greater and lesser fidelity to truth" (ix). And yet fidelity might well prove difficult to gauge accurately. Thus stories that are "not credible will, occasionally, however, turn out to be true, and stories that *are* credible will conversely turn out to be false" (ix–x). Uncertainty thus marks the experience we have with stories, and perhaps the experience we have with experience as well. Why should we believe the film's prefatory text? But, then again, why should we trust the witness of our eyes? How do we in fact *know* anything?

The binary oppositions that figure in the preface to the film and the screenplay (familiar/unfamiliar, credible/incredible, reportage/fiction, truth/lies) figure in the narrative as an encounter between two modes of being, normality and abnormality, or the "homey" and the "exotic," as the Coens put it. The plot sets into conflict "ordinary" people of modest ambitions, the salt of the earth who show up for work and raise families, and the sociopaths they live among, people who, out of greed, pathology, or resentment, or even their own incompetence, commit the most horrible crimes. But the sociopaths are hardly exotic. They too are "trivial," in the sense that their exoticness is grounded in everyday concerns. As *Fargo* details, the killers eat pancakes, get bored with one another's company, find frustrating a television set that gets bad reception, and throw tantrums when a parking lot attendant insists on getting paid. Before he rushes outside in his long johns to murder Carl with the ax he's been using to chop firewood, Gaear puts on his hat. After all, the weather has been cold, and we are, I suppose, impressed by his self-concern (or is it simply a reflex?). We are reminded of Marge at the initial crime scene. Before launching the investigation, she reminds her deputy that she has to pick up some night crawlers for Norm's ice fishing. The everyday envelops the exotic, expressing and yet suppressing its strangeness. And here is the film's political point: contemporary American culture, even in its most mild-mannered midcontinental version, manifests a Hobbesian underside that can erupt at any time into homicidal fury.

Fargo offers a series of scenes that advances the plot fairly economically and with the relentless causality so evident in both *Blood Simple* and *The Man Who Wasn't There.* And yet each scene is also freighted with irrelevancies and sometimes consists only of those excesses and misdirections that, while so typical of lived experience, fiction normally excises because it is invested in shaping its materials in accord with generalities. *Fargo,* as contemporary literary theory would have it, is heavily laden with "reality effects." Jerry meets Carl and Gaear in a Fargo bar, where he is to deliver to them a new car as down payment for the kidnapping they are to perpetrate in Brainerd, Minnesota. But instead of discussing the arrangements, he finds himself arguing with Carl about the time the meeting was set for (Carl insists that Jerry is an hour late). The thugs stop at a motel and hook up with prostitutes; after wild sex, the two couples settle down to watching the *Tonight* show in a scene almost touchingly domestic. Arriving at Jerry's house, Gaear shatters the picture window to get inside, but Carl simply walks through the unlocked front door. Jean is kidnapped while watching the blandest of morning news programs. Hot on the trail of murder suspects, Marge takes time off to make a date with an old boyfriend. Carl buries the hard-won ransom money beneath a snow-covered fence line, whose absolutely identical posts provide no guide to future recovery. Returning to pay off Gaear, Carl gets into a pointless fight with his erstwhile partner about splitting the car, even though he has come into possession of $920,000 more than he had any reason to expect. The disproportionate revenge Gaear exacts makes the joke even darker and more memorable.

These "irrelevancies" or "excesses" function either as reality effects (with their pointlessness a proof of the text's "authenticity," a fictional effect, we might say) or as characterization/description. On a higher level, however, the rhetorical pattern in *Fargo* emphasizes the juxtaposition of the exotic and the everyday as cultural themes. These realms of experience are completely permeable in their absolute divergence from one another, and this paradox creates the incongruity essential to black comedy. *Fargo*'s strangeness is actually its typicality. The world it limns is a not inaccurate representation of contemporary America, where the homey and the exotic interpenetrate to a degree that is, perhaps, worthy of the kind of commentary it receives in this film. The heartland proves home to unsuspected savagery, which can be discovered in the very midst of ordinariness. Gaear's conversion of the wood-chipper to an unimaginably grisly purpose is a most fitting image of the inseparability of, yet distinction between, the everyday and the extraordinary. Such incongruity points to an uncomfortable truth about the society we inhabit, but it is also humorous, prompting a laughter that, because it must acknowledge a pervasive sociopathy, is itself incongruous. To laugh, we must, even more than does Marge, withdraw from what we witness. Black humor is always, for this reason, a joke on us as well. Unlike her, however, we discover an incongruity, disposing as we do of a more complete knowledge of the film's pointed contrasts. Thus, if Marge is not the film's moral center, she functions as its emotional barometer.

But our experience is also strongly differentiated from hers. Even though she solves the case, Marge cannot fully understand all that has happened. The film offers a triple focus on Marge, Jerry, and the kidnappers, with viewers always knowing much more than any character. Though given the safe haven of dramatic irony, we find ourselves denied a stable point of identification. In other words, the completeness afforded by a point of view above the characters is necessarily fragmented, divided among the characters, whose desires are complex and competitive. Only the spectators are positioned, through their sweeping knowledge of a field of disparate events, to find equal places for the homey and the exotic. Only we can thereby comprehend the depth of their interpenetration. Or, to put this in the epistemological and ontological terms *Fargo*'s preface proposes, only spectators, who are told they are watching a story that is true, find themselves deliberately suspended between belief and incredulity.

Such a complexity, which is undecidable for all those without access to the screenplay, may perhaps be best understood as a postmodern gesture. Interestingly, even the screenplay renders only a sort of an answer, as the Coens go on to problematize the very certainty they propose to bestow. After all, postmodernism, to quote Linda Hutcheon, is characterized by a "wholesale, 'nudging' commitment to doubleness or duplicity."[7] The point is "to de-naturalize some of the dominant features of our way of life," a central one of which being a firm distinction between the fictional and the nonfictional. Thus, postmodernist doubleness often "juxtaposes and gives equal value to the self-reflexive and the historically grounded; to that which is inward-directed and belongs to the world of art (such as parody) and that which is outward-directed and belongs to 'real life'" (2). We can also understand this duplicity as prompting interpretive questions. Is the film's strangeness, the truth distorted to the point of risibility, simply the sign of comic intent? Or, with its rejection of generalities (the comforting, ideologically grounded categories in which we seek to fit all experience), is that strangeness the sign of a commitment to truth telling (to telling the truth *about* fiction *with* fiction)? In other words, is the bloody wood-chipper, and all it represents, either a pretext for grim humor or (in the condensed form of an enigmatic symbol) a proposition worthy of serious consideration? The Coens' postmodern point, which is by no means apolitical, is that it is both.

Notes

The epigraph is from Albert Camus, *The Myth of Sisyphus and Other Essays* (New York: Vintage Books, 1955), 7.

1. Geoff King, *Film Comedy* (New York: Wallflower, 2002), 186.
2. Camus, *Myth*, 7.
3. Hilary Radner, "New Hollywood's New Women," in *Contemporary Hollywood Cinema,* ed. Steve Neale and Murray Smith (New York: Routledge, 1998), 256. Subsequent references will be noted in the text.
4. Lennard J. Davis, *Factual Fictions: The Origins of the English Novel* (Philadelphia: University of Pennsylvania Press, 1996), 21.
5. Ethan Coen and Joel Coen, *Fargo* (London: Faber and Faber, 1996), x. Subsequent references will be noted in the text.
6. Aristotle, *On Poetry and Style*, trans. G. M. A. Grube (New York: Bobbs-Merrill, 1958), 180.
7. Linda Hutcheon, *The Politics of Postmodernism* (New York: Routledge, 1989), 1. Subsequent references will be noted in the text.

5. The Artist, Mass Culture, and the Common Man: *Barton Fink* and *Raising Arizona*

I'm a comic writer and it seems impossible to me to handle any of the "big things" without seeming to laugh or at least smile.

—Nathanael West

I was beginning to gain that sense of power that an artist feels by subduing his materials, the power he gains over the whole world — the real freedom in other words. But that was last year, perhaps the year before. Now I have a sense of sitting in a cell with all the obscenities of life in my lap.

—Clifford Odets

Writers come and go. We always need Indians.

—Producer Ben Geisler in *Barton Fink*

Fargo advertises itself as a "true story," ostensibly eschewing thereby any intertextual connections with other works, cinematic or literary. The film's invisible stylization avoids much that often in Coen brothers films alerts spectators to the knowing presence of their creators: unmotivated camera movements, intrusive voice-over narration, unusual graphic matches, and premonitory dream sequences replete with obscure spokesmen and arcane symbols. The distinctive look of *Fargo* has little to do with photography or editing, but depends mainly on an astute manipulation of mise-en-scène, with the blankness of the Siberia-like exteriors matched by an art design that admits only earth tones and dull greens or grays in costuming and interior decoration. Such drabness is expressionistic. It is the perfect visual correlative not only to the harsh monochrome environment, but also to the characters' embodiment of those northern European Protestant values (especially the dislike of ostentation in all its forms) that define the culture of the American Middle West. *Fargo*'s "natural" mise-en-scène is also an extended reality effect, textual proof of the storyteller's conformity to accepted protocols of truth telling, especially his announced undertaking to change nothing but the names.

Yet despite the film's commitment to hiding its fictionality (as we have seen, it entirely lacks the self-reflexivity so much a feature of the postmodern aesthetic), *Fargo* is deeply generic in its themes and characters. As often happens in the classic film noir, *Fargo* traces the interpenetrating encounter between two opposed but complementary versions of American life. The law-abiding respectability pursued by Marge and Norm, among others, finds its moral central in constant self-governance. They are subjects who, in the description of the Marxist sociologist Louis Althusser, "work by themselves." Marge and Norm, in other words, are so unaware of the ideological rules that govern their behavior that they cannot imagine not obeying them. Their pursuit of (limited) financial success thus keeps close to the straight and narrow, not only because there is much to lose, but also because there is so little (thus it seems to them) to gain. As Marge suggests, the value of money must be measured against (and found wanting compared to) the plain wonders of God's creation: a day of clearing weather, beautiful ducks to serve as an artist's models, and a baby on the way. In contrast, the malefactors in this noir world include those who, like Jerry, want to live the right kind of life but whose moral failure brings financial disaster—as well as those who, like Carl and Gaear, want the "good life" as defined by middle-class values (the first fruit of their crime, we remember, is a brand-new, American-made sedan, a "family" car). If desirous of the appurtenances of respectability, they are unwilling to play by society's rules to obtain them, and this is what Marge does not (perhaps will not) understand.

Such a bourgeois view of crime and criminality is often a feature of the classic film noir. In Fritz Lang's *The Woman in the Window* (1945), for example, Richard Wanley (Edward G. Robinson), a respected middle-aged college professor and family man, gazes upon the portrait of a woman in a gallery window and, suddenly, as if in response to his unspoken desire, the same woman appears behind him—beautiful, unattached, and welcoming. After sharing a drink, they proceed to her apartment. There Wanley is attacked by her lover, the rich and powerful man who keeps her in such good style, and he kills the man in self-defense. Though innocent of murder, Wanley is guilty of a disastrous moral indiscretion. Informing the police would mean the end of his career and marriage, or so he thinks. Hence, like Jerry, Wanley is forced into committing other crimes to cover his malfeasance, betraying the other relationships in his life and forfeiting his self-respect. Even so, all attempts to cover up his involvement in the crime fail. It seems likely yet another opportunistic male, who is attempting to blackmail him, will turn him over to the police.

Yet just as Wanley is about to commit suicide (and so avoid the shame that will follow detection), a dissolve reveals the entire story of his weakness and downfall to be a dream. The professor had simply fallen asleep while reading the kind of book a man in his position might find provocative, the Bible's Song of Solomon. The respectable man's unconscious dramatization of his inner life offers a perfect illustration of self-governance, with his transgressive wish fulfillment (a Pygmalionesque vivification of an artist's image) generating its own narrative of shamefulness and punishment. Wanley is thereby issued an effective warning against surrendering to whatever temptations the waking world puts in his path. And he immediately shows that he has "learned his lesson" when, walking by the same gallery window that had appeared in his dream, he looks at the beautiful portrait and is approached by yet another woman (less elegant in appearance than the artist's image, of course, because she is "real," not the projection of his desire). He flees from her in a terror that is abject and yet still polite, a pointedly comic image of his weakness and unshakable conventionality. A similar kind of humor figures in *Fargo*. Though under terrible pressure, Jerry never loses his composure where others can see him. Instead, he vents his frustrations only when alone, throwing his arms around like a spoiled child in his office, impotently flinging a windshield ice scraper into the snow in an empty parking lot as a protest against bad fortune and his own fecklessness.

Like Professor Wanley in his nightmare, Jerry finds himself in a morally impossible situation once his financial indiscretions have involved him in an illegal act. Jerry can preserve his respectability only by making contact with the very forces that destroy it, and with such unintended ease. Though "true," Jerry's story is deeply noir, especially in its imagining of the underside of American culture in moral rather than economic or social terms. Jerry and Marge, after all, claim membership in the same broadly conceived middle class; no apparent difference of access or opportunity divides them. The dark city of noir film often deploys the signifiers of poverty or the lifestyle of the lower orders. And so it is in *Fargo*. With their uneducated speech, disreputable appearance, and dubious manners, Gaear and Carl are self-evidently "trash." Yet such visual elements evoke not class warfare but rather the failure of virtuous self-restraint. Significantly, Gaear kills Carl in a sudden fit of anger after the bungling kidnappers have managed to blunder into success, exemplifying the suicidal energies of the morally ungoverned.

The connection of the noir "underside" to a failure of character is most clear, perhaps, in the alternative "world without George Bailey" sequence from Frank Capra's *It's a Wonderful Life* (1946). In this waking nightmare, the good man is put under erasure (for the hypothetical world includes him only as a literal nobody), and this present absence generates the threatening cityscape of the noir vision, with its economic stagnation, moral hopelessness, distrust of strangers, unbridled self-indulgence, and sexual frustration. In a similar vein (which is in the indicative rather than the subjunctive), *Fargo* shows what happens when the moral failure of the good family man plays out in the real world. If George Bailey is rescued from his financial troubles by the generosity and goodwill of his neighbors, Jerry has realized, as the narrative begins, that no one, especially his father-in-law, has any interest in saving him from a similar disaster. The film is in fact thoroughly noir, belonging like *Blood Simple* to a prominent classic and contemporary subgenre, those "melodramas of mischance" whose reappearance in neo-noir has been effectively anatomized by Foster Hirsch. In such narratives, as Hirsch puts it, "bourgeois characters are sucked into a criminal undertow," a description that suits *Fargo* perfectly.[1] In this respect and others, the Coens' film shares much in common with other productions of the last two decades, including *Cape Fear* (1991), *Nick of Time* (1995), *The*

Morning After (1986), *Someone to Watch over Me* (1987), *Breakdown* (1997), and *The Net* (1995), among numerous others.

Most, but not all, Coen brothers films are genre exercises. *Barton Fink* and *Raising Arizona* prove exceptions to the general rule. Though they are dissimilar in other respects, these two productions are intriguingly self-reflexive, in the sense that each thematizes storytelling. *Raising Arizona* offers, in flashback narrative, the main character's first-person account of his life, including its "projected closure," that is, his end as he imagines and hopes it might be. *Barton Fink,* in contrast, is dramatic rather than confessional. Much like *The Man Who Wasn't There,* the film is a historical recreation. This postmodern pastiche takes as its subject matter, in complex ways to be explored below, two renowned writers of the 1930s and 1940s who were employed by Hollywood and whose works offered an influential critique of commercial filmmaking and, more generally, of mass cultural production.

Such a resurrection and reconfiguration of the past (with particular attention paid to the era's representations of itself) is a not uncommon postmodern project, with Stephen Daldry's mounting of *The Hours* (2002) providing an especially close analogue. Daldry's film probes the interpenetration of Virginia Woolf's life and fiction, dramatizing the composition of her novel *Mrs. Dalloway.* But *The Hours* also traces the influence of the book and Woolf's contradictory experiences (her relentless creativity yet eventual suicide) on women of two later generations. It is not the intention of the Coens or Daldry to provoke some false sense of nostalgia through this kind of parody. These films do not in any sense flatten out the past, eliminating the depth of its otherness for comic effect. On the contrary, *Barton Fink* and *The Hours* amply exemplify the view of Linda Hutcheon that, *contra* Jameson, postmodernism (of, at least, the sort that the Coens and Daldry practice) "does not deny the *existence* of the past; it does question whether we can ever *know* that past other than through its textualizing remains."[2] It is with "remains" of this kind that the Coens confect *Barton Fink.*

Set in late 1941, *Barton Fink* traces the crisis, both personal and professional, of a successful Broadway playwright turned Hollywood screenwriter. The film thus engages with the aesthetics and institutions that govern the production/consumption of cinematic narrative in American culture. The historical moment recreated in *Barton Fink* is the growth to classic perfection of the sound cinema in the years immediately preceding America's entrance into war. By 1941, Hollywood had completed the most profound change of its early history: the development of a radically different kind of textuality after the precipitous fall into obsolescence of the silent cinema, with the displacement of that medium's nearly exclusive reliance on the communicative power of images. Because actors now talked and, talking, could be provided with more complex and engaging forms of narrative, Hollywood all at once needed writers of proven talent and popularity. With much money at their disposal, the major studios proved quite successful in hiring the most popular and acclaimed on the American scene away from the writing of plays and fiction. *Barton Fink* deals with one result of the inevitable cultural collision: the encounter of modernism (in its different modes ranging from social realism to superrealism) with the formula-based genres of popular narrative, which had been adapted to the requirements of Hollywood's most reliably profitable form of repetition, the star vehicle.

The difference between such forms can be theorized expressively, as the distinction between personal and impersonal forms of fictionalizing, or in terms of readability, with the generally opaque modernist text offering a more demanding experience than its popular counterpart. But for our purposes a more useful way of distinguishing between modernism and mass cultural narrative has been proposed by Fredric Jameson. Jameson argues that only by failing to historicize these two forms properly can we indulge in the "valorization of traditional modernist high art as the locus of some genuinely critical and subversive 'autonomous' production."[3] Instead, the emerging commodification of art in modernity has meant that "high and mass culture . . . [are] twin and inseparable forms of the fission of aesthetic production under capitalism." Thus "from a historical point of view the only form of 'high culture' which can be said to constitute the dialectical opposite of mass culture is that high culture production contemporaneous with the latter, which is to say that artistic production generally designated as *modernism*" (15). Mass cultural and modernist texts, it follows, thus work over the same social materials, but in contrasting fashions and to different ends: "Both modernism and mass culture entertain relations of repression with the fundamental social anxieties and concerns, hopes and blind spots, ideological antinomies and fantasies of disaster, which are their raw material; only where modernism tends to handle this material by producing compensatory structures of various kinds, mass culture represses them by the narrative construction of imaginary resolutions and by the projection of an optical illusion of social harmony" (25–26).

In the Coens' oeuvre, *Barton Fink* exemplifies the modernist narrative project, which, in dealing with its contradictory and threatening ideological materials, does not resolve them in the interest of "social harmony" and the pleasure such an "optical illusion" might afford the spectator. Instead, the story of artistic development and frustration that it limns ends without an easy or satisfying resolution that, nonetheless, is indeed a form of "compensation." By way of contrast, *Raising Arizona* projects into a certainly unrealizable future an impossible moment of stifled conflict and hard-won reconciliation. It thereby emphasizes its affiliation with the utopianism, however disavowed, that it is the project of the mass cultural text to provide.

Barton Fink, in a typically modernist gesture, does not allow its eponymous protagonist to transcend his artistic crisis. Neither high nor mass cultural aesthetics answers to Fink's needs for personal expression and meaningful intervention in the class struggle, even though he manages, under great pressure, to combine the forms, producing after seemingly endless struggle the script for a "wrestling picture" that has social significance. But the studio head who had commissioned the project deeply faults Fink's efforts to infuse entertainment with heartfelt seriousness ("We don't put Wallace Beery in some fruity movie about suffering"). So much for Barton's experience with penning what, in contemporary terms, seems very much a "commercial/independent" text—like the films the Coens themselves make. There is a striking contrast between the Coens' experience with the industry and that of their textual other. Like most independent films that take Hollywood as their subject (such as Robert Altman's *The Player* [1992]), *Barton Fink* plays for laughs the divergence between its own evident freedom of expression and the constraints that haunt the harried characters in its fictionalized Hollywood, an imaginary locus that seems nothing less than a wilderness of intellectual life ruled by Neanderthal moguls and Philistine producers.

As it happens, Barton is rewarded in another way for the dubious triumph of finishing the assignment. Having reached a dead end in his personal and professional lives, he finds compensation in both a glimpse of a natural world beyond representation and insight into "the life of the mind," which is metonymically contained in an enigmatic package—and this, so it is hinted, contains a significant totemic object, perhaps the severed head of a great writer. Barton never opens the package, in a suspended gesture that suggests nothing so much as the film's resolve not to resolve its several enigmas. Thus, the film offers its protagonist, as a final possibility, a welcoming space beyond the meditation of representation where he is permitted to remain, if only for a while, in erotic/aesthetic contemplation. There, in a literalization of the concept of "closure," Barton reaches a spot where further movement, physical or spiritual, seems impossible. Somehow he stumbles onto a California beach, at the margin between land and sea. In this way, he completes the journey from the East Coast of high cultural art (the Broadway theater) to the West Coast of cultural production (the Hollywood cinema). But where *does* he go from there? Is there some space that offers the opportunity for a meaningful engagement with "the common man," who is conspicuous by his absence on this beach? And what formal tradition is he to follow if he wishes to address his plight? Such questions find no answers in the film.

Because it is ostentatiously rich in cultural connections, *Barton Fink* demands a more complex response than *Raising Arizona*, to which I will return briefly at the end of this chapter. While *Barton Fink's* intertextual reach is primarily literary, the Coens do not neglect the cinematic. Roman Polanski's two character studies of claustrophobic psychopathology, *Repulsion* (1965) and *The Tenant* (1976), are an acknowledged and obvious influence, especially in the Coens' presentation of the hotel as a kind of horrid, living organism (in a bit of good fortune, Polanski happened to be serving on the jury at Cannes that awarded the brothers the Palme d'Or for this film). Stanley Kubrick's *The Shining* (1979) also shaped the film's mise-en-scène and themes, providing a connection that bears a bit more analysis. In his famous essay on *The Shining*, Fredric Jameson expresses a puzzling admiration for Kubrick's historical re-creation, *Barry Lyndon* (1975), whose "very perfection as a pastiche intensifies our nagging doubts as to the gratuitous nature of the whole enterprise."[4] For him this exquisitely hollow production exemplifies the problem of meaning in an era that is experiencing a "waning of histori-

Writer's block afflicts would-be Hollywood scenar-
ist Barton Fink (John Turturro). (Courtesy of the
Academy of Motion Picture Arts and Sciences)

cal affect." But the same director's *The Shining* may be read as a critical statement, as a "meditation on the issues raised by his previous film and on the very impossibility of historical representation" (92).

Much like the Coens' *Barton Fink, The Shining* tells the story of a failed writer whose compositional block (actually an endless repetition of the same, brief "expressive" formula, an indication of deep resentment at the imperative to work) opens him to both violence within and, shall we say, other voices and presences without. With its self-reflexive analysis of an artist's frustrating, then apocalyptic encounter with Hollywood, *Barton Fink* encourages the same kind of reading. In the Gothic tradition, the Coens' film also offers a nightmarish rendition of what Harold Bloom terms "the anxiety of influence." Both films trace encounters with a human malevolence (especially a violent misogyny) that may be real, but, alternatively, also seems a fabulizing projection of the writer's own insecurities, anger, and sense of rejection. Unlike *The Shining*, however, the Coen brothers' film designates a complex literary intertext, and it is a telling comment on the Coens' indifference to being properly understood (itself a modernist pose) that their references have proved too obscure to decode for most reviewers and commentators—and undoubtedly for the majority of viewers as well.

Another point of divergence is that in *The Shining* the physical and spiritual emptiness of the present (the deserted hotel, the unresolved tensions of family life, the would-be writer's inability to find anything worthwhile to say) contrasts with the living nightmare of a more attractive but destructive past. This is a convention of the gothic followed in the Coens' film as well, where the threatening dwelling (yet another hotel) is likewise the source of meaning, a site where recognition, especially in the sense of self-awareness, can be achieved. If the protagonist of Kubrick's film feels desire, it is something along the lines of what Jameson proposes, "a longing to believe and the nostalgia for an era when belief seemed possible" (95). Such a reading emphasizes how *The Shining* reflects a postmodern sense of cultural deadlock, of pervasive absence, of the unsupportable pressure from an all-devouring history. In contrast, *Barton Fink* is not located in a present ever looking backward, but in a past moment, carefully reconstructed and yet marked as a construction, that aims to provoke a historiographic curiosity as a bygone era whose depths have yet to be fully explored. The Coens' hotel does not contain the ghostly traces of a better era. It houses, instead, a representative "common man," who demands, appropriately enough, meaningful engagement in the here and now.

Which is to say that *Barton Fink* shares the traditional aims, if not the social realist aesthetic, of historical fiction. In fact, the film's mise-en-scène, art design, and even acting are more expressive than naturalist. This slightly exaggerated richness is a constant reminder that *Barton Fink* offers a constructed evocation of, not a clear window onto, the past. Along with its unresolved enigmas, such constructedness can be read as a sign of the film's modernist intentions. One recalls James Joyce's prophetic boast that he had left enough puzzles in *Ulysses* to keep the professors busy for decades, or T. S. Eliot's appending of arcane footnotes to *The Wasteland*. *Barton Fink*'s hermeneutic obscurantism thus appears to be a key modernist element, and this is the principal way in which this film differentiates itself from the Coens' other efforts, which are much more *lisible*.

The three films we have examined thus far exemplify one aspect of the postmodernist aesthetic of the Coens, their *retro* engagement with classic genericity. As we have seen, each film thereby establishes a unique fictional world, of which the artists, who are perhaps no longer "originary powers" in the classic sense, seem something on the order of impersonal "facilitators." In contrast, *Barton Fink* and *Raising Arizona* can be read as commenting directly and specifically on the Coens' filmmaking career. We might say that the two films exemplify, and with no little irony, formal paths otherwise not taken: the modernist art film (with its depiction of a layered crisis, personal and artistic, perhaps even vaguely autobiographical, in the manner of Fellini's $8\frac{1}{2}$) as well as the conventionally impersonal entertainment production (here in its guise of something like a screwball comedy).

If it differs from the ordinary Hollywood movie in its striking stylizations (mostly jokey special effects of various kinds that further the film's antirealist, even cartoonish mode of representation), *Raising Arizona* is hardly postmodern in any other sense. In fact, it is the only Coen brothers film that responds to a current social issue prominent enough to have been taken up by mainstream Hollywood productions of the time: an anxiety-ridden preoccupation on the part of an increasingly yuppie younger generation with the discontents and debatable joys of family life, especially fertility and fatherhood. *Raising Arizona's* intertextual reach is thus limited to its connection with a short-lived, late 1980s comedy series that includes *Baby Boom* (1987), *Three Men and a Baby* (1987), and *Parenthood* (1989).

It seems that a reading of the Coens' oeuvre as a portfolio of fabulizing possibilities uncovers both inclusions and exclusions—and not only in the obvious sense, that is, as choices of form or artistic mode. For their oeuvre, as a "whole" in progress, also may be read symptomatically, as offering a description of the situation of the artist in postmodernity, who can no longer choose between positions that were once mutually exclusive: high-cultural art, on the one hand, or formula production for the mass public, on the other. In terms of practice, what this would mean is either a critical distance from the increasingly totalizing commercial culture or complicity with its institutions. With a great deal of irony and humor (directed particularly at those with social pretensions), *Barton Fink* dramatizes that dilemma by tracing it to its historical roots. The main character is a Jewish playwright of vague, if deeply held, leftist convictions who, having achieved a notable success on the New York stage with a play about the urban poor called *Bare Ruined Choirs,* has decided to accept a "temporary position" as a Hollywood screenwriter. Though he is obviously attracted by the possibility of a fabulous salary, Fink convinces himself that he also decamps in order to further the fortunes of the financially strapped theatrical collective with which he has been hitherto associated.

Barton Fink is in fact a fictionalized but quite recognizable version of Clifford Odets, the leading American dramatist of the 1930s (behind Eugene O'Neill), who in one *annus mirabilis* of artistic/critical success (1935) saw four of his plays in simultaneous Broadway production. Odets is primarily remembered today for his connections with the Group Theatre, founded in New York in 1931. The Group was a loose organization of actors, playwrights, and stage directors: in addition to Odets, most prominently, Harold Clurman, Cheryl Crawford, Lee Strasberg, John Garfield, and Elia Kazan. Beyond developing a more effective style of naturalist acting (the so-called "Method"), its principal aim was to create, as a permanent feature on the Broadway scene, an American theater in which works of social significance rather than shallow entertainment should be most prominent. Its greatest commercial successes were achieved, under Clurman's leadership, in their Broadway mounting of Odets's early plays, particularly *Waiting for Lefty* and *Golden Boy*. By 1941, with the departure of both Clurman and Odets for Hollywood, the Group ceased to be much of a collective presence on the American scene, though its individual members, especially Clurman, Strasberg, and Kazan, continued to play prominent roles in Hollywood and on Broadway. In an artistic sense, however, Odets never moved far beyond this formative experience. As Malcolm Goldstein states with no little irony in regard to his later work, "as late as 1949 he continued to write the best American plays of the thirties, and nothing else."[5]

Odets, as Goldstein suggests, failed to adapt to different institutional circumstances and a profound evolution in popular taste, as the American theater became, in Norma Jenckes's revealing formulation, "the house of mirrors of the American family . . . the territory of the tormented psyche."[6] Eugene O'Neill was the first to explore these new themes, to be followed then by Arthur Miller, Tennessee Williams, and William Inge, among lesser others, in the later 1940s and on into the 1950s. Though his plays eschew the psychological for the political and the social, the Coens' version of Odets's experiences in Hollywood, ironically enough, certainly explores "the territory of the tormented psyche." Such a treatment is justified in biographical terms, very roughly speaking, and it was undoubtedly suggested to the filmmakers by what they came to know about the turning point of Odets's life, of which he left a detailed and intimate record. In 1940, only five years after his greatest commercial and critical successes, Odets was in deep crisis. His marriage to the Hollywood actress Luise Rainer was failing, while his latest play, *Night Music,* in which he abandoned the social realism of his earlier successes for a kind of picaresque romantic comedy, had resoundingly flopped. For a year he lived off the considerable money he had made thus far in his career, staying in hotels and traveling, while he pondered what artistic direction to take. Odets was also increasingly puzzled by his irrepressible and promiscuous sexual desires (for his soon-to-be ex-wife and a number of other women, married and single).

Sensing that this period would be a turning point in his life, Odets compiled a detailed journal of his experiences (including sexual encounters with women he invited to his hotel room, a practice that finds its echo in the Coens' film). He recorded numerous trysts, elaborate sexual fan-

tasies and dreams, and many anguished meditations on the painful pleasures of love. It was the only journal of this kind he ever kept. The result
makes for interesting and revealing autobiography, a mixture of kiss-and-
tell reportage and philosophical speculation (Odets was an autodidact
prone to engage in somewhat banal meditations, much like his counterpart in the Coens' film). The publication in 1988 of what had come to be
known as *The Time Is Ripe: 1940 Journal* was an important literary event.
Although the Coens have never admitted, at least in print, that they had
recourse to it as a source for the screenplay that was to become *Barton
Fink*, the dependence of their film on *The Time Is Ripe: 1940 Journal* is
easily demonstrated (though it is not the only literary text that provided
them with ideas for this unusual story, of which more below).

Interestingly, it was in 1988 that the script for *Barton Fink* began to
take shape. The Coens had been occupied with writing the gangster story later filmed as *Miller's Crossing*, but they were having trouble finishing the script because the narrative turned out to be especially complicated and not easily resolved. And so to divert themselves from this
trouble, they started work on *Barton Fink*, whose composition they completed before returning to *Miller's Crossing*. In an intriguing autobiographical twist, the film takes as its subject the similar compositional
difficulties experienced by a screenwriter from the classic studio era,
another East Coast Jewish intellectual similarly lost in the intricacies of
a genre script he was writing for the pictures. *Barton Fink* and the *1940
Journal* are thus connected in several interesting and revealing ways.

Odets managed a resolution of sorts for the uncertainties and anxieties of that watershed year. He divorced Rainer soon afterwards and
went on to spend two decades in Hollywood building a successful career as a screenwriter. The change of address and focus did cost him his
Broadway reputation, although Odets was to write again, and successfully, for the stage. *The Big Knife* (1949), *The Country Girl* (1950), and
The Flowering Peach (1954) all enjoyed Broadway runs, and the first two
of these plays were also adapted, with some success, for the screen.
Odets's fictional counterpart does not fare so well. Barton Fink first finds
failure in a world of false, readymade culture. Unlike his real-life model, he simply cannot write well within popular genres. A worse threat to
his sanity and freedom is in store, however, as a psychopathic insurance
salesman introduces him to both "the common man" and "the life of the

mind." Mild mannered and friendly (if given to self-pity), this salesman turns out to be the perpetrator of horrific violence, the apparent reflex of deep resentment at his sense of social marginalization.

In *The Big Knife,* Odets gives his experiences in Hollywood a quite different shape. In this play, he dramatizes the deep disappointment, and eventual suicide, of a once-talented writer who has sold himself to manipulative, inhumane studio moguls in return for financial success. His profitable sojourn as a screenwriter offers little happiness and no possibility for self-respect. Odets's drama of moral disintegration ironically unfolds in settings that suggest power and accomplishment: studio offices and the lavish homes of Beverly Hills. By way of contrast, *Barton Fink* is largely set in a seedy hotel. With its suggestion of impermanence, dislocation, and alienation, the hotel, as well as the grotesquerie that, as a mode of representation, elicits a dark humor from what takes place there, seems drawn from a different literary model, perhaps the era's most famous portrait of Hollywood culture, Nathanael West's *The Day of the Locust* (1939). West's novel is set in an apartment complex that has seen better days and is populated by would-be performers and other hangers-on. Like Odets's agitprop plays of the 1930s such as *Awake and Sing* (barely disguised in the film as *Bare Ruined Choirs*), West's most renowned work is deeply political, but in a radically different sense.

Certainly, like Odets, West was a committed critic of the capitalist system, which he saw as heartlessly exploitative of the workers whose blood and sweat made enormous profits for the very few. But the real danger to American society, West thought, might come from another direction, as the critic Jonathan Veitch observes: "instead of following the official line of the Popular Front, which saw fascism as 'contamination from abroad' or 'conspiracy from above,' West's narratives suggest that if fascism were to emerge in America, it would most likely emerge from below, from the people themselves, or in the case of *The Day of the Locust,* from the sadomasochistic rage of mass man—the result of his disenchantment from the spell of commodity fetishism."[7] Interestingly, a main theme of *Barton Fink* is "sadomasochistic rage," which has two distinct but connected manifestations: first, the mordant, guilty frustration that Barton Fink, novice screenwriter, experiences at having to write within an inflexible set of generic conventions he cannot seem to personalize effectively; and second, the murderous rage, and self-hatred, that

Charlie Meadows (John Goodman), Barton's next-door neighbor and the film's "common" or "mass" man, feels not only at the demeaning nature of his job (the door-to-door selling of insurance to the unwilling and the disdainful), but, more important, at his inability to get his story told, to be part of the cultural flow rather than simply its exploited object.

As West's fiction suggests, the crisis of the 1930s and 1940s, the exclusion that gives rise to the kind of anger felt by Charlie, is more properly ideological than economic. Or, to put it more accurately, in West's view a thwarted politics of representation lies at the heart of the era's inequities and widespread anomie, the discontent that made the advent of a homegrown fascism a frightening possibility. *Barton Fink's* engagement with sadomasochistic rage is structured by an inverse parallelism. For Charlie's frustration is the mirror reflex of Barton's. His is a voice from below stifled by institutional indifference rather than a voice from above that, confronting a semiotic tangle of "readymades," can find nothing to say about them.

Such stifled or unheard voices abound in *The Day of the Locust,* and there they exemplify the mass frustrations with a popular culture that turns the charismatic and acclaimed personality into a commodity to be desired. This erotic urge for possession, whose underside is a deep resentment, erupts finally in an apocalyptic violence directed at Hollywood's glittering stars and picture palaces, which figure as the purveyors of irresistible fantasy. As the mob seems to recognize, these are the sources par excellence of a debased and inauthentic flow of cultural product, keystones of the new economic system soon to be known as consumerism. As one character remarks in *Barton Fink,* Hollywood can be imagined as "the great salt lick," attracting beasts from far and wide. For Nathanael West, Hollywood figures also a kind of shrine, attracting the disaffected with a contradictory promise: they are to become part of the powerful flow of images and meaning even as they merge with the chorus of those admiring the inimitable aristocracy of the culture industry. But once Hollywood's false appeal is unmasked, as Veitch remarks, "there is no Heavenly City . . . unless one counts the thwarted, utopian aspirations that lie buried in the cheap artifacts of mass culture" (xiv).

While borrowing heavily from West's ideas, *Barton Fink* notably expands the novelist's critique. Showing its site of production (a Broadway theater dominated by greedy "angels" and grasping agents) also to be thoroughly penetrated by capital, the Coens unmask the supposed autonomy of the high-modernist position of critical, even disdainful distance that West, as the self-appointed chronicler of cultural decline, arrogates to himself. As represented in *Barton Fink*, the Broadway theater objectifies and sentimentalizes lower-class experience in order both to arouse the momentary, inauthentic sympathy of well-dressed, affluent ticket buyers and also to turn a profit for unappreciative investors of the same social class. Not confronted so starkly with the "mode of production" that defines and contains his art, the novelist can pretend more easily than the playwright that he is indifferent to popular taste and questions of "affect," broadly defined. Fink leaves Broadway in part because he finds his experience there artistically frustrating. He cannot connect with "the common man," who, for the author as for his well-heeled audience, is more political concept than existential reality. In fact, neither the theater nor the movies proves adequate to the task of representing these experiences to his satisfaction.

The film opens backstage as what apparently is the opening performance of *Bare Ruined Choirs* is ending. We don't see the actors, but a figure in formal evening dress stands in the wings, mouthing the words they speak. He is obviously the author, and when the curtain falls to thunderous applause, he will be acknowledged by the enthusiastic audience with a standing ovation. The drama that is just concluding, as his miming suggests, is a direct expression of his experience and talent. To judge from the terms of its ending, the story is a kind of *künstlerroman*, a portrait of the artist as a young man that concludes as he is about to leave behind the poor neighborhood where he has grown up, "these four stinkin' walls," as he proudly proclaims. Success (which apparently also includes a finer set of four walls) is just around the corner, as Maury, one of his interlocutors, predicts: "We'll hear from that Kid. And I don't mean a postcard."

On one level, this brief set of dramatic exchanges establishes the literary intertext for the knowing spectator. The model for the film's play is clearly Odets's *Awake and Sing*, upon which the Coens' dialogue plays an interesting riff ("I'm *awake* now, *awake* for the first time. . . . Let 'em *sing* their hearts out. . . . Take that choir. Make it *sing*") [emphases mine]. And this connection is solidified by the appearance of a bespectacled, curly-haired, high-foreheaded John Turturro as Barton Fink. The physical resemblance to Odets is striking. On another level, *Bare Ruined Choirs* provides a narrative model against which to measure Barton's search for professional accomplishment. In his dramatized autobiography, the desire of the Kid is for an escape to parts yet unknown.

This desire (for upward mobility? for the critical distance necessary to represent what the artist knows?) is a conventional element in the *künstlerroman* so prominent as a genre of modernist fiction (Joyce's *Portrait of the Artist as a Young Man*, D. H. Lawrence's *Sons and Lovers*, W. Somerset Maugham's *Of Human Bondage*, among others). And that desire is ironically fulfilled in the decamping of the Kid's creator for Broadway and, afterward, for Hollywood. With the lyrical optimism of its projected closure, *Bare Ruined Choirs* differs from the less sanguine resolution of *Barton Fink*, whose ending rejects the transparencies and conventional politics of social realism, including any simpleminded celebration of the "cult" of the committed writer. The Kid's proletarian family is resigned about his imminent departure from their midst, an absence more than compensated for by the success the artist is certain to achieve elsewhere, in that place where art can be produced, consumed, and (one presumes) properly compensated.

If the Kid is imagined as an artist alone, freed for a life of self-expression by a decision to leave the place of his birth behind, the reality of Barton's life is quite different. After the performance of his play (subtitled, in the tradition of Westian irony, as the "Triumph of the Common Man"), Barton goes to a fancy restaurant to meet with his rich backers. They confess to being moved by Fink's dramatization of the life of common fishmongers, even though, as Barton quips, "the only fish you've ever seen were tacked to the wall of the yacht club." Though disgusted that he has employed his art, which should be in the service of "the common man," only to make the wealthy wealthier, Barton finds himself tempted at the prospect of profiting further from the portrayal of the class struggle by shifting allegiance to a mass medium.

The success of his play has resulted in an offer from a Hollywood studio at a salary of two thousand dollars a week (incidentally, just what Odets was paid upon his arrival on the West Coast). Barton's agent urges him to accept, but the playwright cannot see how a sojourn in Hollywood will serve his artistic aim, which is the "creation of a new, living theater of and about and for the common man." His agent responds that "the common man'll still be here when you get back. What the hell, they might even have one or two of 'em out in Hollywood." The playwright apparently agrees. A straight cut shows him arriving in Hollywood, where he deliberately chooses a run-down hotel as his place of residence. There, as it transpires, Fink does meet "the common man" with whom he wants to get in touch (no common men are evident in New York, of course, save for the actors "playing" at their endurance of poverty and exploitation). In large measure, the story the film traces is defined by the transformation of "the common man" from an easily manipulated abstraction and a ready object of pity to a dominating figure that threatens, with the revelation of his desires and discontents, destruction by fire and the sword (or its modern equivalent).

For Fink, the move to Hollywood is a descent from high to commercial culture. It entails not only the abandonment of political themes and rhetoric (however much such art actually does little more than serve the commercial interests that "back" it). This new world also requires the artist to create "impersonally." He must abandon the neo-romantic protocol of expressiveness. In this older and now, for Barton, displaced model, the artist finds the truth in his talent and experience, while his achievement is measured by formal perfection and thematic seriousness. Meeting with the studio head, Jack Lipnick (Michael Lerner), a kind of composite of Louis B. Mayer and Jack Warner, Fink finds himself reduced to the strange status of an honored hack craftsman. His assignment has been determined by Lipnick's reading, which is more or less accurate, of his writing expertise ("They tell me you know the poetry of the street. That would rule out westerns, pirate pictures, screwball, Bible, Roman . . .").

But what he is required to work on will also be shaped by the studio's need to make use of properties it has purchased (in this case, a story published in *The Saturday Evening Post*), while the salient formal features of the film are determined by what, within a given formula, will work with the star who is being showcased. In fact, the only real question that the construction of the screenplay raises, at least according to Lipnick, turns on an answer to this question: is Beery too old for a female costar? "Wallace Beery is a wrestler. I wanna know his hopes, his dreams. Naturally, he'll have to get mixed up with a bad element. And a romantic interest. You know the drill. Romantic interest, or else a young kid. An orphan." Fink demonstrates his lack of familiarity with Hollywood conventions by suggesting that the film feature both a romantic interest *and* a kid. Lipnick is obviously disappointed with this result, but he still has great hopes for his new screenwriter's career, that he will give his studio's films what he somewhat mysteriously calls "that Barton Fink feeling." One gets the feeling that the studio head has run this shtick by the other writers whom the studio has attempted to bend to its needs.

In any case, Lipnick gives voice to the structuring dialectic of Hollywood production: its need for the new (hence a relentless search for the different, the personal, and the innovative, the welcoming of artists wooed away from the other arts); but also for constant recourse to the conventional (the usual twists, turns, and resolutions of popular narrative, the recycling of appealing performers, the textual verification of common sense). What undoes Fink, at least temporarily, is the pressure to create within a web of readymade ideas and under the severe time constraints of a Taylorized production schedule ("I'd like to see something by the end of the week," Lipnick tells him on their first meeting). "I don't go to the pictures much," Fink protests to Lipnick, learning, perhaps too late and to his dismay, what this new job will involve. The playwright obviously needs a quick lesson in how to write for this different medium. Barton's first efforts go nowhere because he has not yet left behind the subject matter of his Broadway success. In fact, he can get no further than typing in the setting for *Bare Ruined Choirs* ("a tenement building on Manhattan's Lower East Side") as the location for the first shot of the shooting script. But this is not an unpromising beginning. From this perspective, perhaps the playwright can truly tell the story of "the common man" that *Bare Ruined Choirs* handles only unsatisfactorily. In any case, and perhaps ironically, Barton's own experiences in Hollywood follow the pattern outlined by Lipnick. The writer's pursuit of "hopes and dreams" will indeed be defined by encounters with "a bad element" and "a romantic interest."

Inspiration does not come easily, but the opportunity to attain greater knowledge does. From an adjacent room in his hotel, Barton hears the sounds of a man weeping, perhaps hysterically laughing. But he does not extend the hand of friendship to another lonely soul. Instead, he calls the front desk to complain about the noise. Its source, the insurance salesman Charlie Meadows, soon appears at his door. Barton invites

Charlie in for a drink, and the conversation soon turns to Barton's career. Informed that his new neighbor has taken a job writing for the pictures, Charlie is impressed ("Hell, *you've* got it made!"). Accepting this admiration, Barton tells Charlie that people like him are his subject matter: "Strange as it may seem, Charlie, I guess I write about people like you. The average working stiff. The common man." The aim of his career, Barton tells Charlie, is to go beyond mere objectification to "create a theater for the masses that's based on a few simple truths— not on some shopworn abstractions." Barton congratulates himself on his "commitment" to a genuine workers' art because he is unlike the "many writers [who] do everything in their power to insulate themselves from the common man." As a result, their work "suffers, and regresses into empty formalism." Even more patronizingly, Barton opines that "I don't guess this means much to you."

Charlie, however, does understand. He has a voice that, were it heard, might provide Barton with some authentic material for a people's theater. He declares, "Hell, *I* could tell you some stories," but Barton cuts him off with "and that's the point, that we all have stories." It seems, however, that Fink isn't interested in listening to the ones that an actual "common man" might have to tell. In their encounter, with its edgy friendliness largely a product of the Charlie's salesmanly bonhomie, we recognize one of the Coens' characteristic themes. Like Marge in *Fargo,* Barton lives life in accordance with his ideas about other people. He fails to listen properly to others or engage with them sympathetically. Barton misunderstands Charlie because of a class-bred underestimation of the power of "the common man," stereotypically a figure of weakness, not strength. A prisoner of his patronizing political attachment to the poor and struggling, Barton misreads the weepiness and shaky self-confidence that dominate, but only at first, Charlie's demeanor.

Hints of another side to this pathetic figure are certainly there to be noted. Charlie throws Barton violently to the ground, ostensibly demonstrating how a "wrestling picture" works. Surprised, Barton does not understand the kind of help Charlie has offered. A playwright whose medium has always been words, he does not consider that the movies work with images as well as with dialogue, hence the need to describe actions authentically. Charlie's demonstration, however, also offers proof of his physical superiority, his readiness to take action rather than discuss; and, perhaps, it evidences his resentment of Barton's higher rank in society. As later events show, Charlie's insurance salesman's pitch hints at his familiarity with random disaster: "fire, theft, and casualty are not things that only happen to other people." Indeed, he shows himself to be the messenger of the grim news that the worst can happen, even casting doubts on our own innocence. At the close of this scene, Charlie again offers to say more about himself: "Well, I can tell you some stories." Barton's response is, as before, insultingly dismissive: "See you, Charlie."

Rejecting Charlie's offer of technical assistance and story material, Fink looks to other writers to help him out. Working at the same studio is W. P. Mayhew (John Mahoney), a middle-aged Southern writer. Mayhew is a shortish man, slightly built, with beautiful white hair, dressed in Deep South finery (white linen suit and a bow tie), who conducts himself with a consciously affected genteel manner. Mayhew is a strange combination of the grotesque and the fastidious, using his handkerchief to kneel on the floor when, in the midst of an alcoholic binge, he carefully throws up in the studio bathroom. Mayhew seems to be making fun of the very image he takes pains to project. The physical resemblance to William Faulkner is striking, and Fink clinches the historical reference when he addresses Mayhew with great respect, calling him "the finest novelist of our time." Barton confesses to his difficulties in writing within the genre of the wrestling picture, and Mayhew offers him assistance, but when he goes as agreed to Mayhew's studio office, the great author is roaring drunk, raging and weeping rather like Charlie. But Barton does make the acquaintance of Mayhew's "assistant," a beautiful young woman named Audrey (Judy Taylor) whom he finds sympathetic. Fink starts to romance her, but Audrey immediately, even rapturously, confesses, "Bill and I are . . . in love."

Audrey, it turns out, has for some time been doing Bill Mayhew's writing for him. The great novelist's plight is obviously a warning of what can happen to Fink as well, now that he too is a fish out of water, cut off from the sources of his inspiration and art. Mayhew has been reduced to alcoholic self-pity by his sellout to the studio, while his career and reputation are kept barely afloat only by the exertions of a talented and dedicated woman. Back in his hotel room, Barton, still suffering from writer's block, is interrupted again by Charlie. A woman is heard moaning (from pain? from pleasure?), and the salesman reveals that he gets "opportunities galore" in his "line of work," a bit of personal revelation that, once again, that does not prompt his erstwhile friend to inquire further. Instead, Barton remains mired in a gloomy sense of self-importance, as he confesses "my job is to plumb the depths, so to speak, dredge something up from inside, something honest . . . and exploring it can be painful."

Such a modernist emphasis on creation as an act of self-analysis, of course, has little to do with the writing of a Hollywood star vehicle. But Barton, it turns out, will break out in a burst of creativity when, with the assistance, so to speak, of Audrey and Charlie, he will in fact "plumb the depths" and in the process "dredge something up from inside." In a sense, Charlie is that something—a nightmare image of "the common man" whom Fink, if he does not create, at least seeks out and then animates through his disdain and patronizing. Charlie is the wrestler, the "large man in tights," as Fink describes him, who is designated as the main character of his assigned script. Like Charlie, the wrestler is a creature from below, driven by resentment and desire, just as the conventions of the genre demand.

Medieval Jewish legend offers an interesting parable of such artistic creation modeled ironically on the Genesis creation story. In order to save his people from a pogrom, Rabbi Löw creates an automaton-like servant from a lump of clay by pronouncing a *shem* (charm) over it. The huge figure that comes to life, this *golem* (Hebrew for an "unshaped lump"), soon runs amuck, requiring the rabbi in the end to destroy it. Despairing of getting an appropriate script from his fledgling writer, the producer, Ben Geisler (Tony Shalhoub), has Barton look at the rushes from another wrestling picture being shot at the same time. What he sees on the screen is a huge man, who speaks with a German accent and moves toward the camera uttering over and over again with terrifying menace: "I will destroy him."

This vision proves prophetic, an anticipation of the *golem* who in the person of Charlie Meadows will turn his anger on those threatening the writer who, though summoning him to life, has refused to give him a voice. In *The Day of the Locust,* violence is collective, a demonstration of the power of a mass society become a mob, whose frustrated desires and aroused bloodlust vent themselves in a mindless assault against the industry of desire. In *Barton Fink,* violence is individual, its source and meaning more ambiguous. But this much is clear: the eruption is (at least in part) from below, just as in West's scenario of an emerging American fascism. A hitherto silenced voice finally has its say, in the process shedding, Superman-like, its everyday, oppressed identity for a new and frighteningly assertive self.

Interestingly, however, the narrative focuses on Barton's difficulties, his lack of inspiration (despite the menacing figure he sees in the rushes, despite Charlie's anguished plea to use him as a model). Instead of looking to "the common man" in both these forms, Barton seeks out the "greatest living novelist" for assistance, showing his allegiance to art rather than to his subject. Or, more accurately, once he witnesses Mayhew's retreat into alcoholic self-destruction, he thinks of the woman who takes care of him. Barton thus rings up Audrey, whom he persuades to come to his hotel room in the middle of the night. Audrey knows what needs to be done ("Look, it's really just a formula. You don't have to type your soul into it. We'll invent some names and a new setting"). But Barton's needs are more psychological and professional, and the pair end the evening making love rather than writing the script. In the morning, however, Barton finds Audrey dead beside him, covered with blood from knife wounds. But who has wielded the knife? Could it be anyone but Barton? But then he has no memory of the crime.

An answer of sorts emerges when Barton, in a panic of desperation, asks Charlie for help. Though shocked, Charlie argues against any report to the police, who would hardly believe Barton, especially since it can be proved he had "sexual intercourse" with the dead woman. Even if he could somehow prove his innocence, Charlie says, "this would ruin you." Much like Professor Wanley in *The Woman in the Window,* Barton must obliterate all traces of the crime and his connection to it. Like an obedient *golem,* Charlie disposes of the corpse while Barton tries to go on with his life, meeting later that morning with Lipnick, who humiliates one of his "yes men" in front of Barton, perhaps as an object lesson. As if to cement their relationship, Charlie, having found a place to dump Audrey's body, leaves a package with Barton, whose contents he explains enigmatically: "Funny, huh, when everything that's important to a guy, everything he wants to keep from a lifetime—when he can fit it into a little box like that." This may be pathetic, as Charlie suggests, but Barton admits to a certain amount of envy, confessing, "it's more than

I've got." Whatever "objects" the box might hide within, their significance is clear: they are the sum total of Charlie's experience, the gift from his subject that the writer should most treasure. Only when Barton, now properly initiated into the realm of tragic mischance, takes Charlie's parcel and puts it on the nightstand near his typing table is he able to make a start on his wrestling picture. He finishes the assignment with remarkable speed and no further trouble. Interestingly, the last word Barton types is "postcard," which is, of course, the last word of dialogue from *Bare Ruined Choirs*. Evidently, his script is simply a Hollywood version of the play. Certainly it must have "that Barton Fink feeling" Lipnick is looking for.

But if Charlie has provided inspiration with his "package," he has more to show Barton. Before he begins his furious work on the script, Barton is visited in his hotel room by detectives who are looking for someone very much like Charlie. Charlie, as Barton learns from them, is actually Karl "Madman" Mundt, a serial killer who dispatches his victims with a shotgun and then cuts off their heads. Mundt's victims have characteristically been women, starting with a "couple of housewives" in Kansas City. Recently, the body of a beautiful young woman (obviously that of Audrey) has been found in Los Angeles, also missing its head. Not long afterward, Mayhew's corpse also turns up headless. Could the last remains of Audrey or W.P. be in the package now in Barton's possession? Has Charlie killed both of them? Has Barton? We never learn.

Fink is about to be arrested when he is saved by Charlie, who has apparently set fire to the hotel. The elevator opens to disgorge its operator clutching his head, which then falls off. Charlie also shoots the two detectives, but not before telling them: "Look upon me! Look upon me! I'll show you the life of the mind." On the one hand, this proclamation is darkly humorous, considering Mundt's fascination with heads. On the other hand, if Charlie or his other, Karl, is the common man, then he also stands in some sense for "the real," which cannot be properly accommodated to the art of either the social realist or Hollywood kind, both of which offer different, though equally inauthentic, versions of the "common man." As Charlie tells Barton, "C'mon, Barton, you think you know about pain. Take a look around this dump. You're just a tourist with a typewriter, Barton. I live here." It seems that Charlie may also have murdered Barton's aunt and uncle back in New York. The irresolvable enigmas pile up, the unopened package serving as their objective correlative.

The next day Barton meets with Lipnick, and his script is angrily rejected as inappropriately elitist, a work about ideas, not a calculated appeal to the emotions. But then the artist, rejected by inauthentic commercialism and chastened by the real in all its brutality, unhappiness, and rage, wins through decisively to a better form of life, stumbling onto the shore of desire. Does art provide him with a disinterested place for the contemplation of beauty, human and physical? Or has he simply gone as far as he can go? Whatever interpretation we choose, this much is certain. In the film's last sequence, Barton finds himself suddenly and inexplicably alone at the very beach shown in the picture that, hanging on his hotel room wall, had been the object of his constant contemplation. And there, in the same pose, is the woman whose portrait therein had so fascinated him. To his question "Are you in pictures?" she gives a confident answer: "Don't be silly." Obviously, on this last beach we are far from "the great salt lick." The film ends with Barton sitting motionless, staring in contemplation at the ocean. Unlike "the Kid" he does not achieve a happy end; instead he gains a point of stasis that, with its mysterious and unfathomable interconnection between representation and lived experience, offers a space freed from artifice and horror. This is compensation of a sort for what Charlie/Karl has shown him about the "true" life of the mind. The package remains unopened, at least for the present. Who knows what work of art its terrible truth might inspire?

In *Barton Fink,* a classic modernist style (its resurrection heavily inflected by a dose of postmodern irony) brings to life a world, problematically historical, in which Hollywood proves an irresistible attraction for artist and public alike. The artist's error, however, is not only that he succumbs to its lure. His is also a failure of sympathy and intellect (criticisms, it might be said, that have often been leveled at Odets, who grew up not in poverty but among the well-off urban bourgeoisie). Lipnick's rejection of Barton's effort is to be expected. The mogul's Philistinism confirms the disdain that intellectuals have conventionally felt for the "values" of the commercial film industry, whose executives would not recognize true art if it came across their desk in a script penned by a famous writer, which it here does. Who would credit the taste or respect the evaluation of such a buffoonish character? But perhaps Lipnick is not wrong in rejecting the unconventionality of Wallace Beery suffering before the inevitable triumph in the final reel. Barton Fink remains at the end, as Charlie quips, a "tourist with a typewriter," who understands little beyond his own self, whether it is the "common man" or the "mass art" designed for his entertainment.

The authentic tale from below, if it does not emerge in full detail in *Barton Fink*, is the focus of *Raising Arizona*, which, in this regard, fills out the former film's failure to generate a story other than the story of that failure. *Raising Arizona*, in contrast, offers the proper kind of wish fulfillment in which the representation of social materials is shaped into that "optical illusion" of social harmony demanded by the mass cultural text. The main character, Hi (Nicolas Cage), is a career criminal, wasting away in prison, and one night he fantasizes what life would be like if, once released, he could marry a beautiful prison guard named Ed (Holly Hunter). Hi's story, which follows and constitutes the bulk of the film, is either that dream or its actualization in real life.

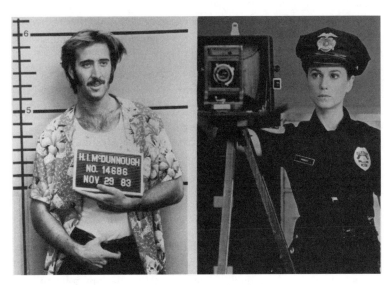

An unlikely romance develops between convicted felon H. I. McDunnough (Nicolas Cage) and his jailer, played by Holly Hunter. (Courtesy of the Academy of Motion Picture Arts and Sciences)

Either way, Hi's story does not shrink from the actual difficulties such a wish would raise: the inevitable return to a life of crime, dead-end jobs, infertility, all daunting impediments to sustaining a marriage in a culture that, to judge from its middle-class representatives of Hi's experience, is more committed to making money and indulging in kinky sex than to family values. And yet Hi is able to imagine—and this is surely the point—a utopian solution to what has threatened his happiness. Love and commitment can indeed be conceived as proving stronger than all other forces. In what may be a dream within a dream, Hi recognizes the utopianism of his musings, but that does not, as far as he is concerned, diminish their enticing power. Such might be his future with Ed: "But I saw an old couple bein' visited by their children—and all their grandchildren too [so much for the barrenness with which the couple is visited]. And the old couple wasn't screwed up, and neither were their kids or grandkids. And I don't know, you tell me. This whole dream, was it wishful thinking? Was I just fleein' reality, like I know I am liable to do?"

In modern American culture, the factory of such flights from the everyday to its perfected realization is Hollywood itself, whose fantasies engage life's problems yet in the end work to transcend them. But this transformation perhaps should not be seen as pure escapism or "sheer manipulation." Jameson argues that such dismissive formulation slights the ideological work of these narratives, particularly the social value of the utopianism they offer, and the unrealizable dreams they project. It is characteristic of the postmodernism of the Coen brothers that, in imagining what the common man might wish for, they can deliver the dream (i.e., produce a pure entertainment film) only when it questions its status as a dream. Even *Raising Arizona*, their simplest, most monologic text, does not eschew the self-reflexive flourish. In the generic polyphony of their other films, save *Barton Fink,* the dream is fractured, reconstructed, and infused with other voices, but it still retains something of its ability to entertain.

Such stories all differ from the nightmare that entraps the committed intellectual in *Barton Fink,* who is saved from the worst that can happen (including the possibility of his own murderous violence) and discovers, if not a utopia, at least a no-place that requires only his presence rather than his continued production. As a form of deliverance from his infertility and discontent, Hi imagines a family from which all dissension has been expunged, a space of such pure (if thoroughly conventional) fulfillment that he must question its attainability. His is the (at least presumed) dream of Hollywood's mass audience, who are thought to desire, as Jameson puts its, an "optical illusion of *social* harmony" (my emphasis). The modernist artist, in contrast, is no family man, but a loner tortured and rewarded by his creativity, by his restless probing of the aesthetic. Thus Barton does not find himself sexualized and socialized by any "constitution of the couple" but makes his way to a landscape of pure contemplation and disconnection, an uninhabited and natural place devoid of texts and the institutions of cultural production, where beautiful women might invite and even welcome the gaze, but are never in the pictures.

Notes

The first epigraph is from Jonathan Veitch, *American Superrealism: Nathanael West and the Politics of Representation in the 1930s* (Madison: University of Wisconsin Press, 1997), xii. The second epigraph is from Clifford Odets, *The Time Is Ripe: The 1940 Journal* (New York: Grove Press, 1988), 152.

1. Foster Hirsch, *Detours and Lost Highways: A Map of Neo-Noir* (New York: Limelight, 1999), 111.

2. Linda Hutcheon, *A Poetics of Postmodernism: History, Theory, Fiction* (New York: Routledge, 1988), 20.

3. Fredric Jameson, "Reification and Utopia in Mass Culture," in *Signatures of the Visible* (New York: Routledge, 1992), 14. Subsequent references will be noted in the text.

4. Fredric Jameson, "Historicism in *The Shining*," in *Signatures of the Visible*, 92. Subsequent references will be noted in the text.

5. Malcolm Goldstein, "Clifford Odets and the Found Generation," in *Critical Essays on Clifford Odets*, ed. Gabriel Miller (Boston: G. K. Hall, 1991), 107.

6. Norman Jenckes, "Turning from the Political to the Personal: Clifford Odets and John Howard Lawson," in Miller, *Critical Essays*, 117.

7. Veitch, *American Superrealism*, xiii–xiv. Subsequent references will be noted in the text.

6. Classic Hollywood Redivivus: *The Hudsucker Proxy* and *O Brother, Where Art Thou?*

The films of Frank Capra and Preston Sturges furnished the Coens with the rich cinematic intertext they explore in *The Hudsucker Proxy* and *O Brother, Where Art Thou?* The latter is by far their most popular film to date and, perhaps not coincidentally, their least serious. It offers an innocently ribald, enormously funny exploration of ethnic and regional stereotypes (this time the Deep South of the 1930s, or at least the cultural mythology about the region in that era, is their target). For the more literate and cine-literate spectator, *O Brother* offers an additional pleasure: an undemanding form of intellectual engagement. In an ironic, perhaps even mocking, postmodern twist, the film takes its title from a "film" within a classic Hollywood film. *O Brother, Where Art Thou?* is the title of the patronizingly committed project that John L. Sullivan, the successful if intellectually dissatisfied director of Tinseltown fluff in Sturges's *Sullivan's Travels*, eventually decides *not* to make. Surprisingly, perhaps, Sullivan's decision comes after he spends some time living like a hobo in order to understand how the country's economic problems have affected the poor. Mischance leads him on an unintended journey to the rural South, where he lands on a chain gang similar to the one from which the Coens' three protagonists make their escape in order to search for buried treasure.

Mythologies of Success

The rich and pampered Sullivan, who had set out in hopes of experiencing "real" life, gets a taste of what happens to those with no connections who run afoul of the legal system. He receives a speedy trial and a harsh sentence. However, it is not long before studio executives secure his release, quickly returning him to more comfortable and familiar surroundings, where, of course, his talent can continue to make them a fortune. Interestingly, however, this harrowing experience convinces Sullivan that politically engaged filmmaking is exactly what the downtrodden and forgotten of the country do not need. In order to serve the mass public, he rededicates himself instead to the making of comedies that celebrate the overcoming (however "imaginary") of life's inescapable harshness, providing momentary refuge from despair and want. Earlier, he has asked studio executives skeptical about his undertaking a serious project: "What's the matter with Capra?" They have no answer for him, but by the end of the story Sullivan has found his own. *O Brother* catches the spirit of this newfound artistic manifesto, reimagining the director's frightening encounter with poverty and harsh justice through another, quite different textual filter. Homer's *Odyssey* is co-opted as a pattern of sorts for the adventures of the Coens' three convicts, the leader of whom just happens to be a determined smart-ass named Ulysses. Like his literary counterpart, this many-minded and long-suffering hero survives many adventures that threaten death and is finally reconciled with his estranged wife after a sudden flood saves him from execution.

O Brother is witty and sophisticated, but, true to Sullivan's theory of a filmmaking dedicated to uncomplicated emotional uplift, it avoids serious questions of any kind. The film contains a political critique of sorts—but of a bygone era's distorted view of the South, whose various stereotypes (from rotund good-ol'-boy politicians to automaton-like religious fanatics) the Coens take great pleasure in "sending up." *O Brother* may borrow its title from Sturges, but the film lacks any sign of his characteristically sharp engagement with social questions. Certainly, the Coens prove uninterested in the unharmonized mixture of tones to be found in *Sullivan's Travels*. Sullivan resolves not to let the real in all its disturbing messiness be a part of his next production. But, unlike his diegetic alter ego, Sturges does something quite different in his film, which offers unforgettable, documentary-style images of the Depression-era poor as the hitherto pampered director, searching for atmosphere and credibility, makes his way among them. Despite its official endorsement of disengagement, the film, moreover, poses nagging and unresolved questions about equality under the law in American society.

One of its most potent scenes is also one of its least comic. Sullivan *does* commit the serious crime for which he is convicted and appropriately sentenced (six years hard labor). Just before he finagles his release, he has this conversation with a trusty in the chain-gang camp:

> SULLY: I haven't got the time to spend six years here.
> TRUSTY: But you were sentenced.
> SULLY: I know that, but I still haven't time.
> TRUSTY: Well, you'll have to *find* the time.
> SULLY: Look, they don't sentence people like me to places like this for a little disagreement with a yard bull.
> TRUSTY: Don't they?
> SULLY: No.

The film's happy ending celebrates Sullivan resuming his successful career, now convinced that what he does has redeeming social value, but Sturges also acknowledges that a very different America exists outside the privileged environs of the Hollywood dream factory. His hero does not challenge the injustices that flow from differences in social class even in a society officially committed to equality under the law. Instead, he unabashedly admits to being part of the problem. *O Brother,* in contrast, does not admit to problems of this kind, while having its fun with the patently artificial world of representations that it conjures into life from the cinematic and literary past.

From this vantage point, *The Hudsucker Proxy* is a more provocative and complex film that bears lengthier comment. Like its models in the dark (and darkly humorous) films of Sturges and Capra, *The Hudsucker Proxy* is full of laughs despite its treatment of more serious cultural issues. Yet the film's elaborately artificial art design, its eye-popping set-piece visual sequences (some using the blue-screen technology developed for action cinema), and its mannerist acting are certainly not in the tradition of either classic Hollywood director, who never made films in which stylization, broadly conceived, similarly dominates. Unlike the films of Capra and Sturges, *The Hudsucker Proxy* is marked by a visual excess that is expressionistic—but also ostentatious. What I mean is that the Coens do not use style as an objective correlative of the characters' worldview, as they do to such good effect in *Blood Simple*. Instead, the self-conscious grandiosity of image in *The Hudsucker Proxy* expresses the filmmakers' detached view of the diegetic world they have conjured into existence.

The Coens' style puts quotation marks around the represented action. Style thus becomes something they use to distance themselves and the spectator from the story, whose key design element, a plain circle traced on a blank sheet of paper, could not in its enigmatic simplicity yet originality provide a more telling contrast. Not naturalized as an element of the story, the film's visual display thus acknowledges the Coens' playful resurrection of the enclosed studio world. It references with its evident constructedness the mode of production from a bygone era, when carefully dressed sound stages conventionally stood in for "the real." Never have the Coens shown themselves to be more "knowing" than in *The Hudsucker Proxy,* which offers an extended, self-conscious homage to one of the most memorable and characteristic genres of classic Hollywood, the screwball comedy, of which Frank Capra and Preston Sturges were the acknowledged masters.

Here also resurrected is a common theme of Capra's: the possibility, always foreclosed, that the hero will end his life after facing either failure or what seems unavoidable public disgrace. Following in this tradition, *The Hudsucker Proxy* also offers a meditation on suicide: specifically the self-destruction that these middle-class characters contemplate when, usually through no fault of their own other than an excess of virtue, they are not only threatened with failure, but also find their reputations besmirched by the villains, who appear constitutionally committed to the undermining of the righteous.

In Capra's Manichean universe (particularly as realized in *It's a Wonderful Life*), self-destruction figures as a moral form of an otherwise immoral action. Given the circumstances these protagonists find themselves trapped by, that is, suicide seems a hardly unheroic protest against the imminent triumph of wickedness. And the reason is that such a death, while prompted by despair or disgust, envisions a restoration of personal honor through the refusal of further complicity. The resolve to commit suicide in these circumstances is one of the qualities that mark out the Capra protagonist as a legitimate hero, for he is someone who refuses to continue living in the absence of a transcendent moral principle. In his screwball comedies, Sturges sometimes entangles his protagonists in troubles that are, potentially at least, just as threatening to personal honor or integrity, but then his characters always turn out to be hollow or foolish. Unprotected by a workable code of behavior, they should prove vulnerable to the unjust, oftentimes cruel world through which they must make their way. And yet these comic figures never contemplate suicide because there is little of the hero in them. Instead of descending into the pathetic to depict their ready destruction by forces they are powerless against, Sturges provides them with unlikely rescues, as circumstances customarily offer them a soft landing. Naturally, these happy endings are thus more form than content, always undermined by the characters' failure to reach beyond their inability, pretense, stupidity, or moral weakness. As not in Capra, an ethical solution to the problems posed never emerges to be endorsed by the emotional overflow of affirming spectators. Instead, the characteristic Sturges plot turning comes from some sort of deus ex machina. And this is usually nothing less, and nothing more, than the good luck bestowed by some well-wishing representative of the goddess Fortuna. Such effects, it goes without saying, are most often transparently fictional, defying the willing suspension of disbelief (the hero's "deliverance" from the law in *Sullivan's Travels* proves somewhat of an exception to this rule).

More cynical about the core values of American culture than Capra, Sturges (if only in his comedies) characteristically retreats from those realities too unpleasant to contemplate, even when he devotes much artistry to depicting them in depth. Paradoxically, perhaps, his films are thus much more comic in the sense that they make light of (or deftly sidestep) life's intractable difficulties. Capra, in contrast, faces the dark side of human experience steadily and with greater seriousness. But, like Capra, Sturges was intrigued by the idea of suicide as an honorable exit from circumstances that promised only needless suffering and humiliation. During his early career, in fact, Sturges wrote two dramatic films (directed by others) in which an ostensibly successful man chooses to kill himself rather than go on living with pain or disappointment even though he is not faced with public shame.

The suicides in these two films acknowledge the emptiness of material success. Tom Garner (Spencer Tracy) in *The Power and the Glory* (William K. Howard, 1933) rises through hard work, determination, and more than a little ruthlessness to become a railroad tycoon. Learning that her husband is having an affair with a younger woman, Tom's wife throws herself in front a streetcar. Some time later, after a strike costs the lives of four hundred of his employees, Tom discovers that his son may be the father of his new wife's child; his anguished reaction is to shoot himself. Perhaps even more tragic is the fate of another self-made man, the eponymous hero (Edward Arnold) of *Diamond Jim* (A. Edward Sutherland, 1935), who, his body ravaged by years of restless upward climbing and self-indulgence, decides to eat a sumptuous meal he knows will kill him when the woman he loves rejects him for the second time.

Just as Capra's beset protagonists are tempted to do, Tom Garner and Diamond Jim choose death over a life that no longer makes sense and, despite substantial prosperity, is otherwise filled with bitter disappointment, regret, and guilt. Such restorative self-destruction has a certain dignity and, it goes without saying, belongs more to a now displaced fictional universe than to the "postmodern sensibility," in which older notions of "character" have given way to "personality." A different mythology of success (one which, motored by narcissism, has precious little to do with honor, personal or otherwise) now holds sway. Interestingly then, in addition to resurrecting a theme from classical Hollywood in *The Hudsucker Proxy*, the Coens put into fictional play the values that once gave it cultural significance. Their film is *retro* in several senses.

This is not to say, however, that *The Hudsucker Proxy* evinces nostalgia for a more meaningful past—even if that past is to be found only in an outmoded regime of representation that can only be displayed, not reinvented. It must be emphasized that this Coen brothers film avoids the "new sincerity" so evident in *The Man Who Wasn't There*. Both these films are historical reconstructions. Yet any sense of authenticity (of, at least, a univocal sort) is deliberately short-circuited in *The Hudsucker Proxy*. Though the action takes place in 1958 (several key events of which are represented or mentioned), the costuming and interior decor belong to the 1930s (or, more accurately, to what Hollywood in that period designated as "contemporary"). Thus these material signifiers better match the period of the production of the films that the Coens reference than the end of the Eisenhower era in which their own is ostensibly set. *The Hudsucker Proxy* in this way juxtaposes two distinct periods from the American past, restaging the cultural politics of a decade that witnessed the supposed "end of ideology" within the conventions of a genre that took definitive shape during the class-based crisis in the capitalist system of some twenty years earlier.

The film offers a potent symbol of that crisis. Dominating both its narrative and visual design is the monolithic Hudsucker Corporation, an organization identified with its impressive New York edifice, where most of the narrative unfolds. True to the American myth of the "robber baron," its founder has built this company through the ruthless pursuit of profit. Hudsucker's employees have little hope for advancement or success as they try to cope with the boss's draconian work rules, which have been carefully Taylorized to control every aspect of their workday— and to their disadvantage. In the mailroom is a wizened old man who, after decades of loyal service, is still hoping for his first promotion. Constantly terrified by the prospect of losing their jobs, all who labor there seemingly serve at the whim of the heartless Hudsucker and his fat-cat directors, who run the business for their profit alone. Those at the top exploit underlings with the unconcern of the factory owners in *Metropolis* (1926), Fritz Lang's horrifying vision of end-stage capitalism, which seems to have provided the Coens with a model both architectural and ideological. Seldom has the gulf between management (here also ownership) and labor loomed wider than in the depiction of modern economic relations featured in *The Hudsucker Proxy*.

The Hudsucker Corporation, in fact, exemplifies Marx's worst-case scenario of that conscienceless exploitation that makes possible the efficient alienation of labor. Such a vision of business figures as a marked anachronism in the postindustrial American 1950s, when developments took a somewhat different turn than what orthodox Marxism had predicted. The immediate postwar era saw the advent and flourishing of quite different theories of "human resource management" that produced the benevolent and conformist corporate culture of deep personal investment anatomized by William H. Whyte in his classic study, *The Organization Man* (1956). This profound shift in how business does business is enshrined in many films of the era, including *The Man in the Gray Flannel Suit* (1956, based on Sloan Wilson's widely read novel) and *Patterns* (also 1956), in which an older-style ruthless businessman is shown to be out of touch with changing times and styles and must make way for his younger, more "progressive" colleague. Though it also features, if only in sketchy form, such a drama of ideological contrast and generational displacement, *The Hudsucker Proxy* is more invested in juxtaposing cultural references than in devising a narrative to connect them. Anachronism, we might say, is the most important element in the film's rhetoric of unstable, polyvalent representation, in its persistent refusal clearly to reference "the world."

Because of such antirealist effects, the Coens' reconstruction of both a different cinema and a bygone era may show us yearning, suffering, despair, and guilt, yet the viewer is prevented from experiencing such feelings in turn, or even empathizing much with the struggles of the characters. Here again the Coens part company with the filmmakers of classic Hollywood in general and Frank Capra in particular, whose films offer deeply sympathetic characters supporting unchallengeable, traditional values. Capra's clear aim, in which he undoubtedly succeeded, was not to leave a single dry eye in the house. Though not much interested in provoking tears or in affirming conventional wisdom, Sturges also offers characters who, despite their foibles and shortcomings, are conventionally likable, if often only minimally so. *The Hudsucker Proxy,* in stark contrast, cultivates emotional detachment in order to promote an intellectual engagement. This "coldness" was often noted by reviewers and evidently had much to do with the film's failure to find an audience, despite a visual *sprezzatura* unrivaled by any other Coen brothers release. Writing about the film in the *Seattle Times,* Jeff Shannon, for example, complained that "not one minute of it registers even the slightest hint of emotional involvement."[1]

There is no disputing this judgment. Perhaps surprisingly, such a disconnection seems a deliberate effect, arguably one better suited to the small independent film than to a more widely released, bigger-budget production. No doubt, it was a miscalculation of sorts—if only in terms of increasing the film's box office appeal—for coldness is not customarily a commercial proposition. The mainstream Hollywood cinema, as Richard Maltby, following the lead of Rick Altman, reminds us, arouses our emotions so that we can "consume," and thereby be purged of, them. What attracts a mass audience to the medium is not an interest in particular forms of narrative and spectacle *in se*. Such compositional elements are simply the means by which the anticipated catharsis is achieved.[2]

But for this affective exchange to work, the emotionality portrayed by the characters must impress us not only as authentic, but also as meriting our empathy. None of the Coens' characters in this film is particularly attractive. Jack Lipnick, the studio head in *Barton Fink*, recognizes that the success with viewers of his projected wrestling picture might well depend on whether Wallace Beery is given a love interest or a charming child to arouse and then reflect his feelings. In fact, Lipnick voices the majority industry view that any film must be built around an attractive character presented sympathetically. The overall design of *The Hudsucker Proxy*, in contrast, conforms to the anti-Aristotelianism of Bertolt Brecht's dramatic theory. Brecht called for an epic theater of ideas rather than feelings in order to promote the spectators' intellectual engagement. The only difference is that in this Coen brothers film it is not just the actors who "speak as if quoting their lines," as Brecht requires. Every element of the film is a quotation in this sense. Though the Coens do not do so, such distanciation might very well be put in service of the "blank parody" of the postmodern pastiche. This is certainly the case in the *Back to the Future* franchise, which features similar elements of stylistic grandiosity and pervasive knowingness.

With their self-mocking resurrections of the past and predictions of the future, these films are similar to *The Hudsucker Proxy,* but only superficially so. As Fredric Jameson suggests, the postmodern pastiche customarily flattens history. Thus, the *Back to the Future* series draws its humor from the incongruous interpenetration of three cultural moments (the third film in the series adds a fourth, the American West of cultural memory and celluloid celebration), destabilizing any firm sense of periodicity by denying depth to the sequence of events. With mannerist acting and the winking deployment of stereotypes, these films also cultivate an antirealism that short-circuits emotional connection except of a minimal kind. Their pasts and futures are points of time that draw all the meaning from the present, being invoked, in fact, as insignificant in themselves. Moreover, as the plots in all three films make clear, the past and future are absolutely contingent. That is, they are infinitely malleable from the perspective of the present, which possesses the means of their continuous rectification or rewriting. And the present, in turn, is itself contingent, subject to a sudden and disastrous instability that can be produced by the carelessness of those who inhabit it.

The Coens' agenda, in contrast, hardly slights the politics of historiography by emptying the past of its alterity or reducing it to *just* another object of reconstruction. With its incongruous juxtaposition of eras (and of representational schemes), *The Hudsucker Proxy* exposes the fault lines in the critical vision of American virtue and national accomplishment of the films that it mimes, measuring that vision against the emerging reality of a consumerist society. Capra's version of good citizenship is shown to have lost its power in an America no longer preoccupied by ideological struggle, but rather easily excited by mindless innovations that are designed for nothing more than passing the time. In launching this critique, the Coens build on the trenchant observations of Sturges about an American culture attracted to image rather than substance. Just as his comedies often engage with the advertising business and its obsession with hype of various kinds, *The Hudsucker Proxy* takes as its theme that most typical of 1950s phenomena: the era's consumer "crazes" for children's toys.

Juxtaposing Capra's optimism with the more cynical views of Sturges, the Coens problematize the inherited thematic content of productions like *It's a Wonderful Life* (1946), what the director, with no little self-mockery about his unabashed patriotism and moralistic politics, called their Capra-corniness. To achieve this end, the Coens avoid even the minimal deployment of sympathy and suspense found in the *Back to the Future* series. The result is a superbly crafted film. *The Hudsucker Proxy* is devoted not to arousing heart-warming emotion, but to offering a cultural critique in which visual design plays an important role. Presumably because the Coens took no interest in creating attractive characters of some depth who become involved in a compelling intrigue, general audiences did not flock to see *The Hudsucker Proxy,* which failed miserably at the box office. Among other moves, making Paul Newman an unappealing villain flew in the face of the conventional logic of the Hollywood system. Certainly, in Capra's films such casting against type (we might even say against "character" in the ethical sense) is conspicuous by its absence.

In Capra's films, the threat of either self-annihilation or, in a minor key, an exile from society motors the restoration of moral balance in the story world. In the narratives that draw a quite clear line between proper and improper ways of life, this restoration depends on the "conversion" of a morally ambivalent character. Such a turning point, energized by an attack of conscience, occurs most famously perhaps in *Mr. Smith Goes to Washington* (1939). In this testament to the American system's accommodation of idiosyncrasy and to the ability of the individual to oppose a malicious collective, the plot turns on the dissolution of the determination of Senator Paine (Claude Rains) to ruin the reputation of Jefferson Smith (James Stewart). In the end, the ambivalent villain cannot continue to oppose a man who is resolved to endure terrible suffering and excruciating humiliation to the bitter end in a good cause.

Capra's *Mr. Deeds Goes to Town* (1936) merits greater attention because it is more directly quoted in *The Hudsucker Proxy*. Longfellow Deeds (Gary Cooper), a poet favored by unfathomable "good" luck, soon finds himself victimized by powerful opponents, the worst of whom are scheming lawyers. They engineer a trial to prove him insane because he has decided to give away a huge fortune he recently inherited. Finding himself surrounded by people of self-serving venality, Deeds determines to found a community for homeless farmers. The lawyers, of course, want their cut. More devastating, perhaps, is the betrayal Deeds suffers at the hands of a Pulitzer Prize–winning reporter, Babe Bennett (played to hard-edged perfection by Jean Arthur). Babe pretends she is a secretary without a job in order to win Deeds's sympathy, and the man soon falls in love with her. In truth, however, Babe is writing a series of "exclusives" for her paper that hold Deeds up to public ridicule as the "Cinderella Man" (a name that, of course, would suit most Capra protagonists).

Contemplating the irony that the exercise of uncommon virtue has led to this existential dead-end, Deeds sits silently as proceedings move toward their foregone conclusion. Despair shows in his uncharacteristic surrender to the power of those who can manipulate a system designed to protect, not unfairly deny, individual rights. And yet, against the odds, Deeds is rescued from the prospect of death in life at the asylum by the good offices of his neighbors and through the assistance of "his girl," who abandons her cynicism enough to appreciate Deeds's genuineness and convert others to her view. The golden rule appears not to operate when the Cinderella Man is punished for his unexpected generosity, but its power is restored after those who have benefited from his kindness and love save Deeds from his own reluctance to struggle. A key to Capra's vision is that the moral equilibrium of society, figured in the protagonist's plight, is reestablished by another character's reclamation of virtue. Yet this can occur only after the good man suffers deeply, almost losing himself in order to save or serve the community.

It's a Wonderful Life (1946) is in some respects a less optimistic film than either *Mr. Deeds Goes to Town* or *Mr. Smith Goes to Washington.* Most notably perhaps, injustice is never therein rectified since the crime committed by the rapacious capitalist that sets the plot in motion is never punished or even revealed (except to the spectator). Here Capra treats not only a reputation ruined by those who resent the selflessness of the good man—and the suicide toward which he is driven by their malevolence and the depth of his shame—but also the discontents experienced as a matter of course by those who live a righteous life. George Bailey (James Stewart) is an average citizen who is exceptional only in his devotion to old-fashioned communal virtues in a world that encourages an "I need to get mine first" philosophy. George, in fact, has suffered all his life from self-denial, not because he has suddenly, like Longfellow Deeds, had a "stroke of good fortune." As the story begins, he has lost his faith in the efficacy of goodness. Worn down by the lack of financial reward for living right, he is pushed over the edge by a terrible misfortune (actually engineered by the villain) that promises his ruin, both public and financial. With symbolic appropriateness, Bailey suffers the theft of money that does not belong to him but has been placed in his trust. And so he begins to despair of the world in which his selflessness plays out, for the community of his birth has come to seem ruled both by the willfulness of the evil-minded (who seem always to have the greater power, even a kind of immunity from bad luck) and also by the apparent indifference of his fellow townsmen.

All his life George has abided strictly by the communalist values of his father, who has bequeathed to his son the stewardship of a small savings bank that is committed to making possible the purchase of that most cherished of postwar middle-class entitlements, the single-family home. Like his father, George assumes the role of resisting the depredations of Mr. Potter (Lionel Barrymore), a local entrepreneur who wants to obtain everything in the town for himself. George, always grudgingly, relinquishes opportunities to travel beyond the small town of his birth in search of self-fulfilling adventure. A close friend goes to the city and there "makes it big," his younger brother becomes a celebrated war hero, but George, barred from military service by a physical handicap (resulting, naturally, from a selfless act), must remain at home in perpetual obscurity and penury. Despite strong urges to live unfettered by responsibilities, he has become a family man, finding that he cannot resist the love he feels for a local girl. As the film opens, George faces the prospect of an upcoming audit by bank examiners that could in fact send him to prison. The town, deprived of its defender, would fall like ripe fruit into Potter's eager hands. But George is thinking only of his own pain and humiliation when he mounts a bridge, intending to leap into the turbulent waters below and thereby end his troubles.

Only divine intervention (which the powers in heaven, debating his fate, certainly think is merited) can save George from himself. God, in fact, does not abandon him in his loneliness, but acts to his benefit by sending an angel to divert him from taking the fatal plunge. Jumping in the water and pretending to be drowning, the angel reminds George that others must be helped before oneself. The angel then shows George the powerful force that George, though unawares, has exerted for goodness. Yet, if this demonstration convinces George of his indispensability, his friends and neighbors must rescue him from impending legal and financial disaster. The vindication of George's virtue, Capra reminds us, plays out in the end on the communal stage, where it has always been exercised to its greatest effect. George's spiritual crisis is resolved internally (Clarence, the angel, disappears once he feels again the desire to live). However, the good man's sullied reputation can only be rectified by a ceremonial enactment of the golden rule, by the unasked and unconstrained flow back to George of what he has given others. George does not need to prove his innocence. Instead, his innocence is manifested to him.

The film's setting is Christmas, and George's friends come to his house with their gifts. Reenacting in a minor key the offerings of the Magi, they join in the singing of a seasonal hymn. The ritualistic bestowal of money and goods, it must be pointed out, has more symbolic than actual value. This collective response literalizes what under normal circumstances remains mostly immaterial: the exchange of goodwill needed to establish and sustain communities. Such an exchange is only barely connected with "payment" in the ordinary sense. Hence any rectification of Potter's theft of the money is irrelevant. The misdeed in fact becomes a kind of Hitchcockian MacGuffin. Ultimately forgotten by the spectator, it provides merely the opportunity for the exteriorization of the gratitude felt by the others for a lifetime of George's charity and helpfulness. The fed-up family man is reconciled to his connection with a loving wife and children, but the mean-spirited capitalist is not expelled from the community, for that would acknowledge his importance and power.

As part of its reworking of Capra's vision of American culture, *The Hudsucker Proxy* similarly focuses both on a thwarted suicide (of sorts) that is attended by a more or less benevolent angel. The reputation of the Coens' protagonist is likewise restored by the conversion of a once cynical and treacherous woman, with Jennifer Jason Leigh doing a superb imitation of Jean Arthur's performance as Babe Bennett in *Mr. Deeds*. Yet the Coens confect something quite un-Caprian with these borrowed elements, infusing them with something of Sturges's cynicism and avoidance of ideological resolution. The film opens with a beautiful nighttime airplane shot of a New York City sparkling with lights (like all the "locations" the city is quite obviously a model, not the real thing). A soothing melody accompanies the camera's graceful glide over the buildings; a voice-over reveals that it is New Year's Eve 1958, and most in the city are preparing to celebrate a fresh beginning, with the rich ready to pop the corks on their champagne. An exception to this general rule of merriment is a desperate-looking young man, stepping out from an office window at the very top of a skyscraper onto the ledge as the camera focuses upon him.

He is Norville Barnes (Tim Robbins), who, like Longfellow Deeds and Jefferson Smith, has become Fortune's child, emerging suddenly (and undeservedly) from anonymity to prominence, only then to find himself betrayed by those he had thought his benefactors and well-wishers. The central questions his plight poses are "How'd he get so high and why is he feeling so low," or at least this is the view of the film's narrator, the maintenance man Moses, who is the building's presiding good spirit and is charged with keeping its huge clock running. Moses's comment motivates a long flashback inquiry, as the circumstances that have led Norville to unexpected heights and delivered him to devastating despair are carefully delineated. In the film's startling climax, we return to the moment of crisis with which it began. Despite the expectation created by the long backward glance of the narrative, Norville's suspension between life and death does not hinge on either some truth that has been now delivered about his character or the revelation of an underlying moral order. Surprisingly, what proves preeminent is that most un-Caprian of principles: pure chance. As the narrative returns to the present, Barnes suddenly slips as he moves gingerly along the ledge, clings desperately for a moment, but then plunges toward the street below.

But this bit of bad fortune turns out unexpectedly well. Norville does not fall to his death but even, before coming to earth, is given to know that the seemingly insuperable problem that moved him to desperate action has already been resolved in his favor. The seeming miracle, however, is, once again, more than a little dependent on chance, on two dei ex machina with their own motives for action, as we shall see. Unlike George Bailey, Norville does not find safety because of his merits— which are debatable at best. In the Capra tradition, he is innocent, even naïve, the archetypal small-town boy who is full of trust and wonder yet cannot resist the lure of a New York inhabited mainly by those quite unlike him: oppressed workers mired in menial jobs, financiers pursuing self-serving schemes, newspaper editors eager for a juicy story of corruption no matter who is harmed by its sensationalizing publication, and a cynical city woman. Like the other fast-talking dames who inhabit the classic screwball comedy, she is intelligent and attractive. And yet, at least under the regime of traditional gender politics, her mannish, even aggressive manner (she can hit you hard with either hand when offended) demands that the hero domesticate and feminize her with his authentic devotion. And this, indeed, is what Norville eventually does.

Unlike most of those around him, Norville (at least generally) intends others no malice as he follows the path toward corporate success that has been illuminated by unbelievably good fortune. His modicum of fellow feeling sharply distinguishes him from the moneygrubbers who have made Hudsucker so profitable and who attempt to make him into yet another instrument to increase their profit. Those at the top are certainly not given to demonstrations of kindness as they maximize the firm's benefit. No doubt, Norville is the film's least unlikable character. And yet the young man, with an irrepressible and ultimately realized ambition to "make it big," no more than superficially resembles the typical Capra hero. Like Longfellow Deeds and Jefferson Smith, he too makes his way to a city that lacks the moral compass of his small-town upbringing. But, unlike these denizens of rural America, he wants nothing more than to become the most successful of city slickers.

The morality-play structure of Capra's films opposes those traditional values nurtured in small towns where everyone knows everyone else to the rapacious individualism that is the product of the modern city, not least the nation's capital, whose corridors of power are crowded by eager self-servers. Though he comes from small-town Middle America (Muncie, Indiana), Norville plans to make New York his home because it is the nation's business center, where he can best realize his dreams of success. Norville takes no interest in what might be called community values, at least if we discount his not inconsiderable nostalgia for high school foolishness, including the football team's silly fight song. Nor is he disgusted, as are Deeds and Smith, by the modern preoccupation with the fervid and often unkind pursuit of wealth and social preeminence, the importance of which it is the thematic project of *It's a Wonderful Life* to debunk. In fact, Norville resembles the careerist executives of 1950s films like *Executive Suite, Patterns,* and *The Man in the Gray Flannel Suit,* who are devoted to ascending the corporate ladder. How to stand out in a crowd of similarly well motivated men on the make? Norville puts his trust in his design for a product that he believes will sell well.

Norville carries the image of his dream with him wherever he goes. On a plain sheet of paper is inscribed a large circle, which looks like nothing more than an emphatic zero, but, as Norville explains rather incompletely to the curious, this design depicts something "for kids." The design, it turns out, is (at least in its first incarnation) for the hula hoop, whose marketing in the decade created one of the first (and most financially spectacular) consumer sensations of the postwar decades. In fact, the hula hoop is a potent symbol of the mindless escapism that appealed

In the *Hudsucker Proxy,* Norville Barnes (Tim Robbins) is pleased by his invention of the hula hoop. (Courtesy of the Academy of Motion Picture Arts and Sciences)

to adolescents of the era, those members of the "Silent Generation," so called because of an at least supposed collective indifference to political enthusiasms of any kind.

Norville is in many ways a caricature of the compliant and uncomplaining young men of the Silent Generation, who aimed no higher than a soft and secure place in the emerging postindustrial corporate order. Having earned his business college degree (the era's newly distinctive ticket to a well-paying job), Norville moves to New York, conforming to a pattern followed by multitudes of his contemporaries. Like goldfish swallowing, phone booth stuffing, and campus panty raids, the hula hoop craze evokes an era often considered innocent in comparison to the two decades to follow. And yet the 1950s can also be construed (and are so here) as an era populated by a new generation that is unproductive, self-absorbed, and frivolous, by the kind of young people happy to stand in one spot and, moving only their hips in a constant rhythm, keep a plastic hoop circling pointlessly around their middle.

In the film's generational scheme, Norville is the "proxy" or stand-in for the founder of a huge corporation, its capacities for profitable manufacturing (of a kind never specified) turned in the first years of an emerging consumerist society toward creating and satisfying a demand for a nothing, for a zero that is, mirabile dictu, in truth a something. For the Coens, the hula hoop craze is a metonymy for the postwar turn toward the making of consumer goods for which a market had to be created. At one point in the film, hula-hooping becomes such a national obsession that President Dwight Eisenhower calls to congratulate Norville personally for the good service he has rendered the country. Here the film constructs a moment that is at once ridiculous and yet strangely plausible. This complex tone is nicely furthered by the deployment of pseudodocumentary techniques, as Norville's newfound celebrity is chronicled in an eerily authentic black-and-white newsreel sequence. Those who lived through the era endured the press's preoccupation with Ike's golfing mania, as he became the first president defined by his leisure-time activity. And so they must wonder if the Coens have in fact, if only for a moment, dropped the mask of fiction. Perhaps Ike really did make such a call to the hula hoop's inventor—or at least thought about it.

In any case, the Coens do follow Sturges more than Capra in rejecting a narrative built around the traditional Horatio Alger virtues of inspiration, hard work, and determination. In many Sturges comedies, such as *The Palm Beach Story* (1942) and *The Lady Eve* (1941), sharpsters and crooks, who are, not coincidentally, the most sympathetic characters, find the surest road to an economic success that is shown to be more or less unattainable by the average, hardworking Joe. Unscalable class barriers provide the central theme in Sturges's *Christmas in July* (1940), where aspiring young people hope for the success that will follow winning a jingle-writing contest. Longfellow Deeds and Jefferson Smith do, in a sense, profit from undeserved breaks as they emerge spectacularly and unexpectedly from obscurity to prominence. Both films work feverishly to demonstrate, however, that such prominence is less of a benefit and more of a challenge. Deeds and Smith must fight to retain the moral equilibrium and reputation they had previously merited by their dedication to traditional (and antimaterialist) values. Success financial and political, in fact, threatens to destroy them.

In a company that seems to offer no hope for success, Norville rises that first day to become its head—precisely because he is considered totally unsuited to the job by those who appoint him. For Capra's hero, the unexpected bestowal of wealth only seems to be good fortune. Money quickly threatens the destruction of Deeds's identity and, ultimately, nearly leads to a loss of freedom. Deeds is first pressured to change his habits and dress, only later to find himself the object of a sinister plot when all he tries to do is rid himself of what had come to ruin the life he had hitherto found completely satisfying. Norville, however, enthusiastically embraces wealth and position after the hula hoop makes him famous. His preoccupation with personal success differs little from those within the company who think to use him to further their own ends. In contrast, Jefferson Smith devotes his time to guiding a troop of young boys, Longfellow Deeds has made his mark as a poet, and George Bailey stands firm as his hometown's strongest defense against Potter's unrestrained schemes of aggrandizement. Norville's "character" (perhaps we should say "personality") offers nothing comparable.

What eventually justifies Norville's success (if only in a limited sense) is that he is a capitalist/inventor in the mold of Thomas Edison and Henry Ford. Like these central figures of modern American life, he proves able to realize his vision and have it endorsed by an eager public. He succeeds when all around him thought his utter failure a foregone conclusion. Norville's enemies do not oppose him on moral grounds. They want what he has been given and has now earned. Were this a film fully in the Capra tradition, Norville would be forced to realize he has chosen a morally bankrupt way of life, becoming a Potter rather than a George Bailey. The Coens have other plans for their protagonist.

Moses's invocation of a tragic rise and fall suggests in its vague moralism that the young man has somehow succumbed to the sin of pride, whose material result can very well be empty accomplishment. As if to exemplify this principle, the beginning of the flashback, in the film's most spectacular sequence, shows us another suicide. The narrative of Norville's life begins with the death that through the strange workings of fate affords Norville his big chance. In the Hudsucker boardroom, one of the officers is reading the latest financial statement to the assembled directors and the president and founder of the company, Waring Hudsucker (Charles Durning), who is sitting at the end of a long table. As Hudsucker absorbs this glowing report of financial health ("In short, we're loaded"), a blank smile flashes across his face. Suddenly, Hudsucker puts down his cigar and mounts the table, down which he runs in order to launch himself out the picture window in a dive that the camera follows right down to impact with the street. This dramatic act of self-destruction seems in context motiveless. What corporate CEO would kill himself upon learning that his company has just achieved a nearly incredible level of financial well-being? Financiers jump out of buildings only when bankruptcy looms. At film's end, however, when Hudsucker reappears as an angel, an explanation is forthcoming: "I have let my success become my identity," he admits, rounding out the cliché with the admission that his personal life has been a failure. The woman he loved spurned him to marry his rival, Sidney J. Mussburger (Paul Newman). This is the same man who, as head of the board, takes charge of the company upon Hudsucker's demise. Thwarted in his attempt to have a happy marriage, Hudsucker became, Scrooge-like, a man devoted entirely to making money, prompting his eventual suicide.

This dramatic demise is intercut with scenes showing Norville's arrival in the city. Clutching a cheap suitcase with a "Muncie, Indiana" sticker, he is dazzled by an electronic board in the window of an employment agency that lists a rapidly changing series of jobs, all of which require the experience that Norville obviously does not possess. Nevertheless, he determines to apply for a mail clerk job at Hudsucker and is just walking in the front door as the company's founder and namesake is "jellying up the street," as the narrator puts it. Meanwhile, up in the executive suite, the company's directors are facing an unexpected crisis. Hudsucker's will requires the sale of his 87 percent of company stock on the first day of the next fiscal year. This means that control of the company will soon pass to the general public. Once again events undermine the incredible success of the Hudsucker Corporation, which could not prevent the suicide of its principal beneficiary and might destroy the power of its directors. The reason is that the executives will not be able to afford the purchase of Hudsucker's holdings with the price of company stock so high after such an outstanding report. The only way to keep the status quo, Mussburger explains, is to lower the share price by hiring as Hudsucker's replacement, or "proxy," some fool whose evident incompetence will shake Wall Street's confidence in the company.

Norville, it turns out, becomes that fool when, just put to work in the mailroom, he is called upon to deliver an important "blue letter" to Mussburger. In the palatial office, the bungling and clumsy Norville manages not to deliver the letter as he sets fire to a wastebasket, loses the pages to an important contract, and almost causes Mussburger himself to tumble out the window to the street below. His display of ineptitude convinces the conscienceless Mussburger that he is the man to lead the company into precipitous decline. This plot is drawn directly from *Mr. Smith Goes to Washington,* in which Jefferson Smith, an unsophisticated bumpkin who spends most of his time working with children, is selected to fill out the term of a recently deceased senator, with the expectation that he can easily be manipulated by party bosses.

At first, Mussburger's scheme seems to be working well, as the company's stock price falls. Ace reporter Amy Archer (Leigh) is dispatched by her paper to investigate this new CEO, who seems so ill-qualified for the position. She is convinced that Norville is a poseur until he invents the hula hoop and takes Hudsucker to previously unimagined heights of profitability and worth, sending Mussburger and his cronies into near despair. No longer an innocent with that one idea that seems utter foolishness, Norville is shocked to find himself in real difficulty. The relentless pressures of producing for the consumer market require him to repeat his success, but, enjoying the time-consuming indulgences suited to his executive position, he can think of no encore. Filled with thoughts of grandiosity and self-doubt, Norville soon perpetrates the same gratuitous cruelty that was his predecessor's trademark. For no good reason other than jealousy, he peremptorily dismisses the firm's elevator boy, who has brought him a new invention (a drinking straw that bends). Norville thereby sets into motion the events that give his enemy within the company, the director Sidney Mussburger, who has his eye on Norville's job, the opportunity to engineer Norville's downfall. The scheming Mussburger forces the desperate young man to prefer death at his own hand to confinement in a mental hospital after the psychiatrist he hires to examine Norville pronounces his would-be patient (and there is some truth in the diagnosis) a "manic-depressive paranoid type B," who "goes from ze peak of delusional GAIETY to ze trrroff of dezBair."

If George Bailey, Longfellow Deeds, and Jefferson Smith do not in the least deserve to be made the objects of malicious plots, Norville finds himself undone by his pursuit of the very kind of success that Capra's protagonists always abjure. George Bailey is persuaded to live again by his hypothetical experience of how terrible the world would be without him. In contrast, Norville, like Ebenezer Scrooge, is afforded yet another opportunity to choose the love of Amy Archer (whose respect he has lost through his arrogance and indolence) over the false gods of profit and renown. Dropping like a stone, Norville suddenly finds himself suspended several stories above the pavement. The Hudsucker clock has been stopped—and, as a result, so has Norville—by Moses, who faces the camera and says "I'm never s'pose to do this, but . . . have you got a better idea?" But, after a visit from Waring Hudsucker, now become an angel, who reveals the full depth of Norville's good fortune and gives him hope for the future (which will bear more comment below), he is launched groundward again when Moses is attacked by his fellow worker and moral opposite, the malevolent Aloysius (Harry Bugin), who sets the clock's gears back into motion.

Appropriately enough, the forces of good and evil dispute Norville's fate, but the issue of that struggle can hardly be termed moral, at least in the Caprian sense of the term. Though Moses wins the fight, sending Aloysius tumbling to his death, the clock keeps running and Norville keeps falling. But then it suddenly stops once again, suspending the fortunate young man just above the pavement. This time Norville is saved by pure chance (Aloysius's false teeth, jarred loose in the fight, catch temporarily in the mechanism). Eventually, Norville tumbles softly to the earth, there to claim the opportunity for a second chance that the angelic Hudsucker has bestowed upon him. He quickly seeks out Amy, who is alone and miserable at "their place" and eager for a second chance of her own (Norville had discovered her playacting and self-serving manipulation), and the couple celebrates the coming of the New Year.

In the film's coda, Amy helps Norville regain control of the company by publishing a heartfelt exposé of the machinations of Sidney Mussburger, who, in a fitting turnabout, is sent to the same insane asylum in which he hoped to confine his rival. Making good use of his second chance, Norville, so Moses informs us in the film's projected closure, regains his position as head of the company and rules with "wisdom and compassion." Having regained his confidence and creativity, Norville finds further inspiration in his circle design for yet another harmless toy: the Frisbee, which is also "for kids." Yet this ending, despite the poetic justice upon which it is based, proves disquieting. No wonder that audiences found it difficult to "feel good" about Norville's triumph; the Coens have provided the characteristic Caprian narrative, but without the Caprian content.

Like George Bailey, Norville is delivered from both suicide and the despair that drives him to the attempt—and yet this is strictly by the operation of chance and caprice. Not only does Moses intervene in a timely, if unenthusiastic fashion, but Hudsucker descends from heaven to inform Norville that he is, by the deepest of ironies, the real Hudsucker "proxy," the man who was (if once again by chance) designated by the founder to succeed him. At the office that first day, Mussburger and the board selected Norville to replace the just departed president because he seemed the perfect, bungling fool. In contrast, the angel diverts George from plunging to his death. Clarence jumps into the river before George has a chance to do so, and George, in a characteristic gesture, rescues him, responding to someone else's need rather than to his own. Paradoxically, then, George saves himself through his selflessness, just as in the end he will, without willing it, reap the rewards of his altruism. Norville happens to be the anonymous proxy designated by Hudsucker's will, as Mussburger is hoisted by his own petard. Norville is Fortune's child, if only (as is now revealed) in an ironically more appropriate sense since Mussburger could have selected himself as Hudsucker's successor.

Norville's deliverance from Mussburger's machinations and his own weakness hardly replicates George's triumph over Potter. While George supports the values of community through a "benevolent" form of business practice, Potter represents the capitalist urge in its most reprehensive and self-aggrandizing form. Potter is interested in acquisition for the sake of acquisition, never giving a thought to how his actions affect others. Mussburger and Norville, in contrast, each want the same thing: control of the corporation and the power, wealth, and position that flow from that control. Norville, Moses tells us, "ruled with wisdom and compassion," but the key fact is that he did "rule." The products that Hudsucker makes under Norville's direction are meaningless diversions and, as in *Sullivan's Travels*, the young man's success leaves unaddressed the several questions that the narrative has raised: the class divisions perpetuated by the modern corporation, journalism's fascination with un-

covering dirt on powerful individuals (a newspaper story becomes Mussburger's main weapon against Norville), and, most of all, the unquestion-
ing devotion of Silent Generation whiz kids to a postindustrial order now
directed toward the manufacture of products for which the market must
also be manufactured. America in the 1950s (at least as this film conjures up its representation through the intertextual web of the then recent Hollywood past) is a culture that merits the full weight of the critique that the Coens mount against it. Here too the happy ending rings
hollow, with the Sturgesian device of the god from the machine humor-
ously realized in a cantankerous, regretful angel who can offer salvation
of a sort only after chance, guiding the hand of Moses, takes control.

The Two Postmodernisms

In his analysis of the most acclaimed films of the Hollywood Renaissance,
from Robert Altman's *M.A.S.H.* to Arthur Penn's *The Missouri Breaks*
(1976) to Kubrick's *2001* (1968), Fredric Jameson observes that "metageneric production becomes, whether consciously or not, the solution" to
the artistic problem faced by the director in a cultural moment "in which
genre in the older sense is no longer possible." What is "metageneric
production"? It is that "all of these films use the pregiven structure of
inherited genres as a pretext for production which is no longer personal or stylistic in the sense of the older modernism." It does seem unlikely,
as Jameson hypothesizes, that metagenericism, in the sense of a necessary return to the representational past, which is then utilized to, as it
were, analyze itself, flows from "the resistance of contemporary raw
material to artistic production."[3] In other words, it is Jameson's view that
filmmakers, debarred from representing the present because it is not a
moment with its own character that can thus be represented in itself,
can only turn to the past since the forms available for their use point them
in such a direction. Certainly, the oeuvre of the Coens suggests otherwise. Even these relentless scavengers of the Hollywood attic can engage interestingly and significantly (and through genre only in the broadest sense) with the present, as they do in *Fargo*. But it seems unarguable
that in metageneric films such as *The Hudsucker Proxy* we can easily
locate what Jameson terms "the historical impulse," taking a shape that
is highly self-reflexive, announcing its status as a "made object" by its

intertextual connections, by its advertising of the forms through which it speaks. Here is a form of postmodernism that, following Jameson, we can endorse as undegraded and still artistically significant, even if in an entirely different way from the modernism so celebrated in our culture.

Jameson suggests that the opposite of the truly metageneric films is pastiche, the blank parody that "confuses content with form, sets down to reinvent the style, not of an art language, but of a whole period." Within the Coens' body of work, the only production that fits into this variety of *la mode retro* is *Miller's Crossing*, which attempts to reconstruct a version of 1930s gangland Chicago, using Dashiell Hammett as a guidebook. *O Brother* does not set itself the task of reinventing "a whole period." Instead, it plays self-reflexively with cultural stereotypes, passing them through an intertextual filter composed, in a gesture of postmodern wit, from sources both high and low. The Coens juxtapose Hollywood screwball comedy to classical epic (with the particular text chosen, *The Odyssey*, being—this is surely no coincidence—the literary archetype celebrated by the greatest of modernism's encyclopedic fictions, James Joyce's *Ulysses*). *O Brother*, instead, belongs to a type of genre film that is, in the formula of Jim Collins, "founded on dissonance, on eclectic juxtapositions of elements that very obviously don't belong together." Such dissonance customarily flows from the "ironic hybridization of pure classic genres," as, in this case, when the comic prison escape film meets the Greek epic of return. Collins connects such confections to changing conditions of production and reception for films in the 1990s, when a "seemingly endless number of texts [became] subject to virtually immediate random access." With this in mind, it becomes possible to offer a reading of this hybridizing: "these stories just might be an attempt to make the chaotic, dissonant cultures of the later decades of the 20th Century somehow more manageable through their presentation of a new mediated landscape." Like Jameson, Collins finds that metageneric films can be seen as harboring an historical impulse: "these genre films involve a meta-mythological dimension, in which the cultural terrain that must be mapped is a world already sedimented with layers of popular mythologies, some old, some recent, but all co-present and subject to rearticulation according to different ideological agendas."[4]

The variety of those "ideological agendas" can be glimpsed in the quite distinct ways in which *The Hudsucker Proxy* and *O Brother* draw

Three escaped convicts led by Ulysses McGill (George Clooney) seek nonexistent buried treasure in *O Brother, Where Art Thou?* (Courtesy of the Academy of Motion Picture Arts and Sciences)

on the films of Frank Capra and Preston Sturges. With no little wit, *O Brother* names itself as the rejected text that will never be (was never meant to be) made, even as it seemingly takes to heart the dedication of Sturges's film "to the memory of those who made us laugh; the motley mountebanks, the clowns, the buffoons, in all times and in all nations." Its engagement with the *Odyssey* is zany and intermittent. The film's version of the Cyclops—John Goodman in an eye patch—is a fast-talking Bible salesman who, standing Homer's point on its head, not only bamboozles Ulysses but beats him unconscious and then robs him blind. Playing constantly with notions of cultural authenticity, the film features a soundtrack of supposedly authentic "Appalachian" music, but there is little in this string of numbers than does not show the homogenizing touch of Nashville. In a nice touch of irony, the film's soundtrack proved a huge commercial success, renewing interest in the "folk sound" that it only supposedly embodies.

In contrast, *The Hudsucker Proxy* critically engages with Capra's moral vision, transposing its drama of despair and salvation to a less worthy decade in which even the small-town innocent winds up complicit with an exploitative establishment. In a transparently fictional finale, borrowed from Preston Sturges films such as *Christmas in July* and *The Miracle of Morgan's Creek* (1944), Norville Barnes is "rewarded" for his devotion to an empty form of production, signified by the zero design he carries with him. Despite his moral failure to be anything other than a "proxy" for the robber baron he replaces, Norville receives a second chance—the benefit that flows from his utter unsuitability for the position to which he is "promoted." The film's clashing schemes of representation (the 1950s refigured in the styles of the 1930s) and its visual exuberance (which alerts the spectator to meaning rather than emotion) hint at deeper levels of cultural instability and developmental misdirection. *The Hudsucker Proxy* makes a gesture worthy of postmodernism's obsession with the representational past, with the world now "sedimented with layers of popular mythologies" all of which cry out for the kind of engaged reinvention at which the Coens during the last two decades have proved themselves so expert.

Notes

1. Jeff Shannon, "A Sleek Machine—Coen Brothers *Hudsucker Proxy* Looks Good but It Doesn't Work Very Well," *Seattle Times,* March 11, 1994, D3.

2. "Audiences go to the movies to consume their own emotions. Movies have to be organized so that viewers will produce their emotions in a sequence and pattern that they find satisfying." Richard Maltby, *Hollywood Cinema,* 2d ed. (Oxford: Blackwell, 2003), 30.

3. Fredric Jameson, "Historicism in *The Shining*," in *Signatures of the Visible* (New York: Routledge, 1992), 83–85.

4. Jim Collins, "Genericity in the Nineties," in Jim Collins et al., *Film Theory Goes to the Movies* (New York: Routledge, 1993), 242, 252, 262.

The Coen Brothers Interviewed

Michel Ciment and Hubert Niogret

Translation by R. Barton Palmer

Interview with Joel and Ethan Coen

(From *Positif*, July–August 1987)

Your two films belong to genres: one to the detective novel, the other to comedy. Do you prefer working within the conventions of a genre?

JOEL COEN: We were more aware of working within a genre in *Blood Simple* than in the case of *Raising Arizona*. *Raising Arizona* seems more unconventional, a mixture of genres. In *Blood Simple*, we were aware that the genre, as a point of departure, unconsciously shaped the film we were making.

ETHAN COEN: In the case of *Raising Arizona*, we did not start off thinking about working with a genre. We intended, in a general way, to make a comedy with two principal characters. Our concentration was on them, rather than on what the film would be in terms of type.

Did you come up with the characters first and then the setting?

JC: In the case of *Raising Arizona*, yes. The story was a way of talking about the characters. In the case of *Blood Simple*, we started out with a situation, the general outline of a plot. The characters came from that. And so it was just the opposite.

In regard to Raising Arizona, *why a second time in the Southwest? You come from Minnesota . . .*

EC: Perhaps in part because we are not from the Southwest, which seems somewhat exotic to us, probably nearly as much as it is for you. It's just a place we find attractive. In regard to our second film, that kind of desert country seemed the right setting to us.

JC: Once again, *Blood Simple* proceeded in a more organized, more conscious fashion. We did not deal with the real Texas, but an artificial version of it, an assemblage of texts and mythologies. The subject is "murderous passion." There have been so many cases of this sort that have occurred in Texas that it has become a part of the public imagination. But what resulted from that was important to us because the film was imagined as a slice of life, a deliberate fiction that it was normal to set within an exotic locale.

EC: All my association with Minnesota, where we grew up, was rather lifeless. It could have been anywhere except Minnesota.

Folk tales have a certain importance in Raising Arizona, *like that of Davy Crockett.*

EC: We decided we'd make a connection with the things of the imagination, and also that the film would not be a slice of life.

JC: When we spoke with the director of photography, Barry Sonnenfeld, about the visual design of the film, we discussed that the beginning the film would be like a storybook, with pretty vibrant colors. That became part of the visual design.

Were your sources then more literary than cinematic?

EC: A film like *Raising Arizona* should make you suspect, I suppose, our admiration for Southern writers like William Faulkner and Flannery O'Connor.

JC: Even if we don't share the same interest of the latter for Catholicism! But she has a real knowledge of the regional psychology of the South, which is not to be found with many other writers. In the case of *Blood Simple,* the influence came instead from the writers of hard-boiled fiction like James Cain.

What you say about Flannery O'Connor is even more striking since a director one thinks of in regard to Raising Arizona *is John Huston because of certain sequences in* Fat City *(1971), and also* Wise Blood *(1979) which is directly adapted from a novel by Flannery O'Connor.*

EC: Right, like the incredible character Stacy Keach plays in *Fat City.*

JC: But in regard to O'Connor, our characters do not have the same mystical obsession as do hers—ours are worldly.

Looking at Raising Arizona *makes you think a good deal about the animation of Chuck Jones as, for example, in the supermarket scene.*

EC: This was very much our intention: those characters who bounce back after colliding, and also the speed of their movements. We tried to give them the energy of the animation in electronic games.

JC: It's funny that you mentioned Chuck Jones since we did not consciously think about him in regard to this film, while, in contrast, his Roadrunner inspired us in the long scene in *Blood Simple* where Ray (John Getz) tries to kill Julian Marty (Dan Hedaya), then bury him. There's some Hitchcock in it, but also some Chuck Jones.

What was the point of departure for Raising Arizona? *The idea of the quintuplets?*

EC: Not really. In essence, after having completed *Blood Simple,* we wanted to make something completely different. We didn't know what, but we wanted it to be something funny that had a very quick rhythm. We also wanted to use Holly Hunter, who has been a friend of ours for a long time. So it really wasn't the story that was the origin of the project, but Holly Hunter, her personality and, by extension, the character we had conceived for her to play. In contrast, *Blood Simple* took shape from an idea for a screenplay.

JC: The idea of kidnapping the baby was really secondary. We weren't much interested in the problem of sterility and about the wish to have a baby, but in the idea of a character who has this kind of desire and who, at the same time, feels outside the law. This conflict enabled us to develop the story line, which is his aspiration for a stable family life, and at the same time his taste for unusual experiences.

EC: Right, this tension in Hi's character was the driving force of the film for us.

How did the other characters take shape, the two brothers who live together for example?

JC: We very much like male couples such as Laurel and Hardy. They're there only to help the story along, that's all. This is very much like an old idea of Dashiell Hammett's: a character from outside intervenes in a situation and then you can observe the reactions he provokes.

EC: At a certain point we said to ourselves: let's bring a couple of uncouth characters into the story and have a look at what effect this will have on the relationship between the main characters.

Was your shooting script very detailed or did you allow yourself a certain freedom during production?

JC: We worked at the screenplay until we were satisfied with it, and during shooting we were overall quite faithful to it. There was little improvisation in the dialogue. What changed a good deal, in contrast, was the visual conception of the film once the actors came in. During rehearsals, we were able to think of other ways of "covering" the scene with the camera. This was especially true of the scenes with dialogue. On the other hand, as far as the action scenes are concerned, they were planned out beforehand, and we followed the storyboarding precisely. As it turned out, we didn't need to refer to the storyboarding during shooting, but it served a psychological purpose. We knew what the visual conception was for the shots. It was down on paper, and that was reassuring.

EC: Sometimes, you look through the camera and discover that the planned layout doesn't work.

JC: For various reasons. For example, the shooting location can pose problems that could not be anticipated. But even if we wanted to improvise during shooting, we couldn't do it because our budgets were very limited. *Blood Simple* was produced for $800,000, and *Raising Arizona* for a bit more than $5 million, which for Hollywood is rather low. In order to make the most of the money, the film had to be meticulously planned out.

Did the actors cause you to change aspects of their characters during shooting?

JC: Absolutely. This was especially true with Nicolas Cage and Holly Hunter. Nick is a comedian with a great deal of imagination. He arrived with a mountain of ideas we hadn't thought of while writing the screenplay, but his contribution was always limited to the situation that the characters we had imagined find themselves in. The same with Holly. But she surprised us less because we already had her in mind when we wrote her role and because we had known her a long time.

EC: She's a stage actress in New York. She appeared a good deal in plays by Beth Henley. For example, she was in the original Broadway production of *Crimes of the Heart,* which Bruce Beresford adapted for the screen.

Could you give me some examples of how the actors participated in creating their roles?

JC: For example, we spoke with Nicolas Cage a long time about his moustache and sideburns. We asked if he should keep them for the entire film or, in contrast, get rid of them at some point.

EC: He was also crazy about his Woody Woodpecker haircut. The more difficulties his character got in, the bigger the wave in his hair got. There was a strange connection between the character and his hair.

And his wardrobe?

JC: That, no, that was not in the script, those Hawaiian shirts.

EC: That's a conventional way of dressing for criminals in the Southwest, these kinds of outrageous clothes.

The motorcyclist character coming out of a dream?

JC: We tried to imagine a character who did not correspond specifically to *our* image of what evil is or of a nightmare come true, but rather to the image of evil that would occur to Hi. Being from the Southwest, he would see him in the form of a Hell's Angel.

EC: We tried to connect the characters with the music. Holly sings a lullaby in the film, and we asked the music director to make it a part of the music theme that accompanies the bounty hunter—it combines Richard Wayne with country music!

Where did you find the actor who plays this role, Randall "Tex" Cobb?

JC: He's not really an actor. He's a former boxing champion. He's appeared in a number of films. In the beginning, he was a kind of Texas street brawler who then tried without much success to make a career out of professional boxing. He's less a comedian than a force of nature. He's not really someone easy to work with, and I don't think I'd be very eager to work with him on another project. He did a good job with his part in *Raising Arizona*, but he did cause us some problems.

What kind of language did you intend the characters to speak? It's a kind of stylized slang.

JC: It's a mixture of local dialect and language that we imagined the characters would get from the kind of reading they probably did: the Bible, newspapers. The voice-over narration was one of our initial ideas for the story. The first part we wrote was the ten-minute sequence that precedes the credits.

In regard to the baby, you establish from the outset a mixture of sentimentalism and ironic distance.

JC: Some people find the end too sentimental. Once again, this does not reflect our own attitude toward life. But, in our view, what he hoped the future would bring was connected to the character's background, and so it fits with his conception of what life is about.

EC: We hide ourselves behind the main character! We weren't the ones who determined how much sentimentality we had to put into this story—it was the characters who guided us.

The two films you have made are very inventive visually. Were there any images that you had in mind before writing the screenplay?

JC: Yes, in some cases anyway. It's a different matter entirely when you write a screenplay for yourself rather than for someone else. In the latter situation, the director generally doesn't want the screenplay to lay out the visual elements for him. When we work for ourselves, however, we allow the visual elements to take the lead in the writing of the screenplay. Sometimes, in contrast, we write the scene and then ask ourselves what might be the best way to convey this information, either to arouse the viewer's emotions or accelerate the rhythm. That's the time we think about the images themselves. But in fact, it's all connected—these are two sides of the same coin. While writing the screenplay, we knew we would be filming with more leeway and on a broader scale than was in the case in *Blood Simple,* which was more claustrophobic.

EC: I remember a specific image that pleased us as we were writing the film: seeing Holly shouting orders at the prisoners. This might seem like a minor thing, but this image played an important role in advancing our writing of the film.

JC: For example, the first setup with the lineup and the character stumbling into the frame was described just this way in the screenplay.

How do you two divide up the work?

JC: We work on the writing together, never separately. We hole up inside a room and we write the screenplay from beginning to end. In the case of *Raising Arizona,* we took three and a half months. On the set, it's pretty much the same as with the writing. We are both always there and never stop consulting one another. The credits point to a separation of tasks that is more rigid than is actually the case. For the sake of efficiency and to avoid confusion, I speak to the actors, and I'm the one who usually communicates with the technical crew, but making decisions about the setups is something we do together. As for Ethan, he is the one who takes charge of production matters.

EC: It's the same with the image and sound editing—collaboration in every way.

And the image of the two characters coming out of the mud?

JC: It's a kind of primitive birth! We thought a long time about how to introduce these two brutes who had escaped from prison. And we suddenly had a vision of this scene, and it seemed an appropriate kind of introduction.

It's curious that you mention James Cain as exerting an influence on Blood Simple, *but Jim Thompson comes more to mind in this regard.*

JC: In fact, at the time, we had not read him. After *Blood Simple* was released, his novels were republished in paperback in the United States, and he began to be rediscovered.

Viewing Raising Arizona *makes you think a bit about Preston Sturges.*

EC: We are crazy about his films. We love *The Palm Beach Story.*

What kind of relationship did you two have as children?

JC: There's three years between us, and that's important when you're a kid. It's only after leaving school that we really began to know one another.

EC: Right, especially while writing together. Joel studied filmmaking in college. Me, I majored in philosophy, God knows why! Afterward Joel worked as an editor.

JC: On horror films! Then we began to write screenplays for other people, and after that we wrote *Blood Simple.* When we were kids, we made films in Super 8. They were abstract and surrealist. Minnesota, where we were born, seemed like an empty, frozen wasteland. The fields were covered with snow, and it had a very abstract look. We also turned out remakes of films we had seen on television like Cornel Wilde's *Naked Prey,* and we shot these in the garden. And *Advise and Consent* too! Now that one had more of an epic dimension to it; it was necessary to build interior sets in the house for it. We saw a lot of films, some from the fifties and the ones that came out in the sixties with Doris Day and Rock Hudson, the worst period for Hollywood.

Where did you study film?

JC: At New York University. Our professors were not well-known directors. They had essentially made a career out of teaching. I was a student there for four years starting in 1972.

And philosophy?

EC: I specialized in the history of philosophy. I wrote a thesis on Wittgenstein. I don't see what connection it had afterward with my career as a filmmaker!

You worked as an assistant director?

JC: No, I worked as assistant editor on the film *Evil Dead,* and I did about a third to a half of the editing work on the film. At that time horror films were all the rage, those with a small budget, produced independently, like *Fear No Evil.* It was always necessary to put *Evil Dead* on the table . . .

In Raising Arizona, *there are several superb editing effects, particularly with the motorcyclist on the road.*

JC: These effects were specified in the shooting script.

You like popular culture, even as you take an ironic attitude to it.

JC: Yeah, sure, that's our view of American popular culture.

EC: We have our opinions about this kind of material and something to say about it. We treat it as a source of humor when we use it.

The characters in Blood Simple *are very different from those in* Raising Arizona.

JC: In *Raising Arizona,* the characters were supposed to be sympathetic. We had a lot of fun creating them. Ed elicits a kind of restrained sympathy, which is very interesting; there is something mature about her. What's not easy is when a character is thoroughly evil and yet, at the same time, you make him rather sympathetic.

There's a dark as well as a comic side to your work. You have no interest in realism.

JC: Some people have been offended by the characters in *Raising Arizona.*

EC: I think it's a pretty savage film.

How did you get the idea for your first film, choosing the film noir genre?

EC: For a long time we've been fans of this kind of story, which is in the tradition of James M. Cain, Dashiell Hammett, Raymond Chandler. It's certainly a genre that is entertaining. And we also picked it for very practical reasons. We knew we weren't going to have a big budget. The financing would not allow it. We could build something on the genre and the appeal it has.

JC: The story gave rise to some special effects, to unusual setups. And we knew we could do a certain number of things on the screen for very little money. It's also a genre that allows you to get by rather modestly in some ways. You can limit the number of characters, put them into a confined set. There's no need to go for large-scale effects or scatter them through the film, and those cost a lot of money. So it was a pragmatic decision that determined what film we would make.

Barry Sonnenfeld, the director of photography, shot these two films.

JC: Yes, he's an old friend, from long before this production. We collaborated very closely. Long before shooting, he looked over the locations. We talked about the filming, about how to shoot in certain locations. He got involved at a very early stage, and this, once again, from a practical point of view, helped us work in a very cost efficient fashion. Once you start shooting, you cannot allow yourself to spend money in an unplanned fashion. Everything was talked through beforehand.

In Blood Simple, *there were setups with some striking effects, like the pistol that shoots through the wall and then the holes become visible from the light that shines through them.*

JC: When you are interested in talking about scenes that started out, in the planning stage, with an image, that one's a good example because in that instance the image dictated the action, which was then elaborated so that this image could be integrated into the narrative at that point.

How was your first film financed? With a lot of shareholders? With independent sources of money?

EC: We had never made a film. We had no credentials. It was difficult to find a producer to trust us and give us the money to make a film. So we approached private investors, a great many of them. For the second film, it was incredibly easier. We went and asked the American distributor for *Blood Simple*, Circle Films, if they were interested in getting involved in the production. They liked the scenario. They said "yes."

What is your position in regard to production? Do you prefer being independent or working with a "studio"?

EC: Producing independently was the result of circumstances, especially in the case of our first film.

JC: In the case of the second, it was the path of least resistance. We could have looked elsewhere and perhaps found the money from a "studio." Because of *Blood Simple,* Circle Films became well known, and so we had confidence in them. It was a natural choice to work with them. There was no ideological position behind these choices. As long as we were able to maintain the kind of control that we wanted to have, we could accept financing from a "studio."

EC: Getting money is the problem.

JC: The problem is that there are strings attached. The whole idea about independent production is that it helps you make the film that you want to make, and in the way that you want to make it. But if the studio allows you to do the same thing, that's fine. Some people do that and manage quite well, even with films that don't fit the "Hollywood formula." Certain directors succeed nicely within this system at making the films they have the urge to make.

How long has the shooting schedule been in the case of the two films?

JC: Eight weeks for *Blood Simple,* ten weeks for *Raising Arizona.*

Your film was released at the same time as True Stories, *which is very different. But there's a deep irony in your film, with its juxtaposition of popular cultural themes and a very modernist visual style.* True Stories *is more static, while yours is more dynamic.*

JC: That's a coincidence. Just as it's a coincidence that John Goodman (the heavier of the two escaped prisoners) appears in both films. We picked him before *True Stories* started shooting, and he arrived on the set just after leaving the David Byrne production.

What kind of distinction would you make between Texas and Arizona as far as characters and themes are concerned?

JC: Arizona does not bring along with it all the baggage that Texas does for American viewers. Texas is associated with many things, which is not the case with Arizona.

EC: Arizona is like many places in the Midwest and Southwest. The stories are just about the same everywhere there.

JC: Once again, Arizona for us was one of those rare states where we could find this type of landscape. That particular kind of desert exists only in Arizona, to some degree in Mexico as well.

With what American directors of the last twenty years do you feel the most kinship? Not which ones you like the best!

JC: It's harder to answer that than to say which we prefer. It's even easier to say which ones we like.

Who do you like?

Scorsese, Coppola, David Lynch.

Kubrick?

JC: Yes.

Kubrick's dark humor?

EC: Yes. *Dr. Strangelove.*

JC: I like Walter Hill a lot. He's done some interesting things.

And Bob Altman?

JC: I like some of his films very much. He did a terrific job with adapting Chandler in *The Long Goodbye.*

EC: Yes, it's a really good film. But I read somewhere that it's one of those he likes the least. I can't understand why.

No, he really likes it a lot.

EC: Really? Okay, then.

In Regard to *Barton Fink*
(From *Positif*, September 1991)

Barton Fink *takes as its theme the writer's block suffered by a screen-writer. How did you come to write this kind of film?*

JOEL COEN: It did not begin to take shape until we were halfway through the writing of *Miller's Crossing*. It's not really the case that we were suffering from writer's block, but our working speed had slowed, and we were eager to get a certain distance from *Miller's Crossing*. In order to escape from the problems that we were experiencing with that project, we began to think about a project with a different theme. That was *Barton Fink*, which had two origins. In the first place, we were thinking about putting John Turturro to work—we had known him well for a long time—and so we wanted to invent a character he could play. And then there was the idea of a huge abandoned hotel. This idea came even before our decision to set the story in Hollywood.

ETHAN COEN: We wrote the screenplay very quickly, in three weeks, before returning to the script of *Miller's Crossing* in order to finish it. This is one of the reasons why these two films were released rather close to one another. When we had finished shooting *Miller's Crossing*, we had a script all ready to film.

Why did you set the action in 1941, which was a key era for Hollywood writers? Fitzgerald and Nathanael West had just died, Preston Sturges and John Huston, who had been screenwriters, had just begun careers in directing.

JC: We didn't know that. In retrospect, we were enthusiastic about the idea that the world outside the hotel was finding itself on the eve of the apocalypse since, for America, 1941 was the beginning of the Second World War. That seemed to us to suit the story. The other reason—which was never truly realized in the film—was that we were thinking of a hotel where the lodgers were old people, the insane, the physically handi-capped, because all the others had left for the war. The further the script was developed, the more this theme got left behind, but it had led us, in the beginning, to settle on that period.

EC: Another reason was the main character: a serious dramatist, honest, politically engaged, and rather naïve. It seemed natural that he comes from Group Theater and the decade of the thirties.

JC: The character had somewhat the same background, in terms of being a writer, as Clifford Odets; only the resemblance ends there. Both writers wrote the same kind of plays with proletarian heroes, but their personalities were quite different. Odets was much more of an extrovert; in fact he was quite sociable even in Hollywood, and this is not the case with Barton Fink! Odets the man was moreover quite different from Odets the writer. There was a great deal of passion and innocence in him.

Have you read the journal Odets wrote during the year 1940?

EC: John Turturro was the one who really read it. But you have to take account of the difference between the character and the man.

JC: Turturro was also interested by the style of the Group Theater plays. At the opening of the film, the voice that you hear off camera is that of Turturro, and, at the end, when he taps out a scene from his screenplay on the typewriter, it is meant to be in the Odets style.

The character of W. P. Mayhew is, in turn, directly inspired by Faulkner.

EC: Yes, the southern writer, an alcoholic. Certainly we chose John Mahoney for this role because of his resemblance to Faulkner, but also because we are very eager to work with him. And yet, that was only somewhere to start, and the parallel between the two is pretty superficial. As far as the details of the character are concerned, Mayhew is very different from Faulkner, whose experiences in Hollywood were not the same at all.

JC: Certainly Faulkner showed the same disdain for Hollywood that Mayhew does, but his alcoholism did not incapacitate him, and he continued to be a productive writer.

Did you get the inspiration for Jack Lipnick, the producer, from Louis B. Mayer?

JC: Michael Lerner looks a little like Mayer, but Lipnick is really an amalgamation of several figures. The incident with the uniform, for example, comes from the life of Jack Warner, who arranged that an army commission be given him and demanded that the studio costume department make him a uniform. Lipnick also has his vulgar side, rather like Harry Cohn.

EC: What's ironic about it is that this colonel's uniform, one of the most surrealist elements in the film, is at the same time one of the few that's drawn from Hollywood history.

One of the most characteristic qualities of your films and of Barton Fink *in particular is the fact that their structures are completely unpredictable. Do you put together your screenplays with this in mind?*

JC: In this case, we had the shape of the narrative in mind from the very beginning. The structure was freer than usual and we were aware that, toward the middle, the story would take a radical turn. We wanted the beginning of the film to have a certain rhythm and to involve the viewer in a kind of journey. When Fink wakes up and discovers the corpse beside him, we wanted this to be a surprise, and yet not clash with everything that comes before.

EC: We were aware that we would be walking a very thin line here. We needed to surprise the viewer without disconnecting him from the story. In the way we presented the hotel, we hint that Fink's arrival in Hollywood was not completely "normal." But it is certain that the film is less tied to the conventions of some film genre, as, for example, *Miller's Crossing* is, belonging as it does completely to the tradition of the gangster film.

At what stage did you start thinking of the picture of the woman on the beach that figures in the last sequence?

JC: That came to us pretty soon after we began to ask ourselves what there would be in Barton Fink's room. Our intention was that the room would have very little decoration, that the walls would be bare and that the windows would offer no view of any particular interest. In fact, we wanted the only opening on the exterior world to be this picture. It seemed important to us to create a feeling of isolation. Our strategy was to establish from the very beginning that the main character was experiencing a sense of dislocation.

EC: The picture of the beach was to give a vision of the feeling of consolation. I do not know exactly why we became fixed on this detail, but it was no doubt a punctuation mark that, in effect, did further the sense of oppression in the room.

With the sequence where Fink crushes the mosquito, the film moves from social comedy into the realm of the fantastic.

JC: Some people have suggested that the whole second part of the film is nothing but a nightmare. But it was never our intention to, in any literal sense, depict some bad dream, and yet it is true that we were aiming for a logic of the irrational. We wanted the film's atmosphere to reflect the psychological state of the protagonist.

EC: It is correct to say that we wanted the spectator to share the interior life of Barton Fink as well as his point of view. But there was no need to go too far. For example, it would have been incongruous for Barton Fink to wake up at the end of the film and for us to suggest thereby that he actually inhabited a reality greater than what is depicted in the film. In any case, it is always artificial to talk about "reality" in regard to a fictional character. It was not our intention to give the impression that he was more "real" than the story itself.

JC: There is another element that comes into play with this scene. No one knows what has killed Audrey Taylor. We did not want to exclude the possibility that it was Barton himself, even though he proclaims his innocence several times. It is one of the conventions of the classic crime film to lay out false trails as long as possible for the viewer. That said, our intention was to keep the ambiguity right to the end of the film. What is suggested, however, is that the crime was committed by Charlie, his next-door neighbor.

From this point of view, the choice of John Goodman to play Charlie Meadows was inspired because he has usually been given more appealing roles and because the viewer sympathizes with him during the first scenes of the film.

EC: This role too was written for the comedian, and we were quite obviously aware of the warm and friendly image that he projects for the viewer and with which he feels at ease. We played on this expectation by reversing it. Even so, from the moment he appears, there is something menacing, disquieting about this character.

The fact that Barton Fink uses working-class characters in his plays obliges him to be friendly to Meadows because if not he would show himself full of prejudice.

JC: That's true enough in part, but Charlie also wins him over completely by his friendly greeting in the beginning.

EC: Charlie is, of course, equally aware of the role that Barton Fink intends for him to play, if in a somewhat perverse way.

While shooting this film, you weren't sure if you would go to Cannes, and even less sure that Roman Polanski would be the head of the jury. It is ironic that it was up to him to pass judgment on a film where The Tenant *and* Cul-de-Sac *meet* Repulsion.

JC: Obviously, we have been influenced by his films, but at this time we were very hesitant to speak to him about it because we did not want to give the impression we were sucking up. The three films you mention are ones we've been quite taken by. *Barton Fink* does not belong to any genre, but it does belong to a series, certainly one that Roman Polanski originated.

One thinks also of The Shining *and of the imaginative world of Kafka, of the black humor and Jewish culture of Central Europe.*

JC: All this is true enough, except that *The Shining* belongs in a more global sense to the horror film genre. Several other critics have mentioned Kafka, and that surprises me since to tell the truth I have not read him since college when I devoured works like *The Metamorphosis*. Others have mentioned *The Castle* and *The Penal Colony,* but I've never read them.

EC: After the insistence of journalists who wanted us to be inspired by *The Castle,* I find myself very interested in looking into it.

How did you divide up work on the screenplay?

EC: We handle this in a very informal and simple way. We discuss each scene together in detail without ever dividing up the writing on any. I'm the one who then does the typing. As we have said, *Barton Fink* progressed very quickly as far as the writing was concerned, while *Miller's Crossing* was slower and took more time, nearly nine months.

JC: Ordinarily, we spend four months on the first draft, and then show it to our friends, and afterward we devote two further months to the finishing touches.

What is your explanation for the rapid writing of Barton Fink?

EC: Perhaps it was because of the feeling of relief that we got from it in the midst of the difficulties posed by *Miller's Crossing.* In any case, it was very easy.

JC: It's a strange thing but certain films appear almost entirely completed in your head. You know how they will be, visually speaking, and, without knowing exactly how they will end, you have some intuition about the kind of emotion that will be evident at the conclusion. Other scenarios, in contrast, are a little like journeys that develop in stages without your ever truly knowing where they are heading. With this film, we knew as a practical matter where Barton Fink would be at the end. Moreover, right at the beginning we wrote Charlie's final speech, the one where he explains himself and says that Barton Fink is only a tourist in that city. It makes things much easier when you know in advance where you're taking your characters.

EC: We have to say we felt we knew these characters pretty well, maybe because we are very close to the two comedians, which made writing their roles very easy.

Now Miller's Crossing *is a film where there are many characters and locations and where several plot lines intersect.*

JC: It is true that *Barton Fink* has a much narrower scope. The narrative of *Miller's Crossing* is so complicated because while writing it we had the tendency ourselves to lose our way in the story.

EC: *Barton Fink* is more the development of a concept than an intertwined story like *Miller's Crossing.*

How did the title come to mind?

JC: We knew we came up with it at the very beginning of our work on the screenplay, but we found we couldn't remember the source. It seems it wound up being what it was by complete chance.

There is a great deal of humor in the film, from the moment when the wallpaper starts peeling off the wall until the pair of policemen arrives on the scene. In fact the combination of drama with comedy is perhaps more evident in Barton Fink *than in the films that preceded it.*

JC: That's fair enough. The film is really neither a comedy nor a drama. *Miller's Crossing* is much more of a drama, and *Raising Arizona* is much more of a comedy.

EC: It seems that we are pretty much incapable of writing a film that, in one way or another, is not contaminated by comic elements.

JC: That's funny because at the start I was imagining *Miller's Crossing,* while *Barton Fink* seems to me to be more of a dark comedy.

EC: As opposed to what takes place in regard to *Miller's Crossing,* here we tormented the main character in order to create some comic effects.

Jon Polito plays a role similar to the one he plays in Miller's Crossing. *In both films, he winds up humiliated.*

EC: Except that in *Barton Fink* the character is mistreated for twenty years. In the end, he gets used to it.

The first image of Hollywood that appears is unconventional for this kind of film: a rock on the beach.

EC: It's funny that you should mention that because we actually filmed other shots that would have made for a more conventional transition, but we decided in the end not to use them. All we needed was a rock on the beach that anticipated the film's end.

This is the second production on which you have worked with your art director, Dennis Gassner.

JC: We shot for at least three weeks in the hotel where half the action of the film takes place. We wanted an art deco stylization and a place that was falling in ruin after having seen better days. It was also necessary that the hotel be organically linked to the film. Our intention, moreover, was that the hotel function as an exteriorization of the character played by John Goodman. The sweat drips off his forehead like the paper peels off the walls. At the end, when Goodman says that he is a prisoner of his own mental state, that this is like some kind of hell, it was necessary for the hotel to have already suggested something infernal.

EC: We used a lot of greens and yellows to suggest an aura of putrefaction.

JC: Ethan always talked about the hotel as a ghost ship floating adrift, where you notice signs of the presence of other passengers, without every laying eyes on any. The only indication of them is the shoes in the corridor. You can imagine it peopled by failed commercial travelers, with pathetic sex lives, who cry alone in their rooms.

You take a look at the Hollywood of fifty years ago, but in a different way you find yourselves confronted by the same problems. Do artists always meet up with Philistines like Lipnick?

JC: We would have to say yes, probably. But in fact *Barton Fink* is quite far from our own experience. Our professional life in Hollywood has been especially easy, and this is no doubt extraordinary and unfair. It is in no way a comment about us. We financed *Blood Simple,* our first film, ourselves, and Circle Films in Washington produced the three next ones.

Each time, we made them the offer of a screenplay that they liked and then they agreed on the budget. We have no rejected screenplays in our desk drawers. There are plenty of projects that we started but then didn't finish writing for one reason or another, either because there were artistic problems we couldn't resolve or because the cost of producing them would have been prohibitive.

Were any of these aborted projects particularly dear to you?

JC: No, because right away you get drawn into another film, and it becomes your sole preoccupation. We would have liked to produce one or two short subjects that we wrote, but it is very difficult to get them made in America because there's no market.

Why did you use Roger Deakins on this project?

JC: Our usual director of photography, Barry Sonnenfeld, wasn't available, and since we had seen Deakins's work and liked it, we asked him to work with us. He seemed right for the film.

EC: We especially like the night scenes and interior sequences in *Stormy Monday*. We also screened *Sid and Nancy* and *Pascali's Island*.

Did you make storyboards, as you had for your other films?

EC: Yes, we did detailed ones, but of course there were a lot of changes once we got on the set. However, we went there with a detailed plan for each shot. This was a film much easier to shoot than *Miller's Crossing*, and the budget ran about a third less, just like the shooting schedule: eight weeks instead of twelve.

Did you shoot any sequences you didn't use in the final cut?

JC: In the case of *Miller's Crossing*, there were whole sequences we shot that did not find a place in the film. This was not the case with *Barton Fink;* we used just about everything. I do remember, however, that we did some shots about life in Hollywood studios, but didn't decide to keep them; they were too conventional.

Compared to your preceding films, which feature bravura sequences like the nighttime shoot-out in Miller's Crossing, Barton Fink *has a much more restrained style.*

JC: We weren't conscious of that. Probably *Miller's Crossing* had so many dialogue scenes that at a certain stage we intended to give the spectator some interesting visual effects. The genre also encourages large-scale action scenes. But in the case of *Barton Fink* this kind of thing did not seem appropriate to us. Stylistic tours de force would have ruptured the film's equilibrium.

The writer victimized by Hollywood is a part of the legend of the cinema.

EC: Right, it's almost a cliché. Furthermore, we gave the two writers in the film the dignity that victims are accorded, something they maybe didn't deserve because Barton Fink is probably not a great artist and Mayhew is no longer able to write.

Do you feel close to any of your contemporaries in the American film industry?

JC: There's no lack of films that we like, but we don't see connections between them and our work. The American film industry is doing quite well these days; a number of directors are succeeding in using the screen to express their ideas. In effect, two kinds of films are being produced these days in the United States: the products churned out by the large production companies, which are most often repetitive although there are exceptions, and the films that certain independent directors manage to make.

Your films contrast sharply with the greater part of the Hollywood films of today. For example, you begin all your films in the middle of a scene without any kind of establishing shot, as in Miller's Crossing.

JC: At the beginning of *Miller's Crossing*, we had two setups: the first was of a drinking glass with ice cubes, then a closeup of Polito. We did not intend to show right away who was holding the glass. You see someone walk off with the glass, you hear the tinkling of the ice cubes, but the character is not visible in the shot. Then you see Polito, you listen to his monologue, and the ice cubes are always part of the scene, but they escape view. Then you see Albert Finney, but you still do not know who is holding the glass, and finally, you get to Gabriel Byrne in the background. All that was set up and laid out in the storyboards.

EC: We intended to create an aura of mystery around the character who was going to become the hero in the film.

JC: Polito is important in this scene because he's the one who provides the background information as he begins to tell the story.

EC: We held back Gabriel's entrance into the conversation. He is the last one to talk, five minutes after the beginning of the film.

How do you explain the relative commercial failure of Miller's Crossing *despite the good reception it got from critics worldwide?*

EC: It is always difficult to speculate about this kind of problem. Perhaps the story is too difficult to follow.

JC: After all the whole plot of *The Big Sleep* was very difficult to understand! It's very difficult to analyze failure at the box office, but in any event we were certainly surprised by it.

(This interview took place in Cannes on May 20, 1991.)

Closer to Life Than to the Conventions of the Cinema
(From *Positif,* September 1996)

Did some news item inspire Fargo, *as the press kit suggests, or is that another false trail that you two have laid?*

JOEL COEN: In its general structure, the film is based on a real event, but the details of the story and the characters are fictional. We were not interested in making a documentary film, and we did no research about the nature of the murders or the events connected to them. But in warning viewers that we had found our inspiration from a real story, we were preparing them to not view the film like an ordinary thriller.

Did this kidnapping of a wife organized by her husband create a good deal of sensation in 1987?

ETHAN COEN: It didn't. In fact, it's surprising how many things of this kind get very little publicity. We heard about it from a friend who lived very close to where the story unfolded in Minnesota, which also happens to be where we are from.

Why did you call the film Fargo *when the important action of the film is set in Brainerd, which is in Minnesota, and not Fargo?*

JC: *Fargo* seemed a more evocative title than "Brainerd"—that's the only reason.

EC: It was just that we liked the sound of the word—there's no hidden meaning.

JC: There was, to be sure, a kind of western connection with Wells Fargo, but that was not part of our intention, and it's too bad that some people should have thought so.

Here you returned somewhat to the territory of your first films, Blood Simple *and* Raising Arizona.

JC: There are some similarities, but also some important differences. These three films are all small-scale productions, their main themes relate to criminality, to kidnapping, and they are also very specific in their reference to geographical locale. Furthermore, Frances McDormand plays a role in *Fargo* and *Blood Simple*. But we have always thought that *Blood Simple* belongs to the tradition of flamboyant melodrama, as given expression in the novels of James M. Cain, along with some influence from the horror film. In *Fargo,* we tried out a very different stylistic approach, introducing the subject in a quite dry fashion. Our intention was also that the camera should tell the story like an observer. The structure of the film also follows from the origin of the story in an actual event: we allowed ourselves more digressions and detours. Each incident did not necessarily have to be connected to the plot. We also allowed ourselves to withhold the appearance of the heroine, Marge Gunderson, until the middle of the film.

EC: This is also a way of signifying to the viewer that he was not watching a genre film, that we were not going to satisfy expectations of this kind. In this way too, the film differs from *Blood Simple*.

What is it that drew you to the subject?

JC: There were two or three things about the actual events that interested us. In the first place, the story takes place in a time and place with which we were familiar and could explore. And then again it features a kidnapping, a subject that has always fascinated us. In fact, we had a screenplay that was quite different from *Fargo* that we would have been very happy to shoot. Finally, this subject offered us the chance to shoot a crime film with characters quite different from genre stereotypes.

EC: It's probably not a subject we would have worked with had it not been connected to this particular context. When we begin writing, we need to imagine in a quite specific way the world where the story unfolds. The difference is that until this point these universes were purely fictional, while in the case of *Fargo* there was an air of authenticity we had to communicate. Since we come from the area, that helped us take into account the particular character of the place.

A "dialogue coach" is listed in the credits. Is that a gag?

EC: No, not at all. Most of the actors come from this part of the country, and they did not need coaching, but Frances McDormand, Bill Macy, and Harve Presnell had to have some training so their accents would blend with the others. This was partly how the characters were developed, and it also contributed to the air of authenticity.

JC: The people there speak is a very economical fashion, which is almost monosyllabic. This seems as exotic to other Americans as it does to you Europeans! In fact, the Scandinavian influence on the culture of that area, the rhythm of the sentences, the accent, all of this is not familiar at all to the rest of America. The story could have just as well taken place on the moon! New Yorkers have a general conception of Midwesterners, but they know nothing about these cultural "pockets," these microsocieties with their idiosyncrasies and peculiarities.

EC: When we were little, we were not really conscious of this Scandinavian heritage that so strongly affects this part of the country simply because we had no basis for comparison. When we got to New York City, we were astonished not to find any Gustafsons or Sondergaards. Certainly, all the exoticism comes from this Nordic character, with its polite and reserved manner. There's something almost Japanese in this refusal to register even the least emotion, in this resistance to saying no. One of the sources of comedy in the story comes from the opposition between this constant refusal of confrontation of all kinds and the accumulating murders.

JC: We didn't need to do any research since this manner of speech, these expressions, these sentence cadences were familiar to us. Our parents had always lived in this part of the country, and that means we returned there regularly and were familiar with the culture. After all, it's this culture that shaped us. Because we had not lived there for some time, we had the feeling of being separated in part from the environment where we had grown up.

The episode between Marge and her old high school friend is a digression from the central narrative, which is fairly compressed.

EC: Someone mentioned to us that in this scene, Frances acts in the very restrained manner of an Oriental, while her Japanese friend is talkative and irrational in the American style. It was certainly our intention while writing this sequence that it should be a digression.

JC: We wanted to provide another point of view on Frances's character, one that had nothing to do with the police investigation. This is also what happens in the scenes with her husband.

EC: Our intention was to demonstrate that this story is more closely connected to real life than to fiction, and we felt free to create a scene that had no links to the plot.

The Hudsucker Proxy *is no doubt your most stylized film. This one, in contrast, is probably your least.*

JC: We wanted to take a new approach to style in this film, to make something radically different from our previous films. And it is true that we were pressured in this direction because the preceding film was the most "theatrical" of them all. But curiously, working from actual events, we came to yet another form of stylization, in the largest sense of that term. The end result was then not as different as we imagined it would be!

A little like Kubrick did with Dr. Strangelove, *you begin with a somewhat documentary presentation, then little by little, with icy humor, everything comes unglued and turns in the direction of the absurd.*

EC: That resulted in part from the nature of the story. There is a plan that is established at the beginning and which in the end changes as the characters lose control of it.

JC: That's an effect implicit in the form of the story. When a character, in the first scene, tells you how things are going to go, we know very well that the unfolding of the story will go in a quite different direction. Others have also made reference to Kubrick, and I see the connection. His approach to the material is very formal, but then progresses regularly from the prosaic to the baroque.

How did you succeed in never falling into caricature, a danger because of the kind of story you work with?

JC: I suppose intuition plays some role with regard to our choice of style, and, even more, it depends a great deal on the actors and their ability to know when they might be going too far. For example, Frances's way of presenting her character is very sincere, very direct. That prevents Marge from becoming a parody of herself. Frances was very conscious of the dangers posed by excessiveness because of the quirk she used of dragging out the end of every sentence.

EC: We worked constantly on the set making adjustments with the actors. They'd give us a fairly wide range of behaviors for their characters, and we never stopped discussing that while shooting proceeded.

JC: We worked a good deal on "feeling." It's hard to say in words why Marge, in the film, is not a caricature, but a real person with three dimensions.

EC: What's certain about this is that when we were writing the screenplay and the actors were interpreting their roles, none of us thought of the story as a comedy.

JC: And that certainly helped, at the same time, to create comic effects and make the characters plausible. The comedy would not have worked if the film had been shot as a comedy, instead of sincerely and directly.

The relationship between Marge and her husband is also quite strange.

JC: We were intrigued from the moment we started casting by the notion of very simple interplay between them and by the impassive expression of John Caroll Lynch, which seemed to suit the tone of the film perfectly.

EC: He is the perfect incarnation of the undemonstrative personality of people from that region. The relations between husband and wife are based on what is not said, and yet they succeed nevertheless in communicating in some sense.

The end seems to be a parody of the classic Hollywood happy ending with the husband and wife on their bed symbolizing the return to order and to the natural.

JC: It is true that this is a return to order, but we did not have the intention of finishing up with a scene that's a parody. There was an article in the *New York Times* in which the writer asked why the people in Minnesota did not like the film's end, even though everything turned out for the best, as they are fond of believing there!

The only point at issue in the ending has to do with money. But isn't money the film's principal subject?

JC: All the characters in the film are obsessed with money.

EC: At the same time, we did not want to be too specific, for example, concerning the debt Jerry owes. It was enough to understand that this character had trapped himself by getting involved in some deal that had turned out badly. Moreover, during the entire film, Jerry is a pathetic loser who never stops improvising solutions in order to escape from the impasses he finds himself blocked by. He never stops trying everything, never stops bursting with activity. That almost makes him admirable!

JC: What we found interesting from the beginning in the character played by William Macy is his absolute incapacity, for even one minute, to project himself into the future so that he might evaluate the consequences of the decisions he has made. There is something fascinating about his total inability to gain any perspective. He's one of those people who build a pyramid but never think for a minute about it crumbling.

Did writing the screenplay take a lot of time?

EC: We had begun it before shooting *The Hudsucker Proxy;* afterward we went back to it, so it is pretty hard for us to estimate the time it all took. But two years had passed. What is certain is that the writing was easy and relatively quick, especially in comparison with our other screenplays, such as the one for *Miller's Crossing.*

Was it determined from the beginning that the wife, once kidnapped, would no longer be a physical presence?

JC: Yes, absolutely. And at a certain point in the story, it was also evident to us that she would cease to be a person for those who had kidnapped her. Moreover, it was no longer the actress Kristin Rudrud who played her, but a double with a hood over her head. In this case, we had no interest in the victim. It did not seem that at any point the husband himself was worried about what might happen to her. And Carl, one of the kidnappers, didn't even know her name.

Did you pick Steve Buscemi for this part before you had settled on Peter Stormare to play the other bad guy?

EC: In fact, we wrote the parts for these two comedians. And it was the same for Marge, played by Frances McDormand. Peter is an old friend, and he seemed an interesting choice for the role. Of course, his character is an outsider in the milieu where he finds himself, but at the same time he has an ethnic connection to it.

How do you work with your music director Carter Burwell?

JC: He has worked with us since our first project. Usually, he screens the film all the way through, then he plays a little bit of what he has in mind for us on the synthesizer so that he can give us some idea of what direction he'd like to go in. Before planning the orchestration, he plays parts of it for us on the piano, and we think about the connections these might have with certain sequences of the film. Then he goes on to the next step.

EC: In the case of this film, the main theme is based on a popular Scandinavian melody that Carter found for us.

JC: This is often how we work with him. For *Miller's Crossing,* the music came from an Irish folk tune that he used as the basis for his orchestration, adding bits he wrote himself. For *Raising Arizona,* he used a popular American tune that Holly Hunter sings part of. On the other hand, for *Blood Simple* and *Barton Fink,* the music is all his own composition; it wasn't inspired by anything else. For *The Hudsucker Proxy,* it was different yet again, a mix of an original composition by Carter and bits and pieces of Khachaturian.

EC: After he completes the orchestration, we go along with him to the sound recording studio. For our last two productions, he directed the orchestra himself. While the film is projected, we are still able to make last-minute changes. All told, the collaboration with him does not last more than two or three months.

How long did the editing take?

JC: About twelve weeks. That was a pretty short time for us because usually we take more, depending on whether we start editing while we're still shooting.

Did the principal photography pose any problems for you?

JC: It was easier for us in this case than with our other films. We talked it over a great deal with Roger Deakins because we wanted to shoot a good many exterior long shots. From the very beginning, we determined to use nothing but shots where the camera does not move.

EC: Afterward we decided that this purist attitude was pretty stupid.

JC: And so we decided then to move the camera sometimes, but in such a way that the viewer would not notice it. We didn't want to make the camera movement dramatic like we'd done in the past because we did not want to emphasize the action, make it seem either too dramatic or irrational.

EC: Roger Deakins worked on this production with a camera operator although, in the past, he was most often his own camera operator, including the two films he had made for us. This time he did not take charge of everything because he was often busy with the camera. On *Fargo,* we had problems with the weather because we needed snow, but the winter when we shot the film was particularly mild and dry. We had to work in Minneapolis with artificial snow. Then, because the snow didn't always work out, we had to travel in the end to North Dakota to shoot the large-scale exteriors. There we found exactly what we were looking for: a sky with a very low ceiling, no direct sunlight, no line marking the horizon, only a neutral and diffuse light.

JC: The landscapes we used were really dramatic and oppressive. There were no mountains or trees, only desolate flatlands extending into the distance. That's what we wanted to put on the screen.

Do you spend a lot of time looking through the camera?

JC: For the first film we made with Roger Deakins, *Barton Fink,* we were constantly looking through the viewfinder. For *Hudsucker Proxy,* less. And even less in the case of *Fargo.* This was no doubt a reflection of the material in each case and of the visual effects we were looking for, but it also resulted from our developing collaboration with the director of photography. When we work regularly with someone, we rather quickly develop a sort of telepathic language. I also think that Roger likes to work with people like us who take an active interest in problems of lighting, rather than with directors who depend entirely on him.

There's a contradiction between what it says in the press kit, which credits you with the editing, and the film credits that name a certain Roderick Jaynes.

JC: Whenever we edit the film ourselves, we use the pseudonym Roderick Jaynes. We prefer a hands-on approach rather than sitting next to someone and telling them when to cut. We think that's easier. In any case, there are two of us in the editing room. As for everything else, we work together, and we never have the feeling of isolation that other people sometimes have. On *Barton Fink* and *Blood Simple*, we were also our own editor. On the other projects, we have used an editor, but we were always there, of course, whenever we could be. But if we called upon Tom Noble or Michael Miller in these other cases, it was because the editing, for reasons of scheduling, had to start while we were shooting.

Your films are set in New Orleans [sic], in New York, in Hollywood, in the West, or the Midwest. It seems you are interested in exploring American geography.

JC: We would like to shoot somewhere else, but, bizarrely, the subjects we come up with are always set in America. That's what seems to attract us.

EC: It's always necessary, or so it seems, that the universe in which our stories take place has some kind of connection, however distant, with us. In the case of *Fargo*, the connection was obviously even closer.

JC: We have a need to know a subject intimately or, at least, feel some emotional connection to it. At the same time, we are not interested unless there is something exotic about it. For example, we know Minnesota very well, but not the people who inhabit *Fargo* or their way of life. On the other hand, in the case of *Barton Fink* and *Miller's Crossing*, the exoticism came from the story's being set in a distant time.

What are your connections with the characters in Fargo, *who for the most part seem somewhat retarded?*

JC: We have affection for them all and perhaps particularly for those who are plain and simple.

EC: One reason for making them simpletons of a sort was our desire to go beyond the Hollywood cliché of the villain as a kind of super-professional who has perfect control over everything he does. In fact, in most cases, criminals belong to social classes that are not well equipped to succeed in life, and that's the reason why they get themselves caught so often. And, in the same sense, too, our film draws more on life itself than on the conventions of the cinema and film genres.

JC: We are often asked how we manage injecting comedy into the material. But it seems to us that comedy is part of life. Look at the recent example of the people who tried to blow up the World Trade Center. They rented a panel truck to use for the explosion and then, after committing the crime, went back to the rental agency to get back the money they left on deposit. The absurdity of this kind of behavior is terribly funny in itself.

What projects are you working on?

EC: At this point we're working on two screenplays but don't know which one we'll finish first or which one will get financing first.

JC: One is also about a kidnapping, but of a very different sort. [This is a reference to *The Ladykillers* project, released in 2004]. The other is a kind of film noir about a barber from northern California, at the end of the 1940s. [This is the project that became *The Man Who Wasn't There.*]

(Only principal cast listed)

Blood Simple, 1984
USA
Production: River Road Productions
Producers: Ethan Coen, with Daniel F. Bacaner and Mark Silverman
Distribution: Circle Releasing
Direction: Joel Coen
Screenplay: Joel Coen, Ethan Coen
Photography: Barry Sonnenfeld
Production Designer: Jane Musky
Editing: Roderick Jaynes (Joel Coen, Ethan Coen) and Don Wiegmann
Music: Carter Burwell
First Assistant Director: Deborah Reinisch
Costume Designer: Richard Hornung
Sound Editor: Skip Lievsay, with Arnold Glassman
Cast: Ray (John Getz), Abby (Frances McDormand), Julian Marty (Dan Hedaya), Visser (M. Emmet Walsh), Meurice (Samm-Art Williams), Debra (Deborah Neumann), Landlady (Raquel Gavia), Man from Lubbock (Van Brooks), Mr. Garcia (Señor Marco), Old Cracker (William Creamer), Strip Bar Exhorter (Loren Bivens), Strip Bar Senator (Bob McAdams), Stripper (Shannon Sedwick), Girl on Overlook (Nancy Finger), Radio Evangelist (William Preston Robertson), Voice on Answering Machine (Holly Hunter)
Color
99 minutes

Raising Arizona, 1987
USA
Production: Twentieth Century Fox, Circle Films
Producers: Ethan Coen, with James Jacks, Mark Silverman, and Deborah Reinisch

Distribution: Twentieth Century Fox
Direction: Joel Coen
Screenplay: Joel Coen, Ethan Coen
Photography: Barry Sonnenfeld
Production Designer: Jane Musky
Editing: Michael R. Miller
Music: Carter Burwell
Costume Designer: Richard Hornung
Sound Editor: Skip Lievsay, with Arnold Glassman
Cast: H.I. or Hi (Nicolas Cage), Ed (Holly Hunter), Nathan Arizona Sr. (Trey Wilson), Gale (John Goodman), Evelle (William Forsythe), Glen (Sam McMurray), Dot (Frances McDormand), Leonard Smalls (Randall "Tex" Cobb), Nathan Jr. (T. J. Kuhn Jr.), Florence Arizona (Lynne Dumin Kitei), Prison Counselor (Peter Benedek), Nice Old Grocery Man (Charles "Lew" Smith), Younger FBI Agent (Warren Keith), Older FBI Agent (Henry Kendrick), Ear-Bending Cellmate (Sidney Dawson), Parole Board Chairman (Richard Blake), Parole Board Members (Troy Nabors, Mary Seibel), Hayseed in the Pickup (John O'Donnald), Whitey (Keith Jandacek), Minister (Warren Forsythe), "Trapped" Convict (Ruben Young), Policemen in Arizona House (Dennis Sullivan, Dick Alexander), Feisty Hayseed (Rusty Lee), Fingerprint Technician (James Yeater), Reporters (Bill Andres, Carver Barnes), Unpainted Secretary (Margaret H. McCormack), Newscaster (Bill Rocz), Payroll Cashier (Mary F. Glenn), Scamp with Squirt Gun (Jeremy Babendure), Adoption Agent (Bill Dobbins), Gynecologist (Ralph Norton), Mopping Convict (Henry Tank), Supermarket Manager (Frank Outlaw), Varsity Nathan Jr. (Todd Michael Rodgers), Machine Shop Ear Bender (M. Emmet Walsh), Glen and Dot's Kids (Robert Gray, Katie Thrasher, Derek Russell, Nichole Russell, Zachary Sanders, Noell Sanders), Arizona Quints (Cody Ranger, Jeremy Arendt, Ashley Hammon, Crystal Hiller, Olivia Hughes, Emily Malin, Melanie Malin, Craig McLaughlin, Adam Savageau, Benjamin Savageau, David Schneider, Michael Stewart).
Color
94 minutes

Miller's Crossing, 1990
USA
Production: Twentieth Century Fox, Circle Films
Producers: Ethan Coen, with Mark Silverman, Graham Place, and Ben Barenholtz
Distribution: Twentieth Century Fox
Direction: Joel Coen
Screenplay: Joel Coen, Ethan Coen

Photography: Barry Sonnenfeld
Production Designer: Dennis Gassner
Editing: Michael R. Miller
Music: Carter Burwell
Costume Designer: Richard Hornung
Sound Editor: Skip Lievsay, with Arnold Glassman
Cast: Tom Reagan (Gabriel Byrne), Verna (Marcia Gay Harden), Bernie
Bernbaum (John Turturro), Johnny Caspar (Jon Polito), Eddie Dane (J. F.
Freeman), Leo (Albert Finney), Frankie (Mike Starr), Tic-Tac (Al Manci-
ni), Mink (Steve Buscemi), Clarence "Drop" Johnson (Mario Todisco), Tad
(Olek Krupa), Adolph (Michael Jeter), Terry (Lanny Flaherty), Mrs. Cas-
par (Jeanette Kontomitras), Johnny Caspar Jr. (Louis Charles Mounicou),
Cop—Brian (John McConnell), Cop—Delahanty (Danny Aiello III),
Screaming Woman (Helen Holly), Landlady (Hilda McLean), Gunmen in
Leo's House (Monte Starr, Don Picard), Rug Daniels (Salvatore H. Torna-
bene), Street Urchin (Kevin Dearie), Caspar's Driver (Michael Badalucco),
Caspar's Butler (Charles Ferrara), Caspar's Cousins (Esteban Fernandez,
George Fernandez), Hitman at Verna's (Charles Gunning), Hitman #2
(Dave Drinkx), Lazarre's Messenger (David Darlow), Lazarre's Toughs
(Robert LaBrosse, Carl Rooney), Man with Pipe Bomb (Jack David Har-
ris), Son of Erin (Jery Jewitt), Snickering Gunman (Sam Raimi), Cop with
Bullhorn (John Schnauder Jr.), Rabbi (Zolly Levin), Boxers (Joey Ancona,
Bill Raye), Secretary (Frances McDormand)
Color
115 minutes

Barton Fink, 1991
USA
Production: Twentieth Century Fox, Circle Films, Working Title Films
Producers: Ethan Coen, with Graham Place, Ben Barenholtz, Ted Pedas, Jim
Pedas, Bill Durkin
Distribution: Twentieth Century Fox
Direction: Joel Coen
Screenplay: Joel Coen, Ethan Coen
Photography: Roger Deakins
Production Designer: Dennis Gassner
Editing: Roderick Jaynes (Joel Coen, Ethan Coen)
Music: Carter Burwell
Costume Designer: Richard Hornung
Sound Editor: Skip Lievsay
Cast: Barton Fink (John Turturro), Charlie Meadows (John Goodman), Au-
drey Taylor (Judy Davis), Jack Lipnick (Michael Lerner), W. P. Mayhew

(John Mahoney), Ben Geisler (Tony Shalhoub), Chet (Steve Buscemi), Garland Stanford (David Warrilow), Detective Mastrionotti (Richard Portnow), Detective Deutsch (Christopher Murney), Derek (I. M. Hobson), Poppy Carnaham (Meagan Fay), Richard St. Claire (Lance Davis), Pete (Harry Bugin), Maitre D' (Anthony Gordon), Stage Hand (Jack Denbo), Clapper Boy (Max Grodenchik), Referee (Robert Beecher), Rustler (Darwyn Swalve), Geisler's Secretary (Gayle Vance), Sailor (Johnny Judkins), USO Girl (Jana Marie Hupp), Beauty (Isabelle Townsend), Voice (William Preston Robertson)
Color
116 minutes

The Hudsucker Proxy, 1994
USA
Production: Warner Brothers, Silver Pictures, Polygram, Working Title Films
Producers: Ethan Coen, with Graham Place, Eric Fellner, Tim Bevan
Distribution: Twentieth Century Fox
Direction: Joel Coen
Screenplay: Ethan Coen, Joel Coen, Sam Raimi
Photography: Roger Deakins
Production Designer: Dennis Gassner
Editing: Thom Noble
Music: Carter Burwell
Costume Designer: Richard Hornung
Sound Editor: Skip Lievsay
Cast: Norville Barnes (Tim Robbins), Amy Archer (Jennifer Jason Leigh), Sidney J. Mussburger (Paul Newman), Waring Hudsucker (Charles Durning), Chief (John Mahoney), Buzz (Jim True), Moses (Bill Cobbs), Smitty (Bruce Campbell), Aloysius (Harry Bugin), Benny (John Seitz), Lou (Joe Grifasi), Board Members (Roy Brocksmith, I. M. Hobson, John Scanlon, Jerome Dempsy, John Wylie, Gary Allen, Richard Woods, Peter McPherson), Dr. Hugo Bronfenbrenner (David Byrd), Mail Room Orienter (Christopher Darga), The Ancient Sorter (Patrick Cranshaw), Mailroom Boss (Robert Weil), Mussburger's Secretary (Mary Lou Rosato), Luigi the Tailor (Ernie Sarracino), Mrs. Mussburger (Eleanor Glockner), Mrs. Braithwaite (Kathleen Perkins), Sears Braithwaite of Bullard (Joseph Marcus), Vic Tenetta (Peter Gallagher), Zebulon Cardoza (Noble Willingham), Mrs. Cardoza (Barbara Ann Grimes), Thorstenson Finlandson (Thom Noble), Beatnik Barman (Steve Buscemi), Newsreel Scientist (William Duff-Griffin), Za-Za (Anna Nicole Smith), Dream Dancer (Pamela Everett), The Hula-Hoop Kid (Arthur Bridges), Hudsucker Brainstormers (Sam Raimi, John Cameron), Mr. Grier (Skipper Duke), Mr. Levin (Jake Kapner), Mr. Bumstead (Jon Polito), Ancient Puzzler (Richard Whiting), Coffee Shop Waitress

(Linda McCoy), Emcee (Stan Adams), Newsreel Announcer (Karl Mundt
[John Goodman])
Color
111 minutes

Fargo, 1996
USA
Production: Gramercy Pictures, Working Title Films, Polygram
Producers: Ethan Coen, with Tim Bevan, Eric Fellner, John Cameron
Distribution: Gramercy Pictures
Direction: Joel Coen
Screenplay: Ethan Coen, Joel Coen
Photography: Roger Deakins
Production Designer: Rick Heinrichs
Editing: Roderick Jaynes (Joel Coen, Ethan Coen)
Music: Carter Burwell
Costume Designer: Mary Zophres
Sound Editor: Skip Lievsay
Cast: Jerry Lundegaard (William H. Macy), Carl Showalter (Steve Buscemi),
    Gaear Grimsrud (Peter Stormare), Jean Lundegaard (Kristin Rudrud),
    Wade Gustafson (Harve Presnell), Scotty Lundegaard (Tony Denman),
    Irate Customer (Gary Houston), Irate Customer's Wife (Sally Winger), Car
    Salesman (Kurt Schweiskhardt), Hooker #1 (Larissa Kokernot), Hooker #2
    (Melissa Peterman), Shep Proudfoot (Steve Reevis), Reilly Diefenbach
    (Warren Keith), Morning Show Host (Steve Edelman), Morning Show
    Hostess (Sharon Anderson), Stan Grossman (Larry Grandenburg), State
    Trooper (James Gaulke), Victim in Field (J. Todd Anderson), Victim in Car
    (Michelle Suzanne LeDoux), Marge Gunderson (Frances McDormand),
    Norm Gunderson (John Carroll Lynch), Lou (Bruce Bohne), Cashier (Pe-
    tra Boden), Mike Yanagita (Steve Park), Customer (Wayne Evenson),
    Officer Olson (Cliff Raker), Hotel Clerk (Jessica Shephard), Airport Lot
    Attendant (Peter Schmitz), Mechanic (Steven Schaefer), Escort (Michelle
    Hutchinson), Man in Hallway (David Loman), José Feliciano (Himself),
    Soap Opera Actor (Bruce Campbell)
Color
99 minutes

The Big Lebowski, 1998
Production: Polygram, Working Title Films
Producers: Ethan Coen, with Tim Bevan, Eric Fellner, John Cameron
Distribution: Gramercy Pictures
Direction: Joel Coen
Screenplay: Ethan Coen, Joel Coen

Photography: Roger Deakins
Production Designer: Rick Heinrichs
Editing: Roderick Jaynes (Joel Coen, Ethan Coen)
Music: Carter Burwell, T-Bone Burnett
Costume Designer: Mary Zophres
Sound Editor: Skip Lievsay
Cast: The Dude (Jeff Bridges), Walter Sobchak (John Goodman), Maude Lebowski (Julianne Moore), Donny (Steve Buscemi), The Big Lebowski (David Huddleston), Brandt (Philip Seymour Hoffman), Bunny Lebowski (Tara Reid), Treehorn Thugs (Philip Moon, Mark Pellegrino), Nihilists (Peter Stormare, Flea, Torsten Voges), Smokey (Jimmy Dale Gilmore), Dude's Landlord (Jack Kehler), Jesus Quintana (John Turturro), Quintana's Partner (James G. Hoosier), Maude's Thugs (Carlos Leon, Terence Burton), Older Cop (Richard Gant), Younger Cop (Christian Clemenson), Tony the Chauffeur (Dom Irrera), Lebowski's Chauffeur (Gerard L'Heureux), Knox Harrington (David Thewlis), Coffee Shop Waitress (Lu Elrod), Auto Circus Cop (Mike Gomez), Gary the Bartender (Peter Siragusa), The Stranger (Sam Elliott), Doctor (Marshall Manesh), Arthur Digby Sellers (Harry Bugin), Little Larry Sellers (Jesse Flanagan), Pilar (Irene Olga Lopez), Corvette Owner (Luis Colina), Jackie Treehorn (Ben Bazzara), Malibu Police Chief (Leon Russom), Cab Driver (Ajgie Kirkland), Private Snoop (Jon Polito), Nihilist Woman (Aimee Mann), Saddam (Jerry Haleva), Pancake Waitress (Jennifer Lamb), Funeral Director (Warren Keith)
Color
117 minutes

O Brother, Where Art Thou? 2000
Production: Buena Vista Pictures, Mike Zoss Productions, Touchstone Pictures, Universal Pictures, Studio Canal, Working Title Films
Producers: Ethan Coen, with Tim Bevan, John Cameron, Eric Fellner, Robert Graf
Distribution: Buena Vista Pictures
Direction: Joel Coen
Screenplay: Ethan Coen, Joel Coen
Photography: Roger Deakins
Production Designer: Dennis Gassner
Editing: Ethan Coen, Joel Coen, Tricia Cooke
Music: Carter Burwell, T-Bone Burnett
Costume Designer: Mary Zophres
Sound Editor: Skip Lievsay
Cast: Ulysses Everett McGill (George Clooney), Pete (John Turturro), Delmar O'Donnell (Tim Nelson), Baby Face Nelson (Michael Badalucco), Pappy O'Daniel (Charles Durning), Big Dan Teague (John Goodman),

Homer Stokes (Wayne Duvall), Penny McGill Wharvey (Holly Hunter), Tommy Johnson (Himself), Junior D'Daniel (Del Pentecost), Pappy's Staff (J. R. Home, Brian Reddy), The Little Man (Ed Gale), Vernon T. Waldrip (Ray McKinnon). Sheriff Cooley (Daniel von Bargen), Man with Bullhorn (Royce D. Applegate), W. B. Hogwallop (Frank Collison), Boy Hogwallop (Quinn Gasaway), Blind Seer (Lee Weaver), Pomade Vendor (Milford Fortenberry), Radio Manager (Stephen Root), Record Store Clerk (A. Ray Ratliff), Sirens (Mia Tate, Christy Taylor, Musetta Vander), Waitress (April Hardcastle), Wharvey Gals (Georgia Rae Rainer, Marianna Breland, Lindsey Miller)
Color
106 minutes

The Man Who Wasn't There, 2001
Production: Good Machine, The KL Line, Working Title Films
Producers: Ethan Coen, with Tim Bevan, Eric Fellner, John Cameron
Distribution: USA Films
Direction: Joel Coen
Screenplay: Ethan Coen, Joel Coen
Photography: Roger Deakins
Production Designer: Dennis Gassner
Editing: Roderick Jaynes (Joel Coen, Ethan Coen), Tricia Cooke
Music: Carter Burwell
Costume Designer: Mary Zophres
Sound Editor: Skip Lievsay
Cast: Ed Crane (Billy Bob Thornton), Doris Crane (Frances McDormand), Big Dave Brewster (James Gandolfini), Frank Raffo (Michael Badalucco), Creighton Toliver (Jon Polito), Freddy Riedenschneider (Tony Shalhoub), Birdy Abundas (Scarlett Johansson), Walter Abundas (Richard Jenkins), Anne Nirdlinger (Katherine Borowitz), Jacques Carcanogues (Adam Alexi-Malle), Persky (Christopher Kriesa), Krebs (Brian Haley), Burns (Jack McGee), The New Man (Gregg Binkley), Diedrickson (Alan Fudge), Medium (Lilyan Chauvin), Bingo Caller (Ted Rooney), Young Man (Abraham Benrubi), Child (Christian Ferratti), Costanza (Rhoda Gemignani), Customer (E. J. Callahan), Sobbing Prisoner (Brooke Smith), Macadam Salesman (Christopher McDonald), Doctor (John Michael Higgins), D.A. (Ricky Scarry), Lloyd Garroway (George Ives)
Black and White
116 minutes

Andrew, Geoff. *Stranger Than Paradise: Maverick Film-Makers in Recent American Cinema.* New York: Limelight, 1999.

Bergan, Ronald. *The Coen Brothers.* New York: Thunder's Mouth, 2000.

Corrigan, Timothy. *A Cinema without Walls: Movies and Culture after Vietnam.* New Brunswick, N.J.: Rutgers University Press, 1991.

King, Geoff. *New Hollywood Cinema: An Introduction.* New York: Columbia University Press, 2002.

Körte, Peter, and Georg Seesien. *Joel and Ethan Coen.* London: Limelight, 2001.

Levine, Josh. *The Coen Brothers: The Story of Two American Filmmakers.* Toronto: ECW Press, 2000.

Lewis, Jon, ed. *The New American Cinema.* Durham, N.C.: Duke University Press, 1998.

Merritt, Greg. *Celluloid Mavericks: A History of American Independent Film.* New York: Thunder's Mouth, 2000.

Mottram, James. *The Coen Brothers: The Life of the Mind.* Dulles, Va.: Brassey, 2000.

Russell, Carolyn R. *The Films of Joel and Ethan Coen.* Jefferson, N.C.: McFarland, 2001.

Tasker, Yvonne, ed. *Fifty Contemporary Filmmakers.* New York: Routledge, 2002.

Woods, Paul A. *Joel and Ethan Coen: Blood Siblings.* London: Plexus, 2000.

R. Barton Palmer is Calhoun Lemon Professor of Literature at Clemson University and director of the South Carolina Film Institute. He is the author of numerous books, including *Joseph L. Mankiewicz: Critical Essays with a Bibliography and Filmography* (with Cheryl Lower); *Perspectives on Film Noir;* and *Hollywood's Dark Cinema: The American Film Noir.* He has recently edited *Nineteenth-Century American Fiction on Screen; Twentieth-Century American Fiction on Screen;* and (with David Boyd) *After Hitchcock: Imitation/ Influence/Intertextuality.*

The University of Illinois Press
is a founding member of the
Association of American University Presses.

———————————————————

Composed in 10/13 New Caledonia
with Helvetica Neue Extended display
by Jim Proefrock
at the University of Illinois Press
Designed by Paula Newcomb
Manufactured by Sheridan Books, Inc.

University of Illinois Press
1325 South Oak Street
Champaign, IL 61820-6903
www.press.uillinois.edu